MISSION READY FINANCES

PROVEN PRINCIPLES TO GUIDE YOUR STORY TO FINANCIAL FREEDOM

LT COL MARCO PARZYCH, USAF (Ret.)

onP INT
— PRESS —

Foreword

The intent of this book is to serve as a financial <u>interruption</u> in your life like an emergency commercial on TV... "we interrupt this broadcast to bring you breaking news." These types of interruptions can be seen as a nuisance, but are meant to break our concentration, get our attention and open our eyes. The same can be said about traffic detours, which are there for our protection and to ensure that we arrive at our destination safely. Interruptions and detours are necessary and can save our lives, depending upon how we respond to them. Many in our country are in desperate need of an interruption, a wakeup call to open our eyes and a course correction to our approach on personal finance to ensure that we arrive safely at our desired destination.

Our modern-day fighter aircraft are some of the most technologically advanced systems in our military. Yet when one of the critical systems on these machines is not functioning properly, the most effective fix is often very simple: turn it off and then back on. For most of us, our management of income is one of our systems that is not working nearly as effectively as it should be. From time to time, even as the most complex and intricate beings in the world, we require a similar reset to one of our systems. We need to shut it down, wipe the slate clean, forgetting what we believe to be true and possible, then restart with fresh eyes and perspective.

My purpose in writing this book is to lead you to a place where you are able to see what I, and many others, have finally been able to see... that life doesn't have to be this way any longer, at least not for you and your household. The objective is to help you improve your life, relationships and productivity by restoring hope in your financial story, reduce stress and marital discord due to financial challenges and ultimately reach your goals of prosperity and generosity. My goal is to reach many, especially those who guard our country, at home and around the globe, and open their eyes <u>before</u> they find themselves under a darkened financial overcast. While pain can be an effective teacher, it also hurts and often leaves a mark. The goal is to help you get on track, ideally before you have to experience the pain, sorrow, and often devastating effects to your household, that will eventually result from the mismanagement of finances.

Regardless of whether you are just starting out, have been going along for a while doing ok, or already find yourself in a financial mess, the principles found is this book will help you do better. Allow me to be your guide, leading you on a fact-finding mission and shining a light onto the path of a bright financial future!

All net proceeds from the sale of this book go to the charitable nonprofit organization,

Mission Ready Finances, Inc.

to help them achieve their vision of financial hope, peace and success for all who bravely serve our nation. Thank you for your purchase and role in furthering their mission! To learn more or to further support this important cause, please visit **missionreadyfinances.com**.

** A Note to Our Nation's Guardians **

If you are currently serving, or have served, as either a member of our armed forces or as a first responder, let me first thank you for your service and dedication to our nation and for defending and protecting all that we hold dear to our hearts. You voluntarily chose to answer the call to serve, putting your own life on the line by running towards events that most run away from so that others may live. Our nation will forever be in indebted to you (no pun intended!) for your selfless service.

Through your service, you have consistently learned to submit to new ways of doing things and exemplified discipline throughout your training and in the workplace. Your level of mission readiness takes on a whole new meaning through your willingness to put your life on the line for others. Now I challenge you to adopt a similar level of willingness to open your mind and learn new ways to manage your finances, with the discipline to put them into practice. You and your families sacrifice far too much to not have mission ready finances. Thank you for all that you do each and every day for our nation.

1

Jets and Finances?

What in the world could fighter planes possibly have to do with my finances? That may be the question that compelled you to pick up this book and start reading. Regardless of what piqued your interest, thank you for giving it a chance. I would encourage you to please keep reading. The level of financial success that you achieve over your lifetime, towards your goals for prosperity and generosity, is depending upon it.

As a retired Air Force fighter pilot turned financial coach, I have had the awesome opportunity and privilege to work with many, guiding them towards a brighter financial outlook. Over the years, I have seen many parallels between the mindset and habit patterns that make a sharp, lethal combat pilot and those that inspire and ensure successful personal finance for any household. Many analogies come to mind, which have proven to be useful working with clients to help them see their misguided financial ways...something that I can definitely relate to.

For many years, in no uncertain terms, I had no clue what it meant to properly manage my household's income and finances. Despite being a well-trained commissioned officer in the United States military, entrusted to fly ultra-expensive single seat fighter planes and lead other Americans in air and ground combat, I had no idea how to be effective with our income. My wife and I sure thought that we were doing fine, and life seemed pretty great overall. We were making a good household income, living in nice houses, driving nice cars, and even eventually had a vacation home. To the untrained eye, we had it all...another shiny example of a family living the American dream. But below the surface, behind closed doors, our finances and balancing of the payments felt more like this -

Car payments, student loan payments, house payments, second house payment and credit card payments with lingering balances from deserved vacations, the latest and greatest electronics purchases and Christmas gifts (snuck up on us again last year). We discovered car leases, which provided us with a new car every few years...how great is that?! We also had a bit of retirement investing going, some years more than others, which we then proceeded to dip into several times to buy bigger homes in nicer neighborhoods with better schools, resulting in loans against ourselves. But it wasn't so bad. After all, we were just borrowing from our own savings, or so we thought.

Yes, we had payments and debt coming out the ears, but the loans all had great low interest rates, minus the credit card of course. But we paid that off every month...ok, most months...ok, some months. Looking back, we may have just been surviving, paycheck to paycheck, month to month, but life felt pretty good financially. We had good income and secure employment with regular raises every few years. Sure, money was tight from time to time, but that was going to change as soon as the next promotion and raise kicked in. We were finally going to get more serious and consistent with saving and investing, just as soon as we got that next income bump.

The plate balancing act became our norm. With a secure job and credit cards providing a backstop for any of life's curveballs, we saw no real need for an emergency fund. Yes, things would get sporty from time to time when life's curveballs exceeded the balance available on our card, throwing an unexpected extra plate in the mix. But it was nothing a quick personal loan with no or low interest for 12 or 18 months couldn't fix. Besides, we convinced ourselves, we would have it paid off with the next tax refund, not to mention the next pay raise over the horizon, so we were good. Unexpected events were easily covered by a credit card or two sitting right there in our wallets. We also had a great credit score...something we took great pride in whenever it came to getting approved for a mortgage or taking on any new debt payment.

After a while, it didn't feel strange anymore. We had accepted the monthly dance of paying bills along with the moderate level of financial stress that came with adulthood. Most couples around us, making comparable incomes, had nice things similar to what we had, which made it seem that this was just how things were here in America.

Perhaps you can relate.... or have a friend that can.

After reading an article about how much money the average American household earns in their working lifetime, I decided to add up our annual income since graduating college. We felt ill seeing how much we had earned so far through our working years despite truly owning very few assets. That's when things started to change

3

for us...a true lightbulb moment. We began to question whether life really had to be like this. We started to realize that despite working hard, earning a decent amount of income throughout our 20s and early 30s and having some great possessions, we really didn't own much of it at all. The banks actually owned most of our big-ticket items and we were basically just reimbursing the bank for the privilege of having them. We were paying the banks and credit card companies a ton of money but didn't have much ownership ourselves. So, we decided to get educated, reading books, blogs and anything else we could get our hands on. We finally learned truths, proven principles that actually worked. Looking back, it boggles my mind how things could have been so squared away and disciplined at work, yet we had such little discipline with our own personal finances at home.

Turns out that it wasn't just us. We were fairly normal in terms of our use of debt, falling right in line with the ways of our country overall. Surveys continually find that money is hands-down the leading cause of stress for Americans, which should be no surprise.[1] The national debt now stands at over $22 trillion.[2] How in the world did our government get us here, we may ask. But before we focus on Washington, we need to take a hard look at ourselves. It's not only our government that is racking up ridiculous amounts of debt. American households are doing the same, with the overall level of national household debt now standing at over $13 trillion.[3] That's right, consumers in this country, just like you and I, are responsible for over $13 trillion of household debt, which includes over $1 trillion of credit card debt.[4]

One trillion dollars in credit card debt...that's insane! Said a different way, that's one million million, or written out... $1,000,000,000,000. It's tough to even get your mind around a number that big. At an average interest rate of 15%, that amount of credit card debt would equate to $150 billion, with a "B," paid in interest each year. Even if we account for half of all credit card debt being paid off each month by cardholders (as many claim but less than 3 in 10 actually do), that would still leave approximately $75 billion paid in credit card interest annually.[5] That's nearly $800 per year blown in credit card interest, every year, when split between half of the estimated number of credit card holders in this country.[6] It should come as no surprise why we get so many credit card offers in the mail! And it's not just credit card companies that are profiting. Interest made from in-store credit cards account for over one-third of profits for some large chain retailers![7]

Other types of debt that surpass credit cards are student loans and vehicle debt. Loans taken out for students now nears $1.5 trillion, while car loans have topped $1.2 trillion.[8] We have become infatuated with debt, embracing a "get it now and pay later" mentality, even convincing ourselves that there is such a thing as "good debt." It should come as no surprise that as our overall debt loads as consumers has continued to rise, it has taken its toll on our stress levels and ability to achieve future goals, with those reaching retirement age becoming less and less prepared for their golden years.

While none of us, individually, can directly target and take down the national debt, improve the nation's budget deficit, or tackle our country's huge amount of household debt, we all hold the power to attack our own household's debt and budget deficits.

So, what exactly is "Mission Ready," and how can it help you to meet your financial goals? Glad you asked...

2

Mission Ready

If you have you ever been to an airshow in America, there is a good chance you have seen one of the U.S. military's flight demonstration teams perform. For the Air Force, it's the red, white and blue Thunderbirds, flying the F-16. The Navy's blue and gold team is the Blue Angels, who fly the F-18. The men and women of both teams fly six fighter aircraft through a variety of close formations and stunts, wowing the crowd below with their precision, speed and power. Both teams put on perfectly choreographed and executed shows as they travel across the country, and often across the globe. The teams showcase America's airpower and serve as ambassadors to the public for their respective military branches. For those who attend these airshows, the Thunderbirds or Blue Angels are typically the last act of the day, the main attraction and highlight of the show.

The thousands of hours of prep work these teams put into practicing their routine, and maintaining the aircraft used to fly in them, results in an inspiring and thrilling showcase. It may not come as a surprise that the formations and stunts flown by these teams don't directly tie into their branch's combat missions. Loops, rolls and tightly flown formations aren't listed in any tactics manual for our services. However, although the maneuvers don't directly represent how the pilots would execute their airborne missions in combat, these elite aerial teams demonstrate the precision, discipline, teamwork, professionalism and readiness of our nation's airpower.

The United States military's capability runs far wider and deeper than what is demonstrated by the aircraft flown in airshows. Most of the public does not get a chance to see the other military branches perform front and center – ships, submarines, tanks, infantry forces, amphibious vehicles, special operators...and the list goes on. Although we may not have the chance to observe other branches perform, all specialties within the services exude a similar level of precision and capability as we see from the Thunderbirds and Blue Angels. We have strong and formidable forces, ready, when called upon, to take down any threats to the freedoms and opportunities that the citizens of this nation are blessed to have.

Regardless of the role being filled, all servicemembers go through immense amounts of training to learn and finetune their skills. Training prepares them for their specialty so that there is no doubt that each will be ready to roll in the event they are called upon by the nation in time of need. Months, and often years, of training are required to be deemed ready for combat deployment. In the Air Force, a pilot certified as being qualified for wartime deployment is distinguished as Combat Mission Ready, or CMR. Most pilots drop the "C" and simply call it "MR" – Mission Ready.

Mission ready is being trained, upon solid time-proven principles, skilled and prepared to meet the mission objectives when and where called upon to do so. Readiness includes a winning mindset and always having a solid plan, unique to the mission at hand. Being MR is not a "one and done" event, but rather a mindset of continuously learning and improving. Lastly, a Mission Ready mindset understands the big picture and how meeting today's objectives brings the team closer to winning the overall campaign.

While qualification for combat operations is certainly unique and encapsulates an entirely different mindset, the concept of completing training and becoming qualified for a specific job reaches far and wide across our globe. Very few are just thrown into a job and told "good luck" or "go figure it out." Just about every paid job entails some level of training, some much more in-depth than others, but a qualification of sorts is reached, nonetheless. Whether it be as a doctor, lawyer, accountant, plumber, mechanic, teacher, salesperson, truck driver, burger flipper, or just about any other job you can think of, there is some level of readiness training completed to qualify an individual for the job at hand. In a sense, we are all trained to become Mission Ready at the specialty that we get paid to do.

Despite being mission ready in our occupations, there is a critical position that we all fill yet almost none of us get adequately trained or prepared for. That would be the role of personal finance manager. We complete tens, hundreds, perhaps even thousands of hours of training for our jobs so that the task at hand can be completed for our employer and we can, in turn, collect a paycheck. For most, we work for companies that ultimately earn a profit due in part to our contributions. In turn, we receive payment for our efforts. Over a lifetime, those paychecks add up to millions of dollars for most Americans. The median household income in the US is currently around $61,000 per year.[1] At that rate, on average, a household will bring in 2 to 3 million dollars over their working years. Regardless of the actual pay, a significant amount of money will pass through your hands when added up over a lifetime.

Despite the inconceivably large amount of money that will pass through our checking accounts, we are woefully undertrained to handle our personal finances. While we may be Mission Ready for our employers, we are anything but when it comes to handling the income that we receive from those jobs.

Take a moment to pause and mull this point over. Most receive at least 12 years of education and graduate high school. Many then go on to either trade school or apprenticeships for several more years, or college for another 4+ years, then on to work for 40-50 years, day in and day out, with millions of dollars passing through their household over their lives. We are trained up in our specialties and work hard over a lifetime, accepting significant amounts of time apart from our families, collecting an income that allows us to support that family, but also making the companies that we work for significant profits. Many may even love their occupation and have the opportunity to make some amazing contributions at work. But regardless of whether you enjoy what you currently do or not, the vast majority of us have had little, if any, training on how to smartly and responsibly handle our personal finances. Not at home, not in high school, not in college, and not at work.

Even for those that did part time work before going to work full time, cutting lawns, babysitting, flipping burgers, or serving customers, you probably made a small fraction of what you do now in your full-time career. We go through school then see an enormous spike in pay, for most hands down the highest jump in income of their entire lives, and suddenly find ourselves making tens of thousands of dollars each year. Of course, that money isn't free and clear. It's needed to support ourselves once we are out on our own...food, shelter, utilities, transportation, clothing, etc. The bottom line is that we aren't <u>trained</u> on how to handle our finances and our financial responsibilities smartly, nowhere near being 'Mission Ready' on the home front.

To look at this a different way, it would be like handing the keys to a Ferrari to a teen, who drove a go-kart as a kid, without any real driving training. Or an F-16 to someone who has taken a few lessons in a small propeller plane. Or sending a civilian into combat without training, or into the role of a police officer, or firefighter, or accountant, or just about any job for that matter...none of which would we ever dream of doing! We wouldn't knowingly put ourselves or others into these types of scenarios. It would be negligent and very likely result in disaster. Yet that is exactly what has happened with most of us in this country when it comes to our personal finances. When we look at it in this light, the fact that many are in over their heads and, collectively, we have racked up significant amounts of debt really isn't all that surprising.

As with any area of our lives that we are not adequately trained for, we are left to learn how to handle our income on our own. As a financial coach, I find that many revert back to what was caught from their parents' handling of money while growing up, which may or may not have been the best example. We are also greatly influenced by the culture and those around us. We watch and observe family, friends and coworkers for tips on what is "normal" for our society and usually emulate some form of what we see. Without being educated on a proven plan that teaches us to be intentional and success-oriented with our income, we go with the flow based upon what we see around us. The problem, as we have all heard many times, is that looks can be deceiving.

3

Jet or Balloon?

A few years back, my family and I went to an airshow where the Thunderbirds were performing. As always, the airshow did not disappoint and was a hit with the kids. A few days later, a business trip brought me to Albuquerque, New Mexico. It happened to be the same week as the annual Balloon Fiesta. Hundreds of hot air balloons participate in this weeklong festival, filling the skies over Albuquerque in an awesome display of balloons floating across the horizon. Two awe-inspiring airshows in the same week! But other than being seen looking up to the sky, these two shows couldn't be more different.

The Air Force F-16s are powerful, precise and intentional with every maneuver, ultimately landing at the runway of their choosing following the show. The hot air balloons are certainly a thing of beauty, nearly silent in comparison to the jets. Those navigating the balloons have much less control of their maneuvers and destination than the jet pilots have. Balloonists are reactive in flight, improvising moment to moment as the winds change direction and velocity. Although experienced balloonists can have some level of control over their landing area by going to different altitudes with varying conditions, they are ultimately reliant on where the winds take them. While they would seem much easier and peaceful to operate, balloons start running out of options quickly when winds pick up or severe weather conditions roll in. The balloonist can't simply turn around as they could in a jet...instead forced to set it down wherever they may be. Balloons also lack a clearly defined forward or backward. You could be facing in one direction in the basket, but actually be moving in the opposite direction, further away from where your eyes are focused.

Most of us go through life financially like we're flying a hot air balloon, aimlessly. Flying our balloon can easily be mistaken as a great opportunity. After all, it takes us airborne with a great view, provides what seems like an amazing ride and looks beautiful to those around us. We look great on the exterior wearing nice clothes, driving new cars, and living in nice neighborhoods in well-decorated houses. Underneath the surface, however, there's often little actual ownership. Our spending habits generally follow the financial ways of our culture, lacking true substance. Without forward thrust or directional controls, we have no clear path or intentionality with our finances to help bring us to a desired destination. Instead, we float along wherever the winds of our culture and our whimsical attitude towards money takes us. The odds of this approach to personal finance taking you to the destination of your choosing, with no clear idea of forward or backward direction, are essentially nonexistent. In fact, floating along is much more likely to take us backwards, further from our hopes and dreams. As author Terry Felber wrote, "if you don't know where you're going, you're not going to like where you end up."[1] And that's exactly the vector, our direction, that most households in our country are heading.

While everything looks rosy around our cultural pack of balloons, the reality is that our society is by and large broke. Recent studies have found that nearly 80% of the households in the United States are living paycheck to paycheck.[2] Living paycheck to paycheck means "living off exactly what you earn with little or no savings to cushion a financial blow," or "constantly scrambling to make ends meet or running out of money before the end of the month."[3,4] Without a solid financial education, we tend to form our views on money from what we see going on around us every day. The takeaway, from what we observe, is likely that everyone else is doing great, using credit to enjoy life and have nice things. But it's all a façade, which our society has become a master of.

Most can't cover basic emergencies, which aren't a matter of "if," but "when," without relying on credit cards. Over 60% of Americans aren't able to cover a $1,000 emergency without going into debt.[5] Many find themselves woefully short on savings as they enter their 60s, forcing them to continue working into their 70s. The majority of Americans over sixty-five depend upon their Social Security paychecks for at least half of their income.[6] Younger adults find themselves on a similar path, with two out of every three millennials (ages 23-38 in 2019) having zero saved for long-term retirement.[7]

Not being able to handle financial emergencies or prepared for retirement is the tip of the iceberg. The dysfunction with our personal finances reaches much deeper, touching just about every aspect of our lives. In study after study, disagreements over finances and the stress that comes with handling money are routinely cited as one of the top causes for marital discord and divorce.[8] The stress that we feel over our finances also impacts our health, how we are as mothers and fathers to our kids and our performance on the job, making us less effective across the board. More and more are also turning to alcohol or other drugs to deal with the increased stress that our finances play a major role in, making the situation even more dire.[9]

At the same time as we enter the workforce, untrained on personal finances yet with tens of thousands of dollars at our disposal, we enter one of the most marketed-to societies on the planet. There is no shortage of ways to spend our income, and we are tempted in thousands of ways to spend our hard-earned cash each and every day. We don't have to look far for ways to spend...nicer cars, nicer furniture, nicer clothing, dining out, nicer house, fast food lane to accommodate our busy lifestyles, and the list goes on. We are a society of convenience and flash.

For most, income is not the issue. Life is abundant in the United States, with the vast majority having much more income at their disposal than most living in other countries. The poverty level in America for a family of four is currently considered to be a household income of less than $25,100 per year.[10] To many that sounds like poverty, and it would be difficult to imagine having to live on such a low income. But if you make an income right at the poverty line, that would put you in the top 2% for income earnings across the globe.[11] Earning a household income of just a bit more, $33,000 per year, puts you in the top 1% of households for income in the world.[12] Unlike many areas around the globe, most Americans don't have to give running water, heat in cold seasons, air-conditioning in hot seasons or even employment opportunities a second thought. These amenities are just there and available and have been for our entire lives. So yes, life is good here in America, and the opportunity in this country is unmatched.

Despite the opportunities at our fingertips, given our well above-average income levels compared to other nations, one would think most would be able to prepare themselves for emergencies and secure a comfortable retirement with relative ease...yet so few in our country do. It bears repeating that *78% of the households in the United States are living paycheck to paycheck*. When we live that way, months turn into years and the stress and burden of our finances continues to grow.

4

Tunnel Vision

Due to their high speed, acceleration and maneuverability, fighter planes subject their pilot to significant gravitational forces, called g-forces, or g's for short. Before new pilots step foot into their assigned fighter aircraft, all must complete g-force training in a machine called the centrifuge. The human centrifuge is a machine that spins a long mechanical arm around in a circle, with a pilot strapped into an enclosed cockpit at the end of the arm. This contraption, dreaded by all who are subjected to it, simulates the high g-forces that a pilot will experience when turning a fighter jet at high speeds, plus what feels like a few more g's for good measure.

For those that have seen the 1980's movie Spies Like Us, starring Dan Aykroyd and Chevy Chase, you have a good visual of what the centrifuge is and what it subjects the human body to. If you haven't seen it (and don't even know who either of those actors are), take a minute to do a quick online search for a centrifuge video – very entertaining.

The experience is not nearly as entertaining for the pilots going through it. Each g multiplies the weight of your body, making a person weighing 200 pounds at 7.5g feel as if their body weighs 1500 pounds. An added bonus is the ability to envision what your face would look like at 100 years old!

Author's Centrifuge Pics (Left at 1g, Right at 7.5g)

Those selected to fly the F-16 had the unique privilege of completing the highest centrifuge profile at 9-g. One of my classmates, who will remain unnamed, picked up the nickname "Old Man" for obvious reasons – instant classic!

"Old Man" Centrifuge Pics (Left at 1g, Right at 7.5g)

The machine spins you around at what feels like warp speed, pulling the blood from your head down into your legs due to the g-forces. Another result of enduring what could easily be classified as a torture device is thousands of burst capillaries in the skin, causing what looks like bright red freckles all over the body. Affectionately known as Geasles, like measles but with a G, these remain as the proof of enduring an experience that literally leaves a mark. But like it or not, it's a necessary evil on the path to becoming a fighter pilot. The purpose of this centrifuge training is to ensure a pilot, when trained on countering the g-forces with proper breathing and muscle contractions, will not lose consciousness while flying their new aircraft that is capable of pulling a similar level of g-force.

One of the primary indicators to the pilot that the g's are increasing, aside from feeling as if bearing the weight of a sumo wrestler, are drastic changes to their vision. As the forces increase, circulation and oxygen flow to the brain is reduced. One of the first senses to go is your vision. The impact to one's vision is usually not instantaneous, but rather in decrements. A pilot starts at 1-g, just as you are experiencing as you sit and read this book, with full color acuity and a field of view extending out to the sides of wherever you are looking. As the g-forces increase, the first symptom is the loss of color vision, referred to as grey-out. Next, your field of view starts to narrow. This phenomenon is called tunnel vision, as it mimics a closing tunnel of vision, from the outside in.

First, you lose your peripheral vision, then the tunnel continues to close more and more, until you feel like you're looking through a soda straw. The soda straw stage of tunnel vision is usually the last thing a pilot remembers if they don't either decrease the g-forces or properly strain their body to counter the g-forces. The potential result is a complete g-induced loss of consciousness (G-LoC, pronounced "G-lock"), which completely incapacitates the pilot. Losing consciousness while flying a high-performance fighter aircraft can have grave impacts, often leading to the loss of the pilot and aircraft when the ground is impacted. (Thankfully many of the newer high-performance aircraft in our military's inventory now have an automatic ground collision avoidance system, which maneuvers the jet away from the ground until the pilot regains consciousness.)

For many of us, we go through a similar type of experience as the centrifuge when it comes to our finances. After reaching adulthood and entering the workforce, we are fired up and feel as if nothing can stop us, with a world of financial possibilities in front of us. We have full color vision and our future looks and feels very bright. As we begin to tack on school loans, then car loans, followed by some credit card debt, our vision begins to grey and the world of possibilities of our newfound income doesn't seem as promising as it once did. Based upon what we hear and observe from others throughout our culture, most accept that this is just the way life is going to be, with monthly debt payments weighing on our shoulders. Hopes of financial grandeur and independence begin to fade.

Before long, we have added on a home loan and possibly a personal loan or medical debt, continuing to walk a tightrope with our finances as we balance an increasing amount of credit card debt to boot. The stress and strain of our bills weighs on us more and more, and we lose our sense of hope and any clear vision for our financial future. Before we know it, much of our vision and financial promise is blacked out, disappearing in a closing funnel. We become focused on only the past and present, juggling our payments each month, living paycheck to paycheck. Our sights are lowered and just getting by from month to month becomes the name of the game. The weight of the payments and debt get heavier and heavier, and slowly our vision for a great financial future completely disappears. Looking through a soda straw, we aim to make it through one month at a time. For some in more dire situations, it can also feel like we're breathing through a soda straw when the money runs out and bills stack up. Our finances bear down on us, frustrate us, dragging down our attitude at work and in our relationships. If nothing is changed with our habits and behaviors, the g-forces of debt become even more grave, often leading to a financial G-LoC in the form of a home foreclosure, bankruptcy or divorce.

We have lost our financial vision as a society. Without the benefit of full-color financial vision, we eventually lose our desire to fly and will to fight, with most accepting that living paycheck to paycheck is just how it's going to be. Many simply become accustomed to living in a gray financial world with our vision tunneled down to only making it through today and paying for yesterday. For the vast majority, it's been so long since living without the weight of debt that we can't even remember the freeing feeling of having none. In the flying world, we are taught that when we lose sight, we will lose the fight. That's where most find themselves financially. Without full sight and vision, we lose hope and ultimately lose the fight.

How in the world did we get here? We have established that most Americans, including our servicemembers, are very well trained and squared away in the workplace. We are well-educated, trained and qualified in our occupations, by and large "Mission Ready" in our jobs. We have mission focus and are disciplined with spending company dollars per the budget, a plan some of you may have even helped build. Most are also doing well in terms of income, by far in the very top percentages for income across the entire globe.

We have an incredible military force, trained and equipped to protect and defend our freedoms. Yet even such a disciplined group is flailing when it comes to handling money. 56% of enlisted military members, who make up the majority of our armed forces, report having difficulty with their finances, and 47%, nearly half, say they are "in over their head" with their expenses.[1] Financial management issues account for approximately 80% of the Department of Defense's security clearance revocations, resulting in involuntary separations that cost us upwards of half a billion dollars each year.[2,3]

As a country overall, how can such an educated, trained, employed and overall rich population be so stressed about finances? Why can't most cover basic emergencies without relying on the use of credit? And why do most households in this country live paycheck to paycheck then end up retiring essentially broke? The answer lies in not implementing the same principles that make us so successful in the workplace or any other area of our lives in which we achieve success.

My hope is that I have stirred up some emotions in you, especially frustration. If so, you stand a fighting chance. We tend to change areas of our lives when we get our eyes opened, get fired up and commit to learning new ways to improve our lives instead of accepting status quo. The choice is yours, and yours alone. Will you become bitter, or instead set your aim on doing better?

"Don't make excuses... make progress!"
- Chris Hogan

5

Yeah, But...

You may be inclined to stop reading, convincing yourself that while the hot air balloon and tunnel vision are interesting analogies, you have better things to do. Perhaps you are being persuaded from continuing due to a "yeah, but" getting in the way. Is your "but" that you don't have the time to continue reading? As a financial coach with the opportunity to work with and guide hundreds of couples and singles, let me be very clear...you can't afford not to! If not now, when?

If too prideful to take a hard look at yourself and your financial habits, what price will choosing not to swallow your pride cost you? And are you willing to accept that cost rather than looking yourself in the mirror and face reality? You get to decide.

If you are in your 50's or 60's, don't be discouraged. Better that you learn to do better now, rather than 10 or 20 years from now. As long as you are alive and here on this earth, it's never too late to make positive changes in your life. Even if you have 10 years or less until you plan to retire, the decisions you make starting today can drastically alter the quality of your retirement and the legacy that you leave for your kids and grandkids.

If you are at the opposite end of the spectrum, just starting out into adulthood, fantastic! Consider yourself very fortunate to have the power of time on your side with many working years ahead. But if you have convinced yourself that you don't have to worry about long-term financial goals until later on in life, I would challenge you to talk with a few people in their 40s, 50s, or even mid to late 30s. Ask them if you have plenty of time on your side before starting to think about financial wisdom and planning. Whether they have struggled or succeeded with money, odds are off the charts that they will all tell you to **start today**! Getting your financial habits and muscles tuned now, no matter your age, will pay huge dividends down the road thanks to the financial gift called compounding interest. Starting early will actually allow you to live more now and later with your family, enjoying a more comfortable and less stressful lifestyle. The bottom line is that all any of us have, financially speaking and in many other regards, is today. Your choices today will significantly change your tomorrow. The earlier you start, the less off course in the wrong direction you will drift, and the more choices you will have.

Many convince themselves that the plate balancing act is worth it, as they would much rather enjoy living in the here and now versus having a bunch of money in retirement. We want to have nice things and enjoy the years that our kids are at home. Tomorrow is no guarantee anyway, right? Been there myself, prioritizing today over the future, justifying irresponsible spending for the sake of the family, unwilling to make sacrifices needed to set ourselves up for the future. The problem with this approach is that we can't help but think of the future from time to time, which brings with it the stress of feeling ill-prepared for retirement. As great as taking a nice vacation or a big purchase may look on paper, it often plants a seed of doubt that manifests itself as stress and a fear of the future. Despite most living with this seemingly easy-going mantra, two out of every three Americans have worries of not having enough saved for their retirements.[1] To try to quell these feelings, this crowd likely falls back on one of two "plans," either counting on Social Security to provide for retirement needs, or accepting that they will just work and earn an income until death. Both arguments are faulty at best.

Social Security is run by the same government that is $22 trillion in debt and is a program that lost money in 2018, for the first time in nearly forty years, paying out more than it brought in.[2] Even if it is still around when you retire, will that paycheck really provide for a desirable lifestyle in your golden years? The average Social Security check paid out in 2018 was just $1408 per month, totaling less than $17,000 for the year.[3] After having little to show for forty to fifty years of working, it is beyond rare to meet anyone "living the dream" on Social Security alone. Instead, the financial stress follows us, and for many gets even worse once the income from work stops, impacting health and overall happiness in retirement. I would challenge those with this plan to ask family or friends in that stage of life if living on Social Security is all it's cracked up to be, or if they have financial regrets of not preparing better.

How about the plan to just work into your elderly years? First off, if you are brutally honest with yourself, does that really sound like an enjoyable way to spend your days in your 70s and 80s? Not so much. Also, and more importantly, what if you simply cannot work as long as you think you would like to? A recent study found that 6 out of every 10 adults have to stop working unexpectedly and are forced to retire early.[4] For most, the choice of when to end their working career is a decision that is dictated versus one that is decided upon.

Others may believe that their situation is different, too deep in debt to escape, or have convinced themselves that living paycheck to paycheck is just how life is going to be. To you I would say, anyone can win financially and the only reason it must stay this way is if you don't choose to change it! Don't fall for the discouraged feeling that everyone else around you is doing great and it's just you with the problem. Remember, eight out of ten of the households on your street are very likely in the same boat, or worse. Beyond living paycheck to paycheck, another recent study found that 80% of Americans between the ages of 30 and 54 didn't believe they would have enough saved for retirement.[5] So don't buy into the façade that culturally we are great at putting on.

Some of you have read along to this point but along the way have convinced yourselves that your financial situation isn't that bad. You're doing ok...good enough to get by. You've got some savings, even a little put away towards retirement, and are doing just fine thank you very much. If you can relate, you are in the majority. Although nearly 80% are living paycheck to paycheck, more than 70% feel that they are doing "ok," accepting that ok is good enough.[6] If you can relate, I would challenge you to ask yourself, is good enough really what I'm aiming for? As the author Jim Collins quipped, "Good is the enemy of great."[7] Very seldom does doing 'good enough' turn into great results. Any great accomplishment in your life was likely the result of hard work and effort on your part. Also, what you think may be ok is probably not setting you up nearly as well for your long-term outlook as you might think.

We generally reap what we sow in all aspects of our lives. Your financial outlook is no different. Good enough shouldn't cut it with your employer, and certainly not for our nation's military. Although we may not look at it through the same lens, as your lives are not physically on the line, the same can be said with our finances and your quality of life. We can either end up on the winning side by being trained, focused and disciplined with clear objectives, or find ourselves on the losing side, reliant on the government to provide, a potential burden to family members, or find ourselves working well into our 60's or 70's without any other options. 'Good enough' or 'getting by' is likely where most Americans would say they are financially....is that where you are? If so, where has your 'good enough' approach taken you to this point and is that where you want to stay? Or do you want to do better?

Many will remain convinced that their financial woes are due to income, and that the solution is simply bringing home more income (as I did for many years!). Unfortunately, as I learned the hard way personally, see as a coach all the time, and is proven year after year by millions, your habits are most likely to remain the same even when your income increases. If you spend all that you earn making $50,000 a year, odds are very high that you would do the same were you to make $100,000 per year.

Take a minute to think back upon the pay raises that you have received as an adult. Unfortunately, our pay increases very rarely look as steep as they did when entering the workforce, or as the example above of going from $50,000 to $100,000. More often, the increases are incremental…a few thousand more here and there, maybe a $10,000 raise or job change if we're lucky.

In the military, I knew when I was getting each pay raise, typically months prior to the effective date. Just about every time, I would have a moment where my financial vision opened back up and seemed bright and colorful once again. I would have great intentions to use the bump in pay to finally get serious about saving more and investing more. Yet way more times than not, it didn't happen. Instead, we found other things we could do with that increase. We could finally afford this or that payment, or go on a great vacation, or buy that perfect house…the list goes on with no shortage of possibilities. Before we knew it, our salary had doubled, then tripled, but we still found ourselves essentially living paycheck to paycheck.

How about you? Have you put all, or even most, of your bumps in pay towards more saving and investing? Or can you relate to my knucklehead experiences with income raises? If so, please learn from my example and those of the hundreds of clients that I meet with each year: income is not your primary problem!

Now some good news. Regardless of what emotions you may be experiencing right now, I'm here to tell you that there is hope. **Regardless of your present circumstances with your personal finances, and regardless of your current income level, you can, without a doubt, DO BETTER and achieve financial freedom.** While you can't go back and change the past, today is the day that you can take charge of your finances and forever change your future path. As author Carl Bard stated, "though no one can go back and make a brand-new start, anyone can start from now and make a brand-new ending."[8] For those waiting on their circumstances to improve or their income to increase, you have to replace your "when, then" attitude with a NOW mentality. It's time to ditch the excuses, take responsibility for your personal finances, regain control of your income, reclaim your financial vision, and become Mission Ready on the homefront!

Life simply doesn't have to be like this any longer. Better is possible, and achievable, regardless of where you stand today. Financial stress doesn't have to remain on your shoulders any longer, if you make the tough decisions to try a new way. The decision is yours, and the ball is in your court. Once you experience the feeling of freedom from debt and financial stress, your financial vision will return, and you will never want to revert back to your old habits again. You may not be able to envision the feeling right now but trust me when I say that you can and will feel free once again. If you won't take my word, take it from the millions of others before you that have come to know true financial peace.

So, stop floating along in your balloon and instead choose to take charge of your course, today. The first step is awareness of the issue, which I am hopeful you now have. Now we need to turn awareness into action.

Are you in?

"Excellence is the gradual result of always striving to do better."
- Pat Riley

DO BETTER

6

Aim High

Regardless of where you stand today with your finances, you can do better. Whether you have no debt, are up to your eyeballs in debt, are in your 20s, 30s, 40s, 50s, 60s, have savings, don't have savings, or even feel you are doing 'ok,' you can do better than you are right now. With the right outlook and training, a brighter financial future is possible. In fact, unless you are living under the poverty level, you have no excuse to not achieve financial independence and be in a position to retire very comfortably. In a culture that often places blames on others or unforeseen circumstance, the bad news, for some, is that no one is going to rescue you...it's up to you. But if you consider that you are the only one that you can truly control, the good news is that it's up to you!

You probably aren't hearing anything that you didn't already know when it comes to the fact that we could all be doing better. Odds are high that you have come face to face with that realization already with your financial standing. You may have even vowed to yourself to do better from here on out. But the reality is that without a plan and intentional path forward, it is highly unlikely that any attempts to improve will take root. We see this all the time with New Years' resolutions and folks' desire to drop some weight. If the plan only goes as far as going to the gym a few times a week from here on out, any goal, in terms of weight loss, is rarely met. By late February the gyms are emptied back out. It's not that we don't have great intentions and goals, but rather often lack the right mindset, specific objectives and a detailed plan to get there. To do better with our financial standing and outlook, we need more than just a desire to improve.

Before we get into the actionable steps to help you to do better, let's start out at the 50,000-foot strategic level and then work our way down, using an example near and dear to my heart.

The motto of our Air Force is "Aim High…Fly-Fight-Win." This is a great motto for our personal finances as well. How in the world could our Air Force's motto tie into succeeding with money, you may ask? Let me explain.

Our journey to financial freedom must first be aimed at something. As author and motivational speaker Zig Ziglar says, "If you aim at nothing, you'll hit it every time."[1] We certainly don't want to hit 'nothing' financially. We have to be intentional and have goals, something to focus on and strive for…a target. You will need to decide your personal financial goals, which we will be getting more into in a bit. Whatever those goals may be, "aim high" when you set them! Very few, if any, end up achieving greater success than what they have set their sights on. Have you found this to be the case in life as well? Or have been surprised when achieving success, wondering how you got there? We achieve in life that which we aim for, remain focused on, and work hard to make a reality.

You have to start by aiming high at the financial destination that you want to achieve, knowing that "winning" financially means reaching that destination. Continuously aim higher and higher, never accepting second best. So how do you ensure that you get there?

Just as with our Air Force motto, the rubber meets the road on our finances with the "Fly" and "Fight." Without the flying and fighting, the goals that we aim high for will never be achieved.

How in the world does one fly and fight with their finances? The way we fly and fight on our financial journey is by having focus and an intentional plan and then executing the plan.

Learning to fly has to come first. Pilots go through years of training to learn how to safely operate an airplane. If the proper training isn't completed, it may very well lead to a catastrophic incident. The same can be said with our finances. Without the proper training, our finances are doomed, and we stand very little chance of meeting our goals. The aim of this book is exactly that, offering the training tools to help you do better.

After being trained to fly, a pilot wouldn't be of much utility if they didn't actually fly. We don't train for the benefit of just learning, but rather with the intention to use our training to push up the power, lift off and fly on our journey. Once you get trained, you must create a flight plan for your journey, utilizing the lessons passed along in training, then pull the chocks, taxi to the runway, push up the throttles and take your plane airborne. If you get trained up but never taxi and takeoff, you will continue to be stuck, coasting along with the winds of our society, forever floating along in your hot-air balloon, and have very little chance of landing at your intended destination! Once trained, you have to use and apply your training and fly your airplane.

Once we takeoff and get airborne, flying has to remain an intentional activity. Intended to reduce workload, all modern aircraft are equipped with an autopilot. This function utilizes onboard computers to maintain the pitch, roll, altitude and airspeed for the pilot. When on autopilot, the person at the controls can sit back and let the jet fly itself. While considered a modern convenience, the autopilot is hands down the least used function in a combat jet. Successful fighter pilots remain on the controls, always ready to maneuver their aircraft to attack, defend and accomplish the mission. Intentionality wins the day.

Those that stay engaged and intentional are those that win financially as well. We don't want to float along or cruise on autopilot. If you do, by the time you realize you were getting off course, it will become more and more difficult to meet your objectives and successfully complete your financial mission. Once you get airborne, you need to continue to fly the aircraft!

The next word of the AF motto after "fly" is "fight." If a pilot gets trained up and takes off on a mission towards their intended destination, but can't fight their way smartly through the battle, he or she is destined to get shot down. Mission objectives not met equals mission failure. Learning to be successful in a combat scenario is typically the last phase before a fighter pilot is deemed Mission Ready. Tactical flying builds upon basic airmanship, teaching pilots how to fight their way in, meet their objectives, and then fight their way back out.

How does fighting in combat relates to your finances? Make no mistake, your financial journey is, and will continue to be, a battle. Once we takeoff on our financial journey, focused on safely landing at our intended destination, we will meet many threats along the way. One of those threats comes from living in the most marketed-to culture in the world. You are hit up by endless of marketers over your lifetime, many of whom spend millions upon millions of dollars to get you to buy their product or service. Advertising is aimed at making you believe that you need, and can't live without, whatever it is they are selling.

In addition to being bombarded by advertisements for ways to spend income, another threat is cultural pressure. There is a perceived sense from others that you should live and experience the same issues and pressures as everyone else does. Those that think or act differently, to include financially, are often ostracized and mocked. Few are willing to stick their neck out and be different from the crowd. Much easier to just go with the flow. But it's definitely not in our best interests to conform financially.

We can also be our own worst enemy to our financial freedom. If we aren't intentional with our income or lose focus of our financial goals, we will always find other ways to spend our income that take us farther away from our goals rather than closer to them. We have to remain cautious of what we accept as truth. The illusion of knowledge is a major threat, and one that we ultimately must control by seeking proven wisdom versus theories.

Another real threat to our financial flight through life are emergencies. Regardless of how much we plan, life is going to throw us some curveballs that we weren't expecting. The good news is that just because we may not see specific emergencies coming, if we're smart, we know they will come and therefore can prepare ourselves for when they do.

When you are properly trained, have a flight plan with objectives, acknowledge and understand your threats, and are able to overcome them with diligence and perseverance, you will win. You may ask, what will winning look like and how do I know when I've arrived? Winning is touching down at your destination of choice, of which there are many to choose from, at the arrival time of your choosing. The sooner in life you start doing better with your finances, the more destinations you will have to choose from and the sooner you will get there. But the time to learn where we will land, financially, isn't upon arrival.

Just as a passenger plane doesn't takeoff, fly around aimlessly and then land when a runway is spotted, that can't be our financial plan. That would make us a balloon, and we don't want to be a balloon. All the effort we put in to prepare and execute must be done with purpose, by putting the end goal in mind first. Although it's the end result, and last word of the Air Force motto, "win" must come first and drive our plan, tying back to the target we aimed at from the beginning. Otherwise, without knowing what winning will look like, how do you know when you've arrived? We know we've won by making our destination the driver to our flight plan before ever taxiing and taking off.

Aim higher, take your jet airborne and fly, fight through obstacles and then win, achieving your financial goals. That is our big picture game plan for financial success at the 50,000-foot strategic level.

"Everyone wants to be a beast…
until it comes time to do what beasts do."
- JJ Watt

7

Thrust, Vector and a Plan

Now let's take it down to the 20,000-foot operational level and get further into the goal of this book…showing you how to *do better* with your finances. We know that simply wishing or hoping for better won't move the needle. Notice that I also didn't say "know better," or "think better," or "get better." Knowing or thinking about how to do something without action doesn't make you much better off than not knowing or thinking in the first place. And getting better implies that we will get it from somewhere or someone else. No, I said DO better. We are after ownership and action… learning and then actually applying the knowledge by **doing**!

Just about everyone wants to build some level of wealth and achieve financial security, peace and success. Everyone wants to be a financial beast…until it comes time to do what financial beasts do. So, if we all want to do better with our finances, and have the ability to do so given our opportunity in this country, why do so few of us achieve a desired level of wealth? As with just about every area of our lives, our failure to achieve results is due to either a lack of thrust, vector or both. Forward thrust and the ability to choose and follow a specific direction, or vector, is what sets an aircraft apart from a balloon. Both fly through the air, but only one can choose a specific destination and navigate to that exact spot. The biggest issue that we have with challenges in our lives is that we stop at just wanting to do better. Without the right mindset and a specific roadmap, with a focused thrust and vector, our efforts fail time and time again.

When I ask clients why they have reached out for coaching, almost every answer I get boils down to the fact that they want to do better. They may not know exactly where they want to go, but often know where they don't want to end up…broke like a parent or family friend that they may know. By reaching out, just like you choosing to read this book, they are taking the desire to do better to the next step of actually learning how.

The three primary obstacles that I see with clients that are struggling to do better with their finances are a lack of vision, a lack of belief and lack of a plan. Vision of where you want to go provides you thrust, motivating you, and a vector for direction. Believing that better is possible is also critical to generating and thrust and sustaining your momentum. Lack of belief acts as drag, the counter to thrust, and fades any vision we may have. Having a detailed plan and roadmap that will deliver you to your vision provides more clarity to our vector. A plan also helps sustain our thrust, as we become more and more confident when we see a clear path ahead and, once we start, that the plan is actually working and bringing us closer each day to our vision. The excellent news is that all three obstacles can be overcome by you, which means your ultimate success, financially, is in your hands.

Here's our flight plan to build your vision, empowering you with thrust, vector and a plan to ultimately reach your financial goals. This is what it takes to **DO BETTER** by letter.

D – Decide

O – Open your eyes

B – Believe

E – Educate

T – Team and Talk

T – Task income

E – Execute

R – Revisit, Revise and Repeat

That's the DO BETTER acronym broken down in a nutshell. Each letter will provide the necessary thrust, vector, or both, needed to be effective with your finances.

The concepts needed to win with money, ultimately allowing you to be prosperous and generous, are not tricky. They are straight forward, but hard to do correctly and consistently. Recall that we live in a society surrounded by broke people in a broke culture, and at the same time living in the most marketed-to society in the world. **Winning with your money will require discipline and intentionality, and an attitude that being different is a good thing.**

A quick word of caution...

All pilot manuals consist of cautions that, if not strictly observed, will likely result in a loss of mission effectiveness and eventual mission failure. I will be using some of these throughout the book to foot stomp important points. Here's the first.

** CAUTION **

Do not gloss through the first three letters of the DO BETTER acronym, as they provide your thrust. Thrust is critical to your financial flight, required to takeoff, keep you airborne, and bring you the distance.

First, you must get your mind right, as you ultimately go in the direction of your thoughts. Our 'fix things quick' culture has likely trained you to skip right to the actionable steps to follow, the vector, without delaying first to cage your mind. A vector is of no use unless you first have thrust to propel you in that direction, and your thrust comes from within you. Your thrust determines your motivation...it's your ignition and drive. You need enough of it to overcome the weight and drag of your present position. It's not a one and done power boost, but rather a continuous need to maintain your momentum.

You can get cleared to taxi, takeoff and know the exact heading you need to turn to, but you first need thrust. Otherwise you will never get out of the chocks.

Many of the amazing individuals that I meet traveling around the country are intrigued not about my being a financial speaker and coach, but rather my experience in the military. Many share that they had a similar dream of becoming a pilot as a child, but it didn't work out for one reason or another. I've probably heard that story at least a thousand times over the years. It has caused me to reflect on how in the world my dream, one shared by many others, actually became a reality for this kid from a small farm town with no other pilots or military officers in my family.

The odds were certainly not in my favor. The acceptance rate into the Air Force Academy was around 10%, of which approximately 80% of those that entered walked across the stage at graduation four years later. After passing stringent medical physicals and a flight screening program, around 40% within the group of newly commissioned officers were selected to attend pilot training, from which only about 15% became fighter pilots. After all was said and done, of the roughly 12,000 that I was competing with out of high school, only around 60, one half of one percent, became a fighter pilot nearly seven years after the application process first began. I certainly don't think that I was that special growing up as a kid, or much different than any other kid for that matter. Also, without question, I am certain that much of it had to do with higher powers much greater than I. But what allowed me, as an average student and athlete, to achieve what was without doubt a highly sought-after profession? Some of my thrust certainly came from witnessing the precision of airpower in Desert Storm during my junior year in high school. That added fuel to my fire, but it goes back much further than that. I attribute the fact that I was able to become an Air Force officer and fighter pilot to a few key events in my childhood that provided the necessary thrust, vector and, in turn, a plan to execute.

The idea was planted during a 6th grade field trip to a nearby National Guard base. We toured an A-10 squadron, get an up-close look at one of their airplanes, and got to meet and speak with some of their pilots. I was instantly hooked and, along with many of my classmates, convinced that I wanted that job someday. Getting to wear a flight suit, which looked more like pajamas, fly a really cool looking piece of machinery around in the air, all while serving the good ole US of A...what wasn't to like? That event planted the seed...a vision. While the vision was the beginnings of developing thrust and vector, it certainly wasn't uncommon, as many kids visit airshows in their youth, so just having the vision wasn't enough.

When I shared my excitement and career plans with my parents that evening of the field trip, they listened and most importantly to me, didn't balk and tell me that the idea was crazy or unachievable. The fact that they were supportive and encouraging of the idea, and even began to share the dream with other extended family members, helped me start believing that maybe my dream wasn't so crazy and could actually happen. Now I had the beginnings of a vision and some belief that it could actually happen.

Over the next year or two, my oldest brother's college roommate was a cadet in Air Force ROTC and was also hopeful of becoming an Air Force officer and pilot. Talking with him started to provide me with a basic vector of the how I could get there as well. I would have to go to college and get a commission as an officer in the Air Force. He was pursuing an engineering degree, and also mentioned having to be pretty good at math and science to become a pilot, both topics that I liked more than others and I felt I did decent at. Talking with him provided the beginnings of a plan and also reinforced the belief that maybe it was actually possible. If he was on a path to do it, why not me?

Between those three events in middle school, I had the beginnings of a vision, a belief that it could actually be possible and a basic plan on what would be required to get there. Initial thrust and vector - check. That was a great start, but I don't think it would have been enough to get me there were it not for two other defining events that occurred early on in high school.

In ninth grade, I struggled a bit in math, ending up with a C. At the end of the school year, we had to choose our level for 10th grade math. I was a little frustrated by my grade, remembering my brother's roommate comment about needing to be strong in math, and decided to challenge myself by signing up for the advanced math class for my sophomore year. Given the C grade in her class, my ninth-grade math teacher, Mrs. Murphy, pulled me aside after class and said she thought signing up for the advanced math class was a mistake. Her comments could have easily discouraged me and convinced me to switch to the basic class. While her feedback did upset me, it actually had the opposite effect. I wasn't going to let this teacher, who I wasn't a big fan of as a student, tell me that I couldn't do anything, especially knowing that taking the basic level would likely put an end to any goal of becoming a pilot. I don't know if that was her true intent, or if she really thought I couldn't do it given my lackluster performance in her class, but it didn't matter. That event lit something inside of me, increasing my internal drive and providing a greatly needed boost in thrust to get off my behind and kick it into high gear. I became determined to prove her wrong.

Not wanting to give someone else that power over me, or give Mrs. Murphy any possible enjoyment of being right, I buckled down in my sophomore year. After applying more effort, I was able to do fairly well in advanced math. Seeing success in a class that I was discouraged from taking helped me see greater potential, and increased my belief in myself, thereby adding thrust.

The last defining event, that in my mind sealed the deal, took place during that same 10th grade advanced math class but was completely unrelated to the math curriculum. Our teacher, Ms. Lyn Heady, who did a great job pushing us all to do continually do better, assigned us a project to be completed outside of class. She asked us to pick a career, explain why we could see ourselves in that occupation, listing specifics on what the job would entail, and then provide a detailed plan on what it would take to get there. The project forced me to research and develop a clear path, with much greater detail, including interviewing a few people that were currently in that career field. Aside from the generic plan that I had in my mind from my brother's college roommate years ago, I had now gotten educated and had a very specific step by step plan to finally follow. In addition to the ROTC path, I learned about the U.S. Air Force Academy in Colorado, which I found would enable a much higher likelihood of becoming a pilot if I could get in. I also learned about the admission requirements, test scores, GPA, involvement in sports, clubs, leadership and volunteering. Thanks to Ms. Heady's project, I now had a crystal-clear plan to make my vision a reality, with renewed confidence that it was possible and now up to me.

Again, the ability to ultimately attain the goal of becoming a fighter pilot required following the plan, a ton of hard work, a good bit of fortunate timing and a whole lot of divine intervention. But I also believe that were it not for these five events over the five years encompassing 6th through 10th grade, I very likely would have never achieved the goal. Together, these events provided a vision, belief that it could be attained, and a plan to get there. These life-changing moments provided me with thrust and vector, and for that reason I will always be grateful for each (even for Mrs. Murphy!).

My hope is that by following through the DO BETTER framework, you will secure vision, belief and a plan, putting yourself in a position to achieve all of your financial goals for prosperity and generosity. Now let's dive in, "get down in the weeds" at the tactical level, providing actionable steps as we expand upon each portion of the DO BETTER flight plan.

"Our lives are shaped not by our conditions, but by our decisions."
- Tony Robbins

DECIDE

DO

BETTER

*"If you don't change the direction you are going,
then you're likely to end up where you're heading."*
- John C. Maxwell

8

Wounded Bird?

When flying in combat, if a plane's systems malfunction or the jet takes on battle damage after being hit by enemy fire, pilots have criteria to decide whether the jet is airworthy and will allow them to continue to complete an effective mission. If the criteria are not met, this series of questions highlights the need to make a U-turn in the sky and abort the mission.

Can I maintain altitude and climb higher if needed?
Can I maintain airspeed and accelerate if needed?
Can I maintain a commanded attitude?
Are the offensive and defensive systems in order?
Can the objectives of the mission be accomplished?

If the answer to any of these questions is no, flights execute an alternate plan to get the broken or hit aircraft, referred to as a 'wounded bird,' safely back to good guy territory.

In a similar fashion, we need criteria to help us determine if we are on track to execute an effective financial mission. If not, is an alternate strategy necessary in order to stay alive, return to base, thereby allowing us the opportunity to get back on track for being effective on future missions? Since many don't consider themselves as needing to do better, this represents our first hurdle.

The first question that you must ask yourself and decide upon is:

DECISION #1	*Are my current ways working, putting me on a path towards financial freedom?*

Your initial reaction may be to quickly answer "yes." Almost every person that I speak to agrees that most Americans find themselves in a financial mess. But not them personally...they are doing ok and not nearly as bad as most. If you feel that you can generally afford your monthly bills and haven't been faced with foreclosure or bankruptcy, many would see that as doing just fine and not being in need of any major improvements. But does that remain your answer when you really take a close look at where you are with your finances today and ask yourself some tougher and more specific questions? Or could you be doing better?

You may have convinced yourself that all is fine with your finances. We have a tendency to downplay our own ineffectiveness to ourselves. Most remain unwilling to let go of this "all is okay" mentality until having an epiphany as retirement nears. Others reach a breaking point earlier, such as becoming unable to make monthly payments or even facing foreclosure. Only then do many finally admit to themselves that things aren't going well. It's often only when we reach the point of no return or hit rock bottom, facing drastic measures such as declaring bankruptcy, that many of us are willing to raise the flag of defeat.

Many never get to the point of hitting a financial rock bottom, but rather become complacent, becoming comfortable with their circumstances, accepting that this is just the way it's going to be. We remain stuck in a constant loop of just getting by for years and years until finally coming face to face with the realization that retirement is right around the corner, for which we are woefully unprepared.

What grade would you give yourself, today, when it comes to the management of your personal finances? When students get a grade on a test or employees receive an evaluation at work, it is typically defined against a standard. When we had annual evaluations in the military, we were scored on a scale, with each score for each category having a specific definition. Same with physical fitness standards. X performance equates to Y score. Without defined standards, what are we grading ourselves against? For too many of us, we have set a woefully low bar in terms of meeting future financial goals, instead remaining focused on the here and now. What bar have you set for yourself? Drive a nice car and live in a nice house? Be able to cover all payments owed each month? Not go bankrupt? Not get foreclosed on? If that's the standard that you are grading against, most Americans would likely score themselves an "A." But if most of us are at an "A" level of financial performance, why is it the leading cause of our stress and found to be a significant contributing factor, or even causal, for a staggering number of failed marriages and appalling rates of suicide? The bar we have set for ourselves needs a major adjustment because what we're doing is clearly not working. But you need to decide that for yourself.

I challenge you to take a moment to really reflect on some questions that you may not typically let yourself dive into. My hope is that doing so will encourage you to see things differently, allowing you to reverse course before hitting bottom or retiring with nothing to show for a lifetime of hard work.

To make the first decision, challenge yourself to dig deeper by honestly answering the following questions.

Do I ever find myself wondering where all of the income is going each month?

Is my primary financial focus on survival, making it through this month and into the next?

Do I ever find myself running out of money, or worried about running out, before the next paycheck arrives?

Do I ever feel stressed about my level of consumer debt?

Do I ever feel stressed about making the monthly minimum payments on my debts?

Do I feel stuck in my job due to my financial commitments?

Do I worry about not being able to put food on the table or even losing my home or going bankrupt if I were to fall ill or lose my job and have no income for a few months?

Are arguments with my spouse over finances a recurring theme?

Are my spouse and I in agreement when it comes to handling our money?

Do I shy away from thinking about retirement due to the associated stress of not being fully prepared, financially, perhaps with concerns if I will ever be in a position to retire?

How many of the things in my possession do I actually own?

What do I have to show for the hundreds of thousands, or perhaps even millions, of dollars that I have earned throughout my years of working to date?

Do I have clearly defined financial objectives for the next 5, 10, and 20-year points? If so, am I on track to effectively meet my financial objectives?

Do I worry about funding, or being in a position to contribute to, my kids' education?

Is what I'm currently doing today and this month getting me closer to where I want to be?

Where have my financial decisions so far in life taken me?

Could I cover a $1000 emergency today with cash, or would I need to rely on the use of credit?

Do I ever feel stress about not being able to cover a popup emergency?

Is regular saving and investing a consistent part of my monthly financial routine?

Do my bills ever feel overwhelming?

Do I rely on part-time or overtime work to juggle my bills?

Is financial stress having an impact on my relationships and effectiveness in the workplace?

Have I convinced myself that things will change, financially, once I get the next promotion or pay raise? If so, have I convinced myself of this before and not seen change?

Have I convinced myself that saving for retirement is something that I could put off a bit longer?

Do I have a desire to increase generosity and give more but feel that I am not in the financial position to do so?

My hope is that after going through this list of questions, you are now ready to make the critical first step by deciding that your current ways are not working as well as they could be. No matter where you may stand today, I am certain that each of us could use somewhere between a tune-up and a major overhaul. How can I be so sure? First, by the fact that you have chosen to read this book. Second, based upon my experience as a financial coach, I am certain that just about everyone could be doing better. I have seen the full spectrum... from a doctor making $300K a year with no retirement savings, to an aircraft mechanic making a modest salary over his working lifetime yet having over $1M in his retirement account. Regardless of their situation, each decided that they could benefit from a checkup, even the one with a million plus net worth.

If your answer to any of the above questions doesn't match where you would choose to be, is that is acceptable? If not, you must agree that your way isn't proving to be as effective as you would like, and, in turn, decide you could do better. Challenge yourself to not accept that this is just the way life has to be...because it doesn't! Like millions of others before you, you can make a U-turn and bring your wounded bird back to base for repair. After some much needed maintenance, you can get back on track to being effective, where you can confidently answer the appropriate response to every single question posed above.

Any area that we look to improve upon in our lives starts with an acknowledgment that my way isn't working as well as I would like it to. The good news is that you, and you alone, are the answer to doing better financially. The first obstacle that stands between you and financial success is recognition that you've taken some battle damage and have a few systems malfunctioning, leading to a decision to get to a place that enables you to start doing better.

Every time a fighter pilot goes out on a training mission, they know by the return flight back to home base whether that day's flight was a success of not. Every day that things don't go as planned, there is a decision to be made. Did my execution of tactics work for me today? The most successful pilots are those that own the failure and commit to making tomorrow's flight better, then get to work to understand and educate themselves on how they can make that happen. That process of learning and getting better all starts with a decision to own that things could have, and should have, turned out better. Granted, the stakes are high, as their success in training directly translates into their success when called into combat. I would contend that your stakes are high as well, for your financial life, which, whether we like to believe or not, greatly impacts many other aspects of our quality of life during our time here on earth.

Change is difficult. Deciding that our current ways are not taking us in the direction that we want is a great first step. Identifying an area of our lives that could use some attention is half the battle. Those who then decide to do something about it are the ones that ultimately achieve success. This first decide chapter should bring you to declare, "enough is enough already!" If what you have been doing is not good enough, what are you going to decide to do about it?

"Begin with the end in mind."
- Stephen Covey

9

The Stakes Are High

Now that you have made the first decision that your way could be improved, the next critical hurdle is to determine why that's not good enough. Knowing that our ways could be improved and actually taking steps to improve them are two entirely different things. Identifying what is at stake, and what those stakes mean to us and our families, is the difference maker and the crucial start of taking us from knowing to doing.

In his book, *Start with Why*, author Simon Sinek highlights the importance of knowing your "why." What's the purpose of doing better? Behavior change is no picnic, requiring sacrifice and discipline, and therefore something we will be unlikely to sustain without a good reason to do so. Doing better financially is similar to losing weight...many want to do it, but few are successful in losing and keeping the weight off until they have identified a strong "why." Perhaps it's a health scare, or not being able to play with kids without getting winded. One thing is for sure, the why has to be important to you, not something you are doing for someone else.

Having a clearly defined financial "why" is a fundamental tenet to long-term success with money. Unfortunately, most gloss over this decision, focusing more on what to do and possibly, for some, how to do it. Of the three pieces, the what, the how and the why, the part we tend to focus on is the "what." This isn't only the case with our finances, but just about any challenge we are looking to overcome. Just tell me what to do, and I'll do it. That works great for short easy-to-fix problems, like fixing a leaky faucet or fixing a flat tire. But primarily focusing on the "what" with long-term challenges, like our finances, requires much more. In fact, when it comes to doing better with our finances, most of us already have a good idea of what we need to be doing – saving and investing more, spending less, getting on a budget, having an emergency fund, paying off debt, saving for kids' college, etc. The problem is that despite knowing, very few actually do those things consistently. Part of the problem is not having a high level of insight on "how" to best do those things. The how is very important, not only to our effectiveness but also to sustaining long-term thrust. If the "how" is painful or we don't start seeing results, that can deflate our efforts as well. But, again, even if we learn the most effective ways "how" to do better, the odds of us actually doing them long-term without a strong "why" are very low.

When I serve as a financial coach for a client, my end goals are to get them to #1 take action and #2 sustain those actions over the long-term. To that end, starting with, and putting a large emphasis on the "why" piece produces the greatest effects for those looking to do better. Your "why" is infinitely important to your financial success. In fact, I would contend that your "why" is hands-down the most important of the three areas. It ignites your fire and serves as the core source of your thrust to do better over the long-term, propelling you around, over or through any roadblocks that arise in your financial journey. Consistently and effectively executing the "what" and "how" are all about having a strong "why." This concept applies to every area of our life that we would like to improve.

Take getting into shape for example. Many set New Years' resolutions to lose weight. We generally know what we need to do in order to accomplish that goal...burn more than we take in. Some may even take it a step further and have their "how" worked out...workout five mornings per week, limit daily calories to a certain amount and then lose a set number of pounds by a certain date. But even with a good idea of what we need to do, and some level of detail on how, most gyms are much less busy by the time Valentine's Day rolls around. What happened? Most don't have a compelling "why" that fires them up and invokes the discipline to keep going. Just wanting to lose weight without a great reason is too weak for most to keep going.

Compare that to an overweight patient who is told that they will likely have a heart attack within six months if they don't lose fifty pounds. Talk about a compelling "why!" If that doesn't provide enough motivation to embrace a much healthier lifestyle, there is likely nothing that will. For many looking to do better with their finances, the problem is no different. We all generally know what we need to do...get out of debt, quit spending so much on junk, etc. Yet most aren't doing it. Some don't know how to best go about doing these things, but the true driver is not having a strong reason. It's not until we can't meet monthly bills or put food on the table that most will finally reach out for help. They finally developed a compelling "why" – to put food on the table and not be taken to court by those that they owe debts to. Does it really take being on the brink of financial ruin to finally build up a strong "why?" For far too many, that is often the case. My goal is to get you to develop a strong why BEFORE putting yourself into a financial corner.

Having multiple "why's" is even better and more powerful. I have found that for myself, and many others, having a "why" that is bigger than you alone is especially helpful in keeping up our thrust. A strong "why" is usually not a physical thing or a quantity of money either...it's much bigger than that.

For those of us with kiddos, we often fall for the trap that providing well for them equates to providing them with more stuff.

Despite things they may ask for, what they really want is you! Stuff will come and go, but what they will remember is the times spent with you, times when you encouraged them, made them feel like you were their biggest fan and were their rock. What are your best memories from childhood? You may have fond memories of a receiving a long-awaited toy or a fun family vacation, but my guess is that the majority of your best childhood memories are those where someone made you feel loved, special in their eye and capable of anything. Think about that before deciding your "why" for your family. More than anything else available on this earth, they treasure you!

That brings us to our next decision:

DECISION #2	*What's my financial "why?" Why <u>must</u> I do better and what's at stake if I don't?*

Here are a few ideas to get you started on some potential "why's":
- An overall lower level of stress and worry?
- Improved health and wellness due to having less stress?
- A better marriage, with improved communication?
- The security of being a more consistent provider for your family, both in the short-term and long-term?
- Being more available to your family and a better parent when carrying less stress from month to month?
- More effective in the workplace and in your career?
- Having the opportunity to change jobs or careers to follow a dream and do something that you are actually excited to do?
- Not being forced to work late in life unless choosing to do so?
- For those serving in the military, no risk of losing clearance?
- For all of our nation's defenders, being more effective and better situated to address and tackle the other unique stresses that come with the dangers of my occupation?
- Having a comfortable retirement without relying on Social Security or our government in general?
- Able to give more generously to causes near and dear to me?

- The ability to have more of a positive impact in the lives of others, through donations of both time and money?

Another way to tackle the "why" question is to propel yourself into the future. Picture yourself with no debt payments, including a paid off house, with a large emergency fund balance in the bank and a significant balance in your investment account. Breathe that in for a minute or two...how would that feel? What issues do you feel melt away? How would that change your relationships...your marriage or your ability to parent better? How about your job...would you choose to stay in the same job if you were in that position? If not, what would you choose to do? What causes would you choose to support if you were in that position and how would that generosity make you feel and change your level of gratitude?

Don't skip ahead until you have really given your "why" a significant amount of thought and written it down! It's not just about reaching financial independence, a certain age or a specific amount of wealth, but rather the "why" behind it. What would achieving this mean to you and what would it allow you to do? If you are married, I highly recommend discussing your "why" with your spouse. If single, share your "why" with a trusted parent, friend or mentor.

** CAUTION **

Failing to identify a highly personalized and motivating "why" will very likely limit your long-term effectiveness, regardless of any other financial principles that you learn.

Identifying your "why" will mean everything to your long-term-term success. Without a strong "why," the draw of spending today will always prevail over saving and adequately preparing for your future. A weak "why" will result in weak thrust, which results in minimal heights attained, or not even getting up into the air at all. The stronger your why, the greater your thrust, and the greater your determination and focus will become. A strong why is what makes the difference for many of those that I coach. It's what fuels the discipline. This is often the catalyst that drives the success of the many that I have had the privilege of meeting with very average incomes...schoolteachers, aircraft mechanics and plumbers that I have coached that are on track to reach their goals. The lack of a long-term why is the same explanation that many of those with very high incomes have almost nothing to show for it in terms of savings and investments. Instead, they find themselves on the fast track to retiring broke and having to work well into their 60s and 70s in order to maintain the high standard of living that has become their focus.

Take some time to think about and write down your "why" in Appendix A. Remain fully aware that whether we like it or not, our financial standing touches every part of our personal and professional lives. The answer is different for everyone and must be yours and yours alone.

Results demand action and, for most, applying new and improved principles in our lives. But change is no fun. It requires focused discipline over a long period of time. As author Andy Andrews says, "Self-discipline is the ability to make yourself do something you don't necessarily want to do, to get a result that you would really like to have." When life gets tough and you start to feel a lack of traction, your "why" is the driver to not turn around and abort your mission. Quitting will no longer be an option when you know what is at stake.

10

Objectives

Combat operations won't be found on any list of life experiences that I would recommend to anyone. Speaking from firsthand knowledge, whether from the air sitting inside a jet or on the ground stuck inside of a Humvee, war is brutal. While I can state with absolute certainty that our nation's services are more prepared than any other fighting force in the world, that doesn't take away from the fact that war is no picnic. Combat operations are intense and can drag on, seeming like they will never end. When added with a lack of sleep, it is easy to start feeling as if living in a fog. When operations start getting dicey, or going differently than planned, staying on task can become a challenge. In the fog, friction and chaos of battle, how in the world do commanders keep their people focused and efforts aligned, day in and day out, in situations that our instinct may be to turn away from instead of running towards? Leadership, training and flat out discipline are certainly important aspects of staying the course, as well attributes needed for financial success as well.

Another critical tenet of any military operation is having clearly defined objectives. From the top down, successful campaigns stay focused on the overall strategic objective which ultimately achieves the "why" of the entire operation. Below the strategic level, there are operational level objectives, followed by tactical level objectives that provide unity of effort for every servicemember on the battlefield. Achieving tactical objectives leads to operational objectives being met, which leads to the strategic objectives being accomplished, achieving the overall "why." When things go haywire, objectives provide the purpose and focus for sustaining every individual component of the combat operation. In the most successful campaigns, each member understands what is ultimately at stake and how their achievement of tactical objectives adds to the likelihood of overall mission accomplishment.

Could you imagine boarding a commercial flight without any specific destination in mind? The pilot announces on the intercom… "morning, folks…we don't really have a specific destination in mind today, so we're going to take it airborne and see where we end up." Is that a flight you would be willing to board? I'm guessing most would hear that announcement, unbuckle and get off that plane! But that is exactly what most of us are doing, day in and day out spending more hours at work than anywhere else, away from our families, with no clear destinations in mind. Any flight we board serves a purpose to bring us to a specific desired location, whether it be for our job, going on a vacation or visiting family. Having a similar specific purpose with deliberate destinations for our financial flight is no different. We have to have objectives, or we aren't going to like where we end up. The purpose of the flight of any military jet or commercial airplane is not to fly around and burn up a bunch of jet fuel…but rather to achieve an objective bringing us somewhere very specific. These goals give us our much-needed direction of where we need to head as well as the unique destinations, so we know when we have arrived.

If we can't tie today's mission objectives back to a strong and compelling "why," our motivation isn't there which means we are much less likely to prevail. But if we can see how it all ties back to achieving our ultimate goals, we become a force to be reckoned with!

Life often becomes a daily grind, throwing us random curveballs from time to time. It can be easy to get bogged down and forget where we are headed. To do better with your finances, you will need to shift your focus from getting by today to aiming high for tomorrow. What was your overall campaign objective...your "why" from last chapter? In order to achieve that why, we need to identify what really fulfills us, and then identify our short, mid and long-term goals and objectives that put us on the path of making our "why" a reality.

Before attacking your goals, it's important to stop and take a hard look at what brings you true fulfillment. Looking back at whatever you chose to spend your last paycheck on, or the last year of paychecks, where did you choose to spend your money and which of those items or experiences do you still consider worth the cost? Which really scratched your long-term itch, bringing you true fulfillment? When we really take a close look, many often find that most of their material possessions really didn't bring the long-term happiness as expected. Instead, it's our quality time with loved ones, life experiences and times that we were able to come to someone's aid that we hold the fondest memories of.

Looking forward, will that next newer and fancier car, or larger house, really fill you up and be worthy of the hit to your wallet? Often what we think will fulfill us ends up being short-lived. Yet we spend our 20s and 30s chasing goals that we may ultimately find didn't really do much for us, which can be quite the letdown as we arrive into our 40s and 50s carrying regrets. So, take a few minutes to think back on moments, events or purchases that fulfilled you for a long period of time. Challenge yourself to avoid setting goals that don't have a history of bringing you contentment and fulfillment, less you reach your later years of adult life feeling as if you have been chasing the wrong objectives all along.

Back to setting objectives. We all need short, mid and long-term financial goals. Doing so unifies our efforts, keeps us focused on the big picture and reminds us of what's at stake if we don't follow through. Goals serve as a vision, providing a constant reminder that impacts our daily decisions. Without raising our sights to clearly defined objectives, our focus is destined to remain in the here and now, which leads us to make decisions that serve us well today, but likely not over the long-term. And when that is the case, our odds of winning long-term financially diminish to just about zero. Sure, there's always that one in a billion chance of winning the lottery or perhaps inheriting a large sum from a wealthy relative, but do you really want to put your long-term financial health in opportunities that carry ridiculously low odds? No, you want to take control of your own financial destiny, which is very likely to increase your odds of winning to 100%.

Yes, living in the here and now is important, but the decisions you make each and every day will have a direct impact on your financial health for years to come. As author and motivational speaker Zig Ziglar says, "if you aim at nothing, you will hit it every time." Again, you're not going to wake up one day with a magical pot of gold in your investment account. Wealth is created by sustained focus on a vision of where we want to get to and then executed over time by taking one step, one paycheck at a time. So, we need objectives that focus our aim, and as with all goals, the more specific, the better! And if we are going to aim at something, let's aim high!

Each goal needs to be uniquely yours, versus what others think your goals should be, and, most importantly, tie back to one of your "why's." For example, a short-term goal to build up an emergency fund that covers between 3-6 months of living expenses, so that I am less stressed about being able to provide for my family in the event of a job loss or a large unexpected pop-up expense. The goal of having a solid emergency fund ties back to being in a stronger and more secure position to provide for my family, achieving my "why" of having less overall financial stress, thereby benefiting my overall health, relationships and performance in the workplace.

What are your goals for the short-term, over the next 3-5 years? Perhaps becoming debt-free? Having a full emergency fund? Purchasing your first home? Beginning to invest a large chunk of your income consistently each and every month? Taking a dream vacation? Starting to give more consistently to a cause that is important and meaningful to you? Whatever the goals may be, they need to be your goals, and as clearly defined as possible. Utilize the SMART method of setting your objectives.... Specific, Measurable, Achievable, Realistic, and Time-based.

For example, one SMART short-term goal could be wanting to be completely debt-free, except your mortgage, in 22 months (assuming you deemed that to be achievable). It can be even more powerful to assign an actual date to goals. For example, by August 1, 2023, versus using a more generic 3 years from now.

Any list of goals that you come up with should be revisited often. If you're not sure what's considered achievable with accurate time-bounding at this point, that's ok. We will be revisiting your objectives in the Educate and Task sections.

Following short-term goals, next we all need mid-term goals next. These cover the period of five years from today until retirement. By retirement I don't mean an age, but rather when you become financially independent, no longer reliant on income from a job. Perhaps purchasing a home is a goal in this timeframe, starting a family, annual family vacations, or funding kids' college. The possibilities are endless.... what are your objectives for this period? Write them down and remember to keep your goals SMART. Generic goals, those without amount or date bullseyes, are rarely achieved.

Lastly, what are your long-term goals? What do you see yourself doing once you become financially independent? What do you want to be doing once you no longer have to work for money? Sit at home on the couch? As nice as that may sound, it's probably not super motivating in the here and now. What would be something you are confident would be fulfilling? What about traveling? Relocating to a home in the country or on a lake? Giving crazy generous amounts of money or time to causes that you believe in? Volunteering to a cause that you are passionate about? These long-term goals are especially important to be specific. Too often we tend to have generic long-term goals.... "I'd like to travel" for example. Author Chris Hogan writes about the importance of dreaming in high definition in his book, *Retired Inspired*. The more clearly defined our goals are, the more likely they will invoke our senses, and the more likely those goals are to keep us focused, motivated and disciplined.

If traveling is your goal, where do you want to travel? What can you imagine yourself doing when you travel there? What kinds of cuisine would you enjoy and which activities would you be doing?

Perhaps your long-term objective is a home in the country, or on a lake. What would the house look like? What would the view look like? What are some of the sounds you would be hearing?

If being in a position to give generously, volunteering your time or even mission work is your goal, which causes would you choose to support and in what locations? How could you see the funds being used or your time spent? Who would benefit from your generosity?

After working most of your adult life, finally achieving the financial independence that you have worked and sacrificed in order to achieve, what activities can you see yourself doing? Being in the position to choose can't be the goal in and of itself. For most, that freedom doesn't provide enough motivation to fight the good fight over decades. Also, those that do achieve independence without specific plans for once they arrive are often let down. Just as with an amount of money being inadequate as a goal, as it typically becomes a moving line and never enough, simply arriving at a destination is not effective. That would be like flying across the world to another airport and then just staying at the airport. The airport is not the goal. The location outside the airport and the activities that we see ourselves doing there are what entice us as the goals.

Regardless of what your unique long-term goals may look like, they will prove to be critical to executing all of the proven principles throughout the rest of this book. You are, and will continue to be, engaged in a long-term campaign between your present and future selves. Without strong long-term goals, your present self is very likely to remain the only victor. In addition to writing them down, which many studies have proven make goals more achievable, I also recommend creating visual reminders of some of your objectives. Print out pictures of some of your goals and hang them in your home, at your office, and in your car. Seeing goals, visually, serves as a great reminder to motivate and encourage us to stay the course.

For some, especially those in early adulthood, long-term goals are tough to nail down. In your 20s, you're still growing and figuring out your likes, dislikes, dreams and desires. This causes many to delay preparing for long-term goals until reaching their 30s and 40s. However, as we will look at more closely in coming chapters, your 20s are the most efficient years for securing your long-term goals. So, what's the best way to stay motivated and tracking towards the long-term when specific objectives are difficult to envision?

First off, I would challenge you to think about the future differently than you may be. Thinking of retirement as being somewhere you will go someday to die isn't super motivating. Instead, think of it as **the sooner you reach financial independence, the sooner you can do what you want to do, when you want, where you want and how you want**. Financial independence is not about an end, but rather a beginning, opening doors and giving you options, and options equal freedom!

For others struggling to envision what exactly independence would look like, clearly seeing what you don't want, or how you don't want to end up, broke and working into old age for example, can be an equally strong motivator. Perhaps you know you don't want to be financially stressed, or stuck with having constant arguments over money, or being at risk of not being able to provide for your family and cover popup emergencies. Looking more long-term, you likely know someone, a relative or family friend, that has continually struggled with money throughout their lifetime. You may know someone that wasn't able to retire and has had to remain working into their 70s. Or someone who retired but had to accept a less than optimal lifestyle, reliant on a small monthly check from Uncle Sam. Is living in sub-par conditions after working your entire adult life, as so many do, where you will allow yourself to end up?

If you are having a tough time connecting your present to the future, consider putting your picture into one of the many aging apps available out there, seeing yourself in 20, 30, 40 or 50 years from now. Visualize how you want life to look for that person, who's you. Ending up broke is a completely unacceptable option and one that is 100% avoidable...IF you decide to act. If not, what's the likelihood of ending up in the same boat as many others?

Without clearly defined objectives, your focus is destined to remain in the here and now. Deciding your goals and objectives will prove to be critical to ultimately achieving your "why," as they provide us with well-defined checkpoints to aim for, as well as further thrust to continually do better.

DECISION #3	*What are my short-term goals for the next five years? Where do I want to be five years from now?* *What are my mid-term goals from the period between five years from now and when I achieve financial independence?* *What are my long-term goals once I become financially independent? What annual income would I need, when do I want to achieve financial independence and what will I do when I get there?* *For every one of your goals, which "why" does it connect back to and ultimately help achieve?*

Take some time, right now, to write down a set of financial goals for the short, mid and long-term in Appendix B.

"The path you take is determined by the decisions you make."
- Unknown

11

If It Is to Be

This will be the shortest chapter you read in this book, but it is also one of the most important, if not the most important.

You have determined why you need to do better and the goals to accomplish to achieve that end state. Now, who is responsible for making those goals a reality? It's not up to your parents, your employer, the government or any other person. Nor does it rely upon events and circumstances outside of your control. Just as gym memberships and GPS running watches won't change your health, your income and raises going forward won't alter your financial path themselves. It's on you - your decisions, your behaviors and your actions. This doesn't mean you have to go it alone. If fact, that's not the best solution. Instead, it's taking ownership for improvement...a personal responsibility for your decisions with money going forward.

DECISION #4	*Do I take personal responsibility and complete ownership of my personal finances?*

*"There comes a time in everyone's life
when a decision is required...a decision to charge,
change your life, change your family's future...charge!"
- Andy Andrews*

12

TTP

Service pilots that fly their aircraft into combat live and die by a rigorous set of tactics, techniques and procedures, or TTP. These manuals of substance aren't chosen individually by each pilot, rather each pilot follows and executes the same set of TTP. Each of the service branches have test units that are continuously developing and refining new TTP based upon the adversaries our nation faces today and their associated threat systems. Once put into print, the guidance gives pilots the necessary tactics, techniques and procedures that they can rely on in combat, thereby allowing them to meet their mission objectives and safely return home. When sent down to the operational units, the TTP is strictly adhered to. If a pilot wants to be effective and live to fly another day, which all do, a firm commitment to the proven TTP must be made.

After going through the questions presented in the first of the Decide chapters, you likely decided that your way isn't putting you on the best path to meet your financial goals. You may have even accepted the realization that your current ways aren't even working for you in the here and now, resulting in stress and fear today, let alone putting you in a solid position years from now. If so, I'm glad to hear it, as that realization is often a necessity to beginning your journey of doing better. Most wish they were investing more towards retirement and overall wealth building, but we know that simply wishing or hoping doesn't bring us around the bases and into home plate. In the end, we all want results, but many will remain unwilling to change. Change and action are required. The ultimate question is, what are you going to do now that you have decided that your way is not bringing you where you want to go?

Many will bury their heads in the sand and pretend the problem will go away. But of course, we know that tactic won't work. Problems don't just go away. Instead, like an untreated wound, they fester and get worse with time.

In order to do better than we have previously done, we are going to have to embrace and commit to doing some things differently than we have always done, adhering to battle tested and proven TTP. In order to win, you will need to pay a price, which all goes back to what's at stake...your "why." How badly do you want it? Your answers to the next questions are equally important to those previously answered.

DECISIONS #5 & #6	*How committed am I to change and embracing new ways, a proven set of effective TTP?*
	What am I willing to sacrifice to achieve my why?

There are typically three possible responses that come from questioning our commitment level, only one of which is sure to put you on the path to financial success.

The first potential answer is fatalistic...thinking that no 'new way' can fix things for me or put me on a path to build wealth. Those that don't believe better is possible for them, have likely already made the decision that they aren't willing to commit to a new way because it wouldn't matter if they did. Too often, our "can't" is actually a "won't." No matter where you stand today, better IS possible, but ultimately up to you!

The second set of potential answers to one's willingness to commit to a new way falls somewhere in between "maybe" and "I'll give it a shot." While those of you in this category certainly have some advantage to the group who have already capitulated and given up hope, your odds of winning long-term are equally dismal. We are creatures of habit, wired with an aversion to change. Even if we know what we've been doing hasn't been working, it's what we are accustomed to. Changing our ways is tough work, so anything less than a complete commitment to a different tried and true way is destined to fizzle out. Perhaps not this month, or even six months from now, but eventually the pull of reverting to your previous ways will likely win out.

The third and final course of action is a complete and total commitment to learning about and sticking to a new and proven way, a set of financial TTP that has worked for my household as well as millions of others. Deciding that you are all in is critical. If you go into this effort with half-effort, you will only ever see that same level of results. A full commitment to doing better is the only way to forever escape the overwhelming pull of our cultural norms and our own previous ways.

If I decide that my current ways are not working, am I ready, determined and committed to a new way? Am I willing to not just doing things a new way, but also thinking completely differently? What am I willing to give up to get there? Doing better starts with a choice...your choice to commit to proven principles. Your decision to adhere to the proven financial tactics, techniques and procedures will ultimately determine your effectiveness and achievement of desired mission objectives. The hardest part is not what you have to do, but what you may have to give up to get there!

Like it or not, none of us can have it all now and later. While everyone can get to a point where they can enjoy some things now and set themselves up for achieving their goals, it may require some tightening of the belt to get to that point. You will either choose to pay a price now, or you will pay the price down the road. The great news is that sacrifices, and things given up, don't have to stay that way forever. When you think of the things you are willing to give up, think of it as postponing. Author and radio host Dave Ramsey encourages listeners to, "Live like no one else now, so later you can live and give like no one else."[1] So what will it be for you? What things are worth delaying the achievement of your "why" and which are not? Each decision will either bring you closer to, or further from, the achievement of your goals. Take a few minutes to reflect upon what you are willing to give up in order to achieve your "why" and add them to the bottom of Appendix A.

The more committed you become, the deeper and more radical you are willing to get, and the more probable and faster your desired results will occur. On a scale of 1 to 10, with 10 being the most committed and intense, where will you choose to fall on the power intensity scale? Are you going to kick it up to a 10, into maximum afterburner? Maybe a 9, still in afterburner but at a reduced level? Or possibly an 8, out of afterburner and into what is called mil power? You get to decide. The higher the level, the faster you will accelerate and get to where you want to go. The lower the power level, the slower you will go and also less likely you will be to get off the ground at all. If your "why" isn't worth at least an 8 level of commitment to you, it's probably in need of another look.

True commitment and deciding to not let anything stand in your way goes back to taking ownership of your future and your "why," - how badly do I want it? Continually remind yourself, what's at stake if you don't commit to a new way? It's not about the number in your bank account, but instead the other parts of your life that are improved with a stronger financial footing. Your stress levels. Your sense of security and protection. Your relationships. Your overall quality of life through the fulfillment of your goals.

Around midway into my Air Force career, I had to learn a new set of TTP. I was given the opportunity to step out of the cockpit for one assignment and instead work with an Air Force ground unit that was embedded with an Army Division. At the time, I wasn't really stoked with the assignment and being stuck on the ground. I had joined the Air Force to fly and fight from the sky and was finally building up some proficiency as a flight lead. But the Air Force powers that be had other plans, and I reported for a two-year stint with the Army.

The unit I joined was charged with providing close air support for the units of the Army division. I had flown close air support missions in the F-16 and felt that I had a great understanding and appreciation of how to best utilize close air support. But my perspective was from the sky, which I quickly learned was very different from the ground. Also, despite being part of the same Department of Defense, the vernacular used by the Army units was akin to learning a foreign language. Very few of the acronyms were the same. I was also now leading groups of enlisted Tactical Air Control Parties (TACPs), which was also a new endeavor. Coming from flying squadrons, the vast majority of my experience was with other officers. In these ground units, while there were a few officers leading, the vast majority of the squadron was enlisted members, and they were the tactical experts, not the officers.

Between the new language, much different perspective and change from officers to enlisted being the tactical experts, I was definitely a fish out of water. After two ops tours in the Air Force, I had to learn a new way of doing business, in many ways different to what I had been doing in the years leading up to that assignment. The other three mid-grade officers and I had a decision to make. Would we push our ways and perspective, or embrace a new language and a new way of doing business, given our change in office from a jet to a Humvee? It wasn't a tough decision to make, as we quickly learned that we would become most effective, and therefore in the best position to achieve our unit objectives, if we committed to learning new ways and tapping into the experience of our NCOs. It also helped having a strong "why," as we prepared to embark on a major combat operation, knowing that our lives, and the lives of the enlisted men we were charged with leading, depended upon it.

That assignment definitely presented some unique challenges and provided a much more up-front view of death and destruction. Thankfully, everyone returned home safely from our deployment. While I was ready to go back to the cockpit after the two years was up, I consider myself very fortunate to have had the opportunity to learn a new perspective and work with some incredibly motivated and talented individuals. The lessons that I learned about effective close air support followed me back to the jet, with a much better understanding of what's at stake when supporting our brethren on the battlefield below.

We are most successful in life when we recognize that our way is not the most effective way and then commit to learning new proven principles from the experts. It takes guts to try a new way, but we have to put aside our pride and go with what works best, remaining willing to be taught by those who have been there, done it and had success. This doesn't mean that we have to enjoy the process. What we always need to remember is where each choice and every sacrifice is leading us...closer to fulfilling the "why." That is what keeps us going, one step at a time, one foot in front of the other.

Success is a choice. Are you going to choose to simply survive, or instead thrive? Will financial readiness and success become a critical mission to you? It all starts with a decision, today, that only you can make. If you want to achieve better results, you are going to have to decide to commit to making better choices and go ALL IN. You can always choose to revert to your current ways, abandoning your "why" and associated goals, but we already know where will lead. Your story will ultimately come down to how strongly your "why" compels you and your associated level of commitment. Yes, effort and discipline will be required, as any accomplishment worthwhile in this life requires a price to be paid. But no matter where you are, or where you have been, you get a chance, right now, to DECIDE. It's ultimately the only thing holding you back. If not today, when?

"When you change the way you look at things,
the things you look at change."
- Dr. Wayne Dyer

D

OPEN YOUR EYES

B
E
T
T
E
R

13

Point of Departure

When my wife and I got married soon after college graduation, a few of our groomsmen decided to save some cash and drive across six states to the wedding instead of flying. Instead of stopping and getting a hotel, they decided to take turns and drive straight through. In the middle of the night, with the others in a deep sleep, one of the drivers noticed a police car turn on their flashing lights and make a U-turn across the highway. Quickly realizing that he had forgotten his license back at home, the driver woke up our friend in the passenger seat, telling him they had to switch seats since he didn't have his license on him. In a matter of seconds, they had switched seats as the new driver was still waking up. When the officer came to the door and asked if he had any idea how fast he was going, he answered, completely truthfully, "I have no idea, officer." I'm sure the cop had gotten that answer before, but in this case, it was 100% true!

To make matters even worse, when they were switching seats, the cup of spit from chewing tobacco had spilled right into the driver's seat. So not only did the driver get a ticket for being "asleep at the wheel," but also got to sit in a nasty puddle of tobacco. We still joke about that story, and I'm sure the first driver will never live it down!

That memory often comes to mind when trying to learn more about where someone stands with their finances.

Me: How much do you make each month?

Client: Not exactly sure.

Me: How much debt do you have?

Client: Not sure.

Me: How much do you spend a month on groceries and eating out?

Client: No idea, but it's probably more than I should be.

Many of us are asleep at the wheel, with only a very general idea of where we stand today. Others have no clue, choosing to live by the motto that ignorance is bliss. In order to do better, our answer to any questions on our finances cannot be "I have no idea." A recent study released by the Federal Reserve reported that many Americans underestimate their credit card debt by about 40% and their student loan debt by 25%.[2] That would be like starting a trip to Atlanta thinking we were in Dallas instead of Albuquerque. It's going to be tough to figure out our path towards our goals without first knowing, with a level of confidence, our point of departure.

After deciding that you are in fact ready to try a new way, your why and the goals that you set out to achieve, the next critical step is to open your eyes to where you stand today. Knowing where you are starting from, your location of takeoff, is a key element to setting your vector. Just as when giving someone directions, you can't even start until knowing where they are starting from. The greater detail, the better. So, where do you stand today? What's your income?

What are your bills? What does your debt picture look like? Any savings or investments?

Let's start with where you stand currently in term of overall financial net worth. You can calculate your financial net worth by simply subtracting everything you owe others from everything you own. Go through the table in Appendix C, which should cover all that you own and owe. This will tell you where you sit today.

Don't be discouraged if you have a negative financial net worth. This would, unfortunately, make you normal, as many Americans owe more than they actually own. As painful as this realization may be to you, ripping off the band-aid and facing our current position is a critical step towards ultimately doing better.

Once you know where you are with your finances, the next step is getting a grasp on what got you there. We need to take a close look at some of our cultural myths, assumptions, contributing factors and root causes, as they serve as an opposing force to our thrust. Taking the time to address our behaviors with money is key in order to avoid improperly treating the symptom, which won't change anything in the long run.

* A Note On Pensions (Also known as Defined Benefit Plans)

Many servicemembers, veterans and first responders receive pensions after completing a set number of years of service. While most pensions are typically not included in a net worth statement (unless there is a cash value you could withdraw today), pensions can have significant value and should definitely be considered. A few points to keep in mind:

- **If you have not yet qualified for a pension, then you should not count on it for income**. You never know what curveballs life may throw at you, preventing you from qualifying for the pension. Do not count on the pension for providing future income until you have fully qualified for that defined benefit.
- To get a feel for the value of your pension, look at it from the perspective of what a civilian would need to have invested to receive the same benefit for the remainder of their life. A general rule of thumb is the ability to withdraw 3-4% from investments each year, increasing as inflation rises, without ever running out of money the rest of your life. Dividing your annual pension by 3 or 4% (which is the same as multiplying by 33 or 25 respectively) gives you an idea of its value. For example, if a pension provides an annual income of $50,000, that would equate to an approximate equivalent value of having $1.25-$1.65 million dollars in investments!
- Once you do qualify and start using the pension for income, **remember that most pensions die with the holder**. This is why pensions are not typically included in net worth calculation. However, since a pension can hold significant value, you will definitely want to include it as a part of your planning, and caveat your net worth appropriately, $200K net worth + a $50K annual pension, for example.

"It ain't what you don't know that gets you into trouble.
It's what you know for sure that just ain't so."
- Mark Twain

14

Seat of the Pants

One of the first things that a pilot learns is that flying by the seat of your pants can quickly get you killed. In pilot training, part of our instruction was reading a large booklet, called The Road to Wings. Page after page is full of powerful examples of pilots reaching their demise by not adhering to the procedures that they were taught. The purpose is to teach that flying is a dangerous business, that the rules and regulations are developed and written through the trials of those that went before you, and if you don't adhere to the lessons learned you will very likely become yet another statistic and page in the book.

In financial terms, our Road to Wings lessons can be seen all around us. Consumer debt levels... loan default rates... bankruptcies... foreclosures... broken retirements.... folks snapping due to financial stress... broken families... the list goes on and on. Yet most households in this country continue to fly by the seat of their pants, following our perceptions, based upon cultural myths, instead of flying in accordance with proven procedures. Truths have been passed along from those that have achieved financially security, peace and wealth before us, many of whom did so with very modest salaries. Yet most continue to fly by the seat of their pants, floating along in their hot air balloon with no clue that they are headed in the complete opposite direction of where they wish, straight into a thunderstorm.

Our journey to a financial awakening continues with opening our eyes to the myths that we are falling for. While making us feel secure, perched in the basket of our colorful balloon, they are leading us into the dark clouds of a nasty storm. That's no small task, however. We believe in what our culture has taught us and have actually become advocates of the same myths we have fallen for. Most of us are also surrounded by friends, family and co-workers who preach the same narrative that we have convinced ourselves of, which only adds to our belief that they are not lies, but rather truths. But we have to remember that nearly 80% of those that we may be taking wisdom from are just as confused and broke as we are. It's a classic example of the blind leading the blind, with most of us too close to our own situation to see right through the holes that cover it. I was right there myself for many years, going with the flow, watching and learning from others just as lost as I was. And then I had my eyes opened, and my financial views haven't been the same since.

Our thrust to do better with our finances is ultimately up to each and every one of us. Just like an airplane flying through the air, the external winds can either slow us down or speed us up. Unfortunately, we are surrounded by many more headwinds that slow us down, versus tailwinds that speed us up. Cultural myths regarding what works or is acceptable, or even required, to "win" with money provide many of the headwinds. Although our thrust is ultimately up to each of us, we want to remove as many of those unnecessary headwinds as possible, thereby helping us go even faster and arrive at our chosen destination sooner. Let's break down the most common and debilitating myths and see if we can remove any unnecessary headwinds to our financial flight path. In an era of an abundancy of information, it has become more difficult to decipher truths. Challenge yourself to look at each of these areas from a different angle than you may have in the past. If you can see each in a different light, you will become more likely to trade flying from the seat of your pants for flying off instruments of truth.

Myth #1: I can delay investing until my income rises and still achieve the same long-term wealth.

Many say, "I know I should be investing, but I can't afford it right now... I will start as soon as I start making more." You cannot afford to wait!

Like trying to climb in altitude in a plane, or for a hiker climbing to a peak, the longer we wait, the steeper and more difficult the climb becomes. Can it still be done if I wait to start my ascent? Possibly. It's never too late to change and start doing better from here on out. But does it become tougher each day that I delay the start of my climb? Absolutely! We can delay the climb, but we can't delay our advance forward in time and the loss of power with each day that passes. The longer that you wait to start, the more daunting and unsustainable the necessary climb will become.

The fact that the climb gets steeper each year is not just about saving up our own money. Much more so, our loss of time is really about our loss of the ability to take full advantage of compounding interest. All this fancy term means is the growth on our money (interest) growing on top of itself. When we put $100 into an investment growing at 10% per year (10% interest), we have $110 after one year. The next year, we don't just make $10 in interest, but $11 ($110 times 10%). That seems like a really insignificant fact, but has huge results long-term, quickly turning the growth on our interest even greater than the money that we originally invested.

In the example of a 10% growth rate, in just over seven years, our original $100 will have doubled, meaning that we now have over

$200 in the account. This means that beginning in the eighth year, we are making more in interest off of our growth than we are from the original amount that we invested! That effect builds stronger and stronger each year, having amazing results over a long period of time. For example, $100 invested today, growing by 10% each year, becomes $4,526 after 40 years.[1] Let's not miss what this means. You put just $100 into a solid investment (like an S&P 500 index fund for example, which has had a rate of 11.56%), and after 40 years, and putting zero additional dollars into the account, it is now worth $4,526. $100 of that was your money, but then you gained $4,426 from compounding interest. Of the $4,526 you now have, only less than 3% of it is the money you actually put in, and the other 97% of your balance is from compounding interest. That's how much your money can work for you over a long period of time...insane!

DO NOT MISS THIS! Go back and reread this last paragraph, and if it doesn't completely shock you and open your eyes, you didn't fully grasp the benefit.

You have probably seen a graph of an example of compounding interest like the one below, showing the power of growth over time.

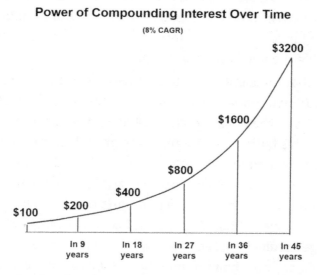

Power of Compounding Interest Over Time
(8% CAGR)

Unfortunately, despite showing the amazing long-term power of compounding interest, it often doesn't do a great job of motivating many that see it. How in the world would this NOT motivate anyone? Turning $100 into $3200, without any effort on our part beyond putting in the initial $100, is like magic. But it's not magic, it's reality. So why wouldn't every single person, especially most in the United States in the top 1% of household income in the world, not be taking advantage of this? Many, especially those just starting out in their 20s see this and their takeaway is something like, "so if I put money in today, which will mean that I have even less to do stuff here and now, it will grow into a lot of money when I am really old and can't enjoy it much anyway... maybe later down the road."

Having a difficult time connecting with our future self, many years into the future, is really tough to do, especially for young adults feeling as if they have lots of lots of life in front of them where they can worry about long-term wealth. Besides, many think, it is already difficult to get by. Most of us convince ourselves that we will start taking advantage of the power of investing down the road when we are more financially secure and making better incomes. Another part of the answer as to why we delay taking advantage of compounding interest lies in our genetic makeup. As human beings, we like to win, but we are often much more motivated by loss. We hate losing even more than we like winning. With this in mind, I find that flipping the compounding interest phenomenon, showing the

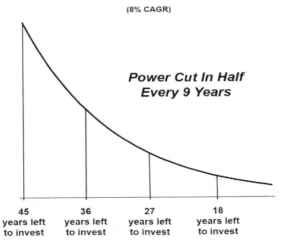

Power of Compounding Interest Lost Over Time
(8% CAGR)

Power Cut In Half Every 9 Years

| 45 years left to invest | 36 years left to invest | 27 years left to invest | 18 years left to invest |

power lost each year, often does a better job motivating those that I coach, regardless of their age, to start taking advantage of this amazing power, today!

Many of us have heard that we should start early, but we don't hear the detail on exactly what delaying will mean to us long-term. Using this example of an 8% compound annual growth rate (CAGR) over time, with a retirement age of 67, **each year that we delay investing, we lose 7-10% of our power of compounding interest in comparison to the year prior.** The average age that Americans start investing for retirement is 31 years old.[2] By this time, we have already lost half (50%) of our power of compounding interest as compared to ourselves back at 22 years old. As shown in the same graph with more detail below, this means that whereas every single dollar invested at 22 turns into $32 by age 67, the same dollar invested at 31 years old only grows into $16. Nine years later, the 40-year old has lost half the power of the 31-year-old, with a power factor of only $8 for each dollar invested.

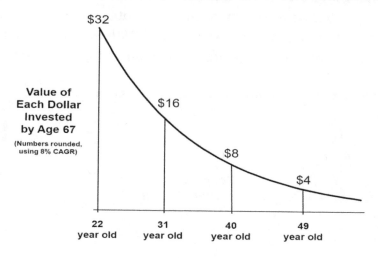

Power of Compounding Interest Lost Over Time

But won't increases in our income make up for the loss of time? While most do see income increase in their 20s and 30s, how many are really consistently seeing eight percent raises every single year?

In 2018, based upon Bureau of Labor Statistics reporting, the median annual income for those 20-24 years old was $29,952. The median income for the 25-34-year-old group was $41,236. While, on average, the percentage jump in income from early 20s to early 30s is one of the highest most see over their working lifetime, 38% for this median income earner, this still doesn't make up for the loss in investing power during the same period of years. To have the same long-term growth end result at retirement, the 31-year-old would have to invest over twice as much monthly as they would have back at age 22. Not only would this represent a higher percentage of monthly take home income for most but would also require many more of our own dollars over the long-term.

The boost in income that most gain from their early 20s to early 30s tends to drop off. For the majority of Americans, our 40s are the decade where income earnings tend to plateau.

Age Group	Median Annual Income	Growth in Income (%)
20-24	$29,952	--
25-34	$41,236	↑ 38%
35-44	$51,272	↑ 24%
45-54	$52,208	↑ 2%

Median income by age group with growth percentage from previous age group[3]

What doesn't change, however, is the increasing amount needed to invest to get to the same end result at retirement age. Assuming the same 8% growth rate after inflation, the amount needed to invest to reach the same goal as our younger selves doubles around every eight years. Given that none of the median age groups increase at that rate, most are fighting a losing battle against time, making it more and more difficult, and much less likely, to build long-term wealth and achieve financial independence.

Our current federal tax code allows those that are over 50 years old to invest more in their retirement account. Called "catchup," the purpose is to help those who delayed to "catch-up" by investing more in their 50s. While it can help a bit, the term "catch-up" is really a misnomer. "Catching up" when you have lost 90% of the power of compounding interest in comparison to your 22-year-old self would require what for most would be considered unachievable amounts. As an example, let's compare one who smartly starts with just $100 per month at 22 years old, to one that delays investing until 50 and tries to catch-up. What would that take?

The 22-year-old that invests just $100 per month from age 22 to 67, with an annualized growth rate of 8% after accounting for inflation, would have just over $500,000 at retirement. Again, that is in today's dollars, since we accounted for inflation, and assumes that this person never increases their monthly investment for 45 years. For someone starting at 50 instead of 22, achieving the same result of having half a million dollars at 67 would require investing $1145 per month for those 17 years! While the one starting at 22 would have invested only $54,000 of their dollars over the 45-year period, the one starting at 50 would need to invest $234,000 of their income to achieve the same result.

Now I know most of us expect, as we should, to be making much more at 50 than what we start out making at 22, but would we really make that much more? Let's say our 22-year-old makes $30,000 per year, just above the median income for that age bracket. The $100 investment would equate to just 4% of their monthly income. With $1145 being 11.5 times greater than $100, in order to achieve the same percentage of income, 4%, our 50-year-old would need to make nearly $350,000 per year, and again that's in today's dollars since we have already accounted for inflation. How many Americans are making that kind of annual salary? Only the top 1% of salary earners in the United States make $350K per year. While many strive to grow their income over the years, the odds are stacked way against us to make that kind of money... and for 99 out of 100 of us, we simply won't.

Another important piece that this example assumes is that the 50-year-old will enjoy the same annualized return over their 17 years of investing as the 22-year-old over their 45 years of investing. The numbers above assumed the same growth rate of 8%, after accounting for inflation, for both investors. But the shorter the period of investing, the less likely that we will achieve a high annualized growth rate. Case in point, for the past 17 year period, from 1 Jan 2002 through 31 December 2018, the S&P 500 has an compound return of just 6.8 percent, and that's before bringing the inflation rate into account.[4] After including inflation, the annualized growth rate was just 4.6 percent these past 17 years.[5] That would mean that the 50 year old gets to enjoy even less annual growth, requiring them to invest much more to achieve the same result of $500K by a retirement age of 67. In fact, using 4.6 percent, the 50-year-old would need to have invested $1600 per month.... Over $326,000 of their dollars to achieve the same result of our 22-year-old who only had to put in $54,000.

One last consideration to bring up. The above examples, comparing our 22-year-old to a 31 and 50-year-old, doesn't take into account any kind of employer match, into a 401K for example. If we bring that into the equation, and assume that our 22 year old would get at least a 4% match all of their working years (never getting a raise for 45 years), that would equate to $200 per month being invested each month, bringing the amount at 67 to an astounding $1,001,822 in today's dollars! Despite only saving $100 of their own income per month, and never getting a raise for 45 years (beyond a worst-case scenario), our 22-year-old turned $54K into over a million dollars at 67. How much more comfortable would retirement be for Americans with $1M in savings? Better than where most sit today going into retirement? Much!

While beginning to invest at any age is nearly always a good thing, are you starting to see the impact of delaying further? Waiting until your 50s, or even 40s, can make reaching your goals of securing a comfortable retirement much more difficult to attain. Those starting later will likely need to choose to either invest significantly greater amounts of their own dollars to catch up, accept having less of a nest egg in retirement or delay retirement, which may or may not be an option. While none of us can go back in time, we can all change our path going forward. You cannot afford to delay and give up any more of the power of time through compounding interest!

So why don't many of us start investing earlier? For a majority of Americans, our levels of debt play a large role.

---

* Note to young servicemembers (and any others who put themselves in a position to begin investing before age 22)

A majority of our nation's servicemembers join the military ranks in their teenage years, shortly after graduating from high school. For this group, beginning to receive reliable income at a young age (coupled with very low living expenses if provided housing and meals on a military installation) offers an amazing opportunity to begin to take advantage of the power of time and compounding interest. The graph below shows the incredible power of starting long-term investing between the ages of 18 to 22. In this example, with the assumptions stated below, every $100 invested at age 18 would grow to an eye-popping $4,300!

Takeaway: even if in small amounts, start as early as possible!

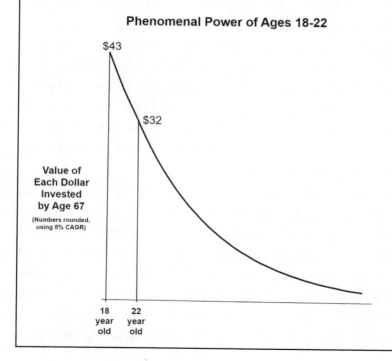

Phenomenal Power of Ages 18-22

$43

$32

Value of Each Dollar Invested by Age 67

(Numbers rounded, using 8% CAGR)

18 year old   22 year old

Myth #2 – Debt is Necessary and Can Actually Help Me

One of the most thrilling experiences in a fighter is the opportunity to fly at low-level. Scorching over the earth's surface, just a few hundred feet over the treetops at over 500 miles per hour is exhilarating to stay the least. While there can be a tactical purpose for flying at these altitudes, living on the edge greatly increases the risk level. Operating at low altitude exposes the pilot to a much greater array of threats, a higher risk of flying into the ground, which takes only a second or two of distraction at that speed, as well as things that present seemingly low risk. Hitting a bird, or flock of birds, which is one of every pilot's worst fears, can turn a good day into bad in a split second. Just one small bird down the intake of the engine can quickly result in engine failure. Flying low-level also significantly limits the jet's range, burning fuel at a much higher burn rate. It also adds stress, knowing that margin for error is much less.

This type of flying also greatly limits the pilot's options to react to unforeseen issues that pop up. To a pilot, altitude equates to options. When flying low, if the motor hiccups or another system malfunctions, the pilot can trade airspeed for altitude, but nowhere near the same amount of flexibility and safety as when flying at high altitudes. For all of these reasons, although flying low is an amazing adrenaline rush, we generally avoid it, as the risk and high potential for a catastrophic ending typically outweighs the perceived benefit.

Our use of debt is a lot like flying low level, allowing just about anyone to live in the fast lane, regardless of income. Being able to purchase expensive things before we have the money in our account is exhilarating, at least for the short term. But it ultimately exposes us, and our families, to much higher levels of risk. Debt also results in us burning much more of our hard-earned income, our fuel, at a higher rate and limits our long-range perspective. Tough to look out over the horizon when our vision is focused on not hitting the ground by running out of cash and not being able to make monthly payments. Debt payments also tend to increase stress levels.

Over recent decades, Americans' use of debt has skyrocketed. Despite having great incomes and opportunity, many of us don't enjoy our positions due in large part to our high use of debt. On average, 10% of household income in this country goes towards consumer debt payments, which doesn't include home mortgages.[6] As a coach, most clients that I see are paying between 15-25% of their monthly income towards minimum debt payments each month. And it's not just a problem for those just starting out with lower incomes. The results of a recent survey by the Federal Reserve, reported in Money Magazine, stated that "people's peak earning years are their peak debt years."[7] Did you catch that? The years that we earn the most, and therefore have the greatest percentages to invest and build wealth, are instead the years in which most choose to carry the greatest amounts of debt! Not only are most not taking advantage of time by starting their investing early on, but many are not taking full advantage of the higher incomes with which they promised themselves they would.

Debt appears to make our lives super convenient, giving us what we want, or at least think we want, right away without having to wait to save up and actually have the money to buy it. No longer is it only for homes and cars, but rather just about everything we consume and buy. Vacations, dinners, groceries, a candy bar... put it all on the card then pay it off. Debt seemingly gives us more sooner, but it doesn't give us anything but more heartache in reality. Like most things that come too easy, debt includes a twist. Remember the saying, "if it seems too good to be true, it probably is?" That summarizes debt... over promise and under deliver. We get to pick up the same standard of living that it took our parents decades to build up to, right now, without the building up to part. Buying with credit makes our debt limit the only obstacle to us purchasing anything our hearts desire.

Every time you use credit, you are, in general, paying someone else for the convenience of having whatever it is right now, before you can probably afford it. That convenience comes at a significant cost for most, ultimately making others rich with our hard-earned income.

If we stop to peel back the layers, it becomes apparent that debt cripples us in many different ways.

First, our use of debt keeps us focused on the past versus focused on the future. Any portion of our income that is stuck paying for yesterday cannot, by definition, also be used to save and help us achieve our financial goals. Our monthly income lost to debt payments is similar to using today's jet fuel for yesterday's mission. Doing so leaves me short on fuel for today, and therefore much less likely to achieve my present mission. Another way to think of debt is like driving a vehicle while focusing primarily on the rearview mirror. We become focused on where we have been instead of where we are going, and it's likely to take us off the road and into the ditch!

Second, the more we have to pay for the past, that equates to less that we have for investing in our future, taking advantage of the magic of compound interest. Every dollar has an opportunity cost, as we are limited to only doing one thing with each. Each dollar that we waste on paying for the past cripples our ability to build for the future. This takes us backwards, floating further away from our desired destination, our goals, in our hot air balloons.

Next, debt weighs and slows us down. It makes us feel like we're flying around with the speed brakes out, slowing our progress down and making our movements sluggish. Debt is a really inefficient use of our income, the fuel of our airplane.

Fourth, debt causes us to pay more, through interest, by paying back on the item over months or even years. Not only does it slow down what I can do with my income today, due to having less of it at my disposal, but the interest also serves as a fuel leak to our airplane. For the convenience of having something today, before I can really afford it, I'm going to have to pay much more for the item. How much more is paid depends on the terms of my payback – the interest rate and how quickly it gets paid back. The higher the interest rate and longer it takes you to pay it back, the more you will pay for the item in the long run. Many of us balk at paying $20 for a nice meal, but then end up paying more than that for a cheaper lower-quality $10 meal that was charged to a credit card and took a year to pay off. We often end up paying more for buying a cheaper thing on credit than a nicer version with cash, without even getting to enjoy the nicer version. That's essentially like accepting a lower quality item for the same price as a much higher quality version, all to have the convenience of getting it now. No wonder we end up with so much junk, but hey, at least we got it sooner! How much sense does that make?

Debt also exposes us to a much higher risk level. The commitments of monthly payments that debt incurs brings on greater turmoil if we were to lose our monthly paycheck, even for a short term. Not only do we have to worry about providing for the needs of our families in the event of a job loss or injury, but now we also have the risk of not being able to make our minimum debt payments, exposing us to legal judgments by debtors, repossession of vehicles, or even foreclosure on our homes. Even if we don't experience that level of income loss, we are still far less able to react to one of life's curveballs when we have less access to our income because of debt. Just like living on the edge flying a low-level, debt payments bring us closer to the margins, with very little room for error. When life happens, which isn't a matter of if but when, we are caught with few options and a catastrophic ending much more likely.

Lastly, and perhaps the worst of impacts, debt increases our stress levels. Living in the fast lane may get our heart rates up due the adrenaline rush, but it also gets our blood pressure up, knowing that we are now ultimately less capable of providing for our families over the long-term and cushion life's blows. Boston University defines financial wellness as one's "satisfaction with current and future financial situations."[8] When we purchase with debt, our aim is to bring ourselves satisfaction in the present. Unfortunately, the high is often short-lived and soon transitions to stress. Now saddled with a payment and less satisfied in the present, our future outlook is darkened as well, now having less to save and invest to meet our goals. All of these downsides of debt bring on stress, which brings down our general outlook on life, our health, our relationships and even our performance on the job.

Financial stress, often times brought upon by the burden of debt, brings us into a vicious downward spiral. When we become stressed, many turn to overindulgence in food, alcohol or the use of drugs, which brings physical and mental health down. Once feeling down, its common to seek more short-term relief through further purchases, which of course brings us further into debt, and the cycle continues.

Let's look at an example of the impact of debt on a typical American family. The median American household income in 2017, according to the US Census Bureau, was $61,372.[9] That's nearly twice the amount that is needed to move a household into the top 1% of the world in terms of income. Based upon the 2017 married filing jointly federal tax tables, a couple at this income would pay just over $8000 in federal tax and around $4700 in FICA (social security and Medicare). Many would also be required to pay an income tax to their state, which varies anywhere from 0 to 13% (with California being the only double-digit state income tax rate). We will use a median amount of 5% for state tax, which would equate to another $2700 paid in tax after an average standard deduction. After federal and state taxes, this would leave our median household with around $46,000 in take home income, or about $3830 per month. As a general rule of thumb, I recommend that no more than 25% of take-home income is spent on rent or mortgage, so we will use a $950 monthly rent or mortgage amount. If this couple decided to give 10% and invest 15% for the future, that would add up to approximately $960 per month. That means that after paying for the roof over their head, giving 10% and investing 15%, this average couple would be left with $1920 per month for the rest of their needs like groceries, utility bills, insurances, phones, clothing, and even some wants like internet service, some meals out, and saving up for a vacation or next vehicle. That all sounds fairly doable and again that is for a median income family, so half of the families would have even more income available each month.

What this example leaves out is consumer debt. If we send a typical amount of income towards debt payments, 20% on average for those I have coached, that robs our monthly income of $770. Odds are high that most don't lower their housing level due to the income lost to debt and still have the same rent or mortgage amount of $950, which now brings us to $2110 left for the month, without any giving or investing. The household still needs to meet their needs, just as they did without debt payments taken out. Most would find it difficult to cover their needs if they still sent nearly $1000 to giving and investing, which would also mean having no wants.

Due to losing nearly $800 to consumer debt payments, something has to give. By definition, it can't be meeting our needs, and for most it's not going to be wants. That means that our giving and investing are the easiest targets to cut out. And that's exactly what most are doing. It's no wonder that as our rates of increased use of consumer debt has directly led to lower overall rates of saving and investing![10] Each dollar that goes to debt payments cannot, by definition, go to saving or investing.

They say that a picture can be worth a thousand words, and for many of those that I coach, the next set of depictions helps open their eyes to the impact that debt is having on their hard-earned income. This first graphic shows a household with full access to their income without consumer debt. As with our last example, most households would find that without debt, they would be in a position to meet needs, save for annual expenses, invest, give and enjoy a fair amount of wants.

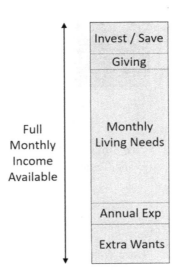

Unfortunately, that's not the case for most households. When we tack on a large amount of consumer debt payments, as most have, the effect is added pressure to other areas of our plan.

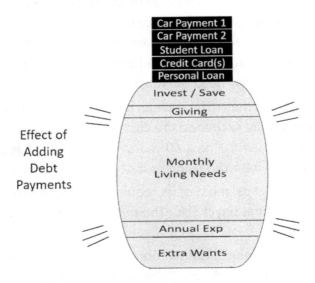

As with anything under pressure, eventually something has to give. Giving up needs is not an option, and most remain unwilling to give up wants entirely, so that leaves our investing, giving and saving for annual expenses.

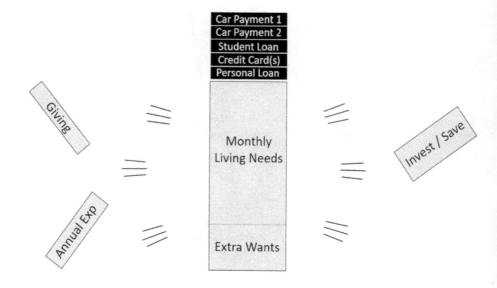

Most see these graphics and agree that the debt has a big impact on their ability to give and invest more but feel as though they don't have a choice. The "cost of things have gone up more than our incomes," "we need a car" and "can't go to college without student loans" are probably the three most common justifications that I get. But what if those weren't true, and instead are what we, and our society by in large, have convinced ourselves?

First, let's address incomes. The median income in the States has kept up with and generally exceeded the cost of living here, measured as inflation, over the past 40 years.[11] So it's not that our salaries haven't kept up with the rising cost of goods and services.

How about vehicles? Yes, most of us require vehicles in order to drive to work and earn that paycheck. The question is what kind of vehicle do we "need?"

The average cost of a vehicle is now more than $36,000, with new car buyers paying an average of over $550 per month for 69 months.[12] That's for one vehicle... many households have two! Considering that a new car will likely lose up to 60% of its value in the first 4-5 years, that would equate to losing nearly $100 per week due to the depreciating value.[13] The result of a new car payment isn't much different than renting a car from the airport every month.

"No, it's different because we own the car." While some is going towards eventual ownership, how much of your monthly payment is really going towards ownership of the car after taking account of the interest and depleting value of most new vehicles? With many taking out six- or seven-year car loans, the vast majority of the monthly payment doesn't even cover the interest and quickly descending value of the car. In fact, most with those loan terms find themselves under water, owing thousands more than the car is even worth. Even those with four-year loans will find that most of their monthly payment is simply covering interest and the value lost each day, just for the privilege of driving a nice car. How is that different than renting a car each month, which most would never consider doing?

Just how much does that staggering car payment add up over time? What is the monthly payment on a new car payment costing you over the long haul? $550 spent monthly from age 22 to 67 adds up to a total of $297,000. But that's just the money spent and doesn't take into account the loss of compounding interest that could have been realized had the money been invested. That same amount put into investments, with a compound annual growth rate of 8%, would have grown into a staggering **$2.8 MILLION** by age 67. That's how much just one monthly payment for the privilege of driving a new car throughout your working lifetime is costing you!

"That's great and all, but I need a car to get to work!" Of course you do, but does it "need" to be a new car that is robbing you of so much of your hard earned income based on the fact that it may be going down in value faster than you are paying it off? While many of us, myself included for too many years, believe that new cars are a need and worth the extra cost, that's usually not the case. Just buying a used car, especially one at least three or four years old, can drastically reduce a monthly payment. A quick example: a new model of a car that we recently purchased was nearly $29,000, but instead we purchased a four-year-old used version of the same model, with just over 40,000 miles, for close to $12,000, just 40% of the cost of a new model. Is the reliability of a car with 40,000 miles much worse than a brand new one? No. Did we save over $17,000 and avoid the worst period of time of depreciating value? Yes. The mileage cost the first owner over 42¢ per mile, and that's without factoring in any interest if purchased with a car loan. Assuming we drive the car until 200,000 miles, which most vehicles are built to last to these days, dropping the value down to $2,000, each mile will have only run us about 6¢. That's one-seventh of the cost in comparison to the first four years. And that's not including any added savings from not paying interest on a new car loan. What about leasing? Leasing has been found to be even worse of a deal, and more costly in the long run, than purchasing a new vehicle.[14]

"Yeah, but now the car warranty is up, and I will spend much more in repairs." According to an article by U.S. News and World Report, the average five-year old vehicle requires $350 per year in repairs, on average, and just $600 per year for a ten-year old vehicle.[15] What about reliability? The same article found that the five-year old car may encounter a problem just once every three years, with the average ten-year old car increasing in frequency to only every 18 to 20 months. So, is the great cost and loss of value with a new or newer car worth it in terms of repair costs? The facts would tell us that, for most, the answer is a resounding no. With all of that said, most could greatly reduce, or through smart purchasing even eliminate, the great burden of vehicle payments on our incomes.

How about student loans? Can't get a college degree without a student loan, right? Once again, that is a myth. Many students are able to successfully graduate with a bachelor's degree completely debt-free, even those without assistance from their parents. The greatest factors for those that are able to do so are school selection, seeking scholarships, and working through college (which reports actually show increases the average GPA[16]). But most are falling prey to student loans, graduating with an incredible amount of debt which puts them starting their adult lives in quite the hole. Tough to see a bright future when starting out in a dark place with an average of nearly $40,000 in student loan debt.[17] Facing a seemingly insurmountable climb out of the abyss, many are defaulting on their loan repayments. In fact, 1 million former students default on their loans each year…. that's nearly 20,000 borrowers defaulting each week![18] How in the world did we find ourselves here? Fortunately, and without a doubt, graduating with absolutely no student loan debt is doable, even without help from Mom and Dad.

A third type of debt that is completely avoidable is carrying a balance on credit cards. With now over $1 trillion in credit card debt, these plastic cards of convenience are suffocating far too many in this country. For most, the intentions of getting a credit card seem legitimate, there for unexpected emergencies. No one that I have ever met got a credit card with the sole intention of just maxing it out. Most have every intention of paying off the full balance each month. But just like weather taking a turn for the worse, the growth of credit card debt is often insidious. They can quickly become a crutch…a purchase here, a Christmas gift there, and before we know it, we are unable pay off the balance at the end of the month. For many, it's a slow but slippery slope and soon there is a balance of several thousand dollars on the card that we are in no position to pay off by the end of the month. I am often told, "we pay off the balance every month," which is also what I used to tell myself. Only you know the truth, and if that isn't the case then you are only fooling yourself. Go back and take a look at the past several years of credit card statements. Did you pay any interest or really payoff the balance every single month? For most, credit cards are like playing with snakes…eventually, just like most snake charmers, you are going to get bitten!

What about those that actually pay off their full balance every single month, and always have? One, you would be in the small minority, as 7 of every 10 card holders carries a balance.[19] Two, I would still challenge whether you actually spend the exact same way were you to be using cash or a debit card, that at least makes you consider whether you have enough in the account to cover the purchase. A recent study showed that we spend 12-18% more when using credit cards rather than cash, simply because we don't think the same, and experience the same hesitation, when using a piece of plastic versus cold hard cash.[20]

But what about covering emergencies? I have to be able to protect my family if life throws us a curveball, at least that is what I told myself for many years. What if you actually had some savings set aside for life's emergencies, which we know aren't a matter of if, but when? There are other options, besides credit cards, that provide us the same protection but have zero chance of biting us and, in turn, sabotaging our monthly income. As an added benefit, these options don't make a bad situation even worse by putting us down into a hole of debt on top of the emergency we face. Ultimately, each of us have to ask ourselves, what are the convenience and supposed rewards of our habitual use of credit cards really costing us, and are they bringing us closer to achieving our long-term goals, or farther away?

For most of us, our homes represent the single largest purchase, and largest debt, we will incur in our lifetime. Unfortunately, as with most decisions that we make impacting our personal finances, we don't have much guidance. We fall prey to what we are told in terms of how much house we can afford by others with a conflict of interest. Realtors, banks and other mortgage lenders, all of whom benefit from us spending as much as possible, entice us. We are often approved to borrow more than expected and are shown homes slightly above our price range. When we see the homes that we could qualify for, which are typically nicer than houses with lower prices, we fall prey to our weaknesses. We want to provide the best possible home for ourselves and our families, and often succumb to the temptation of a slightly higher payment that we can stretch the budget to afford.

That is exactly what happened to my wife and I when we were house shopping for the first time. We had a general idea of the payment that we thought we could make each month, then met with a realtor that helped us turn the payment into a home value. We had access to a VA backed loan and therefore didn't need a down payment. She took us around to maybe ten or so houses, all of which were ok but didn't wow us. Then we went to a home outside of our price range, just to see "what a little extra would look like." To no surprise, we loved the house, which was a notch above all of the others we had looked at. Seeing the home, and the excitement my wife and I shared, my mind went to work to figure out how we could make the higher payment work. Without having a solid plan and sticking to it, my emotions took over and I quickly justified how we could make it happen. There was also an underlying level of guilt that I carried after moving six times in as many years. I wanted to provide the very best for my family, and that's what I thought I was doing when we signed on the line to make the purchase.

Of course, that house payment stretched us too far, as first-time home buyers often overlook many of the costs associated with home ownership. Being stretched, something had to give. Our giving, saving and investing took the hit, and when unexpected things popped up, we relied on credit cards to foot the bill. Two short years later it was time to move again so we put the house up for sale. Luckily, the market had gone up a bit, so we came close to breaking even after closing costs and realtor fees, which are always more than we expect them to be. When we accounted for the loss of not investing, upkeep expenses and added debt in other areas due to the strain of a higher payment, that purchase set us way back financially.

I have seen this same exact scenario with home purchasing hundreds of times as a coach. Folks with good intentions of wanting to provide the best possible home for their families fall prey to what others tell them they can afford. This was certainly a large part of the 2008 housing collapse, with many Americans in homes that they simply could not afford and banks more than willing to make the loans. When our home payment gets to be too high, it takes too much of our monthly income which leads us to be short in other needed or wanted spending areas. Many Americans are "house poor." Despite the shortage of income this creates, most of us don't cut lifestyle in other areas, but instead keep it up or even increase spending. The result is increasing levels of credit card and personal loan debt, putting our households in a downward financial spiral.

Add to that a market downturn, which many are not prepared for after putting as little down as possible, and it doesn't take much to find ourselves under water, perhaps even faced with foreclosure or bankruptcy.

Homes are another area that many believe have gone up in price, thereby causing us to become broke. A 2016 article by the Foundation for Economic Education reported that the price per square foot for new houses remained relatively stable between 1973 and 2015 when adjusted for inflation.[21] Interesting, what has not remained stable is the size of our house. Between the same years, the average new house in the United States grew in size from 1660 square feet to nearly 2700 square feet. The takeaway is that while the cost of new houses has basically remained flat, the cause for the greater pinch on our budgets has been a result of the demand for much larger homes. How about those that rent? Over the past 30 years, from 1987 to 2017, the median gross rent has increased 14% after taking inflation into account. However, median income has also increased by the same amount after accounting for inflation, also up 14%, so no smoking gun there either.

We have got to be smarter when it comes to our purchasing decisions. Stay tuned for smarter ways to purchase vehicles, graduate with a college-degree debt free, put yourself in a position to cover emergencies without a credit card and best purchase a home in the Educate section.

Our over-reliance on debt is dragging us down and preventing us from consistently investing, which is required to build wealth. Our shortest path to wealth is consistent investing which is facilitated by not having debt that robs us of our income and, ultimately, of our future selves. Staggering levels of consumer debt have certainly caught up with us, best illustrated by a recent article from The Simple Dollar group that reported just how much the average American pays in interest each year.[22]

- Auto loan interest: $769 to $895 per year
- Student loan interest: $641 per year
- Credit card interest: $855 per year

That adds up to, on average, over $2300 per year lost just to these three types of debt. If a 22-year-old pays this amount in interest for a ten-year period, from age 22 to 32, what would it equate to in terms of lost wealth at retirement age since these same dollars cannot be invested instead? At an 8% compound annual growth rate, $2300 per year for just this ten-year period could have grown to over a half of a million dollars by age 67! Just for the convenience of having these debts, many are losing out on literally hundreds of thousands of dollars, instead turning over their wealth-building abilities to the banks and credit card companies.

After seeing the impact on hundreds of households over the years as a coach, to include my own, I am 100% convinced that our use of debt presents the greatest hurdle to every American's awesome power to build and achieve long-term wealth. In flying terms, debt payments are akin to fuel leaks, slowly crippling my ability to complete the mission. In effect, we are robbing our future selves and making a strong finish less and less likely. Not only are many not investing themselves, but they are also passing up FREE employer matches in their 401(k) retirement plans. A study by Financial Engines estimated that Americans leave up to $24 BILLION in unclaimed 401(k) company matches...each year![23] I haven't met a client that doesn't want to take advantage of this free money. Rather, they don't We have got to open our eyes and see that we are being played, right into the credit industry's web of deceit, and putting ourselves further away from achieving financial independence.

How did we become so susceptible and willing to make other people and companies rich with our own hard-earned income? When you take a step back and look at debt with fresh eyes, it's easy to see how we fall for it. I can have anything and everything that I want, right now, before I have the money for it? Sold! The new car that I have my eye on and deserve with all of the hours that I have been working? You can have it, today. The bigger, nicer house that you sacrifice so much for and will make you a better provider for your family? Of course! In fact, you qualify for an even nicer house than you thought. What, really? How awesome is that? This all sounds crazy when looked at with fresh perspective, yet the vast majority of us are falling for it, every single day. IF BEING ABLE TO HAVE WHAT I WANT BY USING DEBT TO GET IT SOUNDS TOO GOOD TO BE TRUE, IT'S BECAUSE IT IS! We need to wake up and realize how we are falling prey to making the credit industry the most profitable industry in our country. In doing so, we are holding our own household back from reaching the potential that we all should be.

But don't I need some debt and a credit card in order to build up my credit score? Glad you asked!

Myth #3 – A High Credit Score Equates to Winning Financially

We have become infatuated with our credit score, to the point of being proud of having a score in the high 700s or even 800s. After all, having a high credit score means that we are winning financially, right? Wrong! This is one of the greatest and most pervasive myths in our country. As a recent Forbes magazine article noted, "for years, FICO credit scores have played a disproportionate role in our lives."[24] I could not agree more. Time to open our eyes and seek the truth.

If you peel back the common perception of the mystical credit score calculation, you will find that there are five components of the score. According to the myFICO.com website, the five components of a credit score are: amount of debt owed, debt payment history, type of debts, length of debt history and amount of new debt. Seeing a common theme here? **All five components have to do with your usage of debt**, which we have already established makes others rich with your hard-earned income.

The site goes on to list items not included in your FICO score. Your salary, and any other information not found in your credit report, are not considered in your score. Since any savings or investments are not part of your credit report, those aren't considered in your score either. Yet, the site highlights that the FICO score is "used by 90% of top lenders." So, let me get this straight...when somebody loans me money, they don't care if I actually have a job and income to pay them back? They don't care about my financial net worth and whether I have $2 in the bank or $2 million, both of which have no impact to my credit score? What am I missing here? Perhaps this was part of the reason for what led up to the 2008 housing market crash! It's really no wonder that most lenders use a FICO score to determine whether they should lend money... it shows that you have a consistent history of paying people back, a lot. That probably means that you don't actually own much, which likely means that you won't be in a position to pay off the debt quickly. That all to our lenders making a ton of interest from you on your loans over years and years.

I recently came across an article titled, "How to join the 800 credit score crowd," which highlighted the habits of those with "exceptional" credit scores.[25] Based upon a study by LendingTree, which looked at thousands of credit reports of those with 800+ scores, those that achieve this highly sought after level had average non-mortgage debt amounts of $22,000 and "tended to have a mix of debt products, with an average of nine accounts open." The article went on to state "those with desirable credit scores tended to have long credit histories, with the average around 22 years." Let's break that down. Those with the highest credit scores generally had to carry a bunch of debt that was causing them to pay interest, thereby making others wealthy, and they did so for a very long time. How is that winning or "desirable" again? Another recent news article went as far as recommending that consumers "think twice" about paying off any installment loans early, suggesting loans be kept open for the duration as a strategy to raise your score.[26] Really?

I am not suggesting that anyone intentionally sabotage their credit score by making late payments or skipping them altogether. I am simply asking that you reconsider whether a focus on having a great credit score is bringing you closer to your goals or farther away. For most that I coach, their chase of a great credit score comes at a high cost to their long-term wealth building. Again, any dollars that are lost on debt interest, by definition cannot be used to bring you closer to achieving any long-term goals. Having no credit score is nowhere near the same as having a low credit score. Having a low credit score can present challenges, often caused by having a history of not making payments on time or in full. It will take some time to clean up, which I'm certainly not opposed to as a byproduct of doing better. Just don't allow your score to become the focus.

Although the FICO score only became common for most Americans in the mid to late 90's, we get very defensive of them, as most of us have fallen for the lie that it's not only good, but essential to our livelihood. We have fallen for the fear that we can't live without a high credit score, which puts us right into the hands of the marketers. Triggering fear is one of the most effective ways that we are manipulated, and it's working better than anyone could have ever expected. FICO and the three credit report agencies are excelling, with performance literally off the charts. They make ridiculous levels of profits by collecting information on us, then selling it back to us, banks and credit card companies.

Really brilliant marketing on their part...create an environment where Americans believe that they cannot thrive, or even survive, without their three-digit number. Capitalize on the fear factor while exploiting our weaknesses for spending and convenience, then make us pay for our own data. Genius, yes, but not in a good way. We are made to believe that the only way to achieve financial security and stability is by having a high credit score. Is the notion that we cannot make it without a high credit score really true though? The most common arguments that I get, and actually used to give myself before I had my eyes opened to truth, are the need for a credit score to rent a car or an apartment, get auto insurance, get a job and purchase a home. Let's break each of those down and open our eyes to the deception that many have fallen for, hook, line and sinker.

100

You need a credit score to rent a car or an apartment – both false! I have personally rented vehicles, both in the U.S. and overseas, over a hundred times with only a debit card. The rental company often puts a small extra hold on the card, maybe $200 or so, to protect themselves in the event there is damage. The only additional request that I have received is for my return flight information as verification of departure. That doesn't guarantee that every company will rent to a debit card holder, so double check when you choose a rental company. The same goes for apartments. The vast majority of apartment complexes (and I have called literally hundreds across the country) are perfectly willing to rent to you even if you have no credit history. Most reported that they will charge a slightly higher deposit but will certainly rent to those without established credit histories, either due to their young age or beliefs on the use of debt. Unfortunately, this myth has grown legs, and many that I meet don't even think it is possible to rent an apartment without a credit score. Not buying it? I would challenge you call some apartment complexes in your area and check for yourself.

You need a credit score to get auto insurance – false! While most insurance providers do consider a credit score as a part of your overall "insurance score" and insurability rating, I have not found one that will not provide insurance to someone without a credit score. Again, different story for someone with a low credit score. Some companies will charge a slightly higher rate to someone without a credit score, but it will not prevent you from getting insurance. Three states, Massachusetts, California and Hawaii, have banned the practice of using credit-based insurance scores as a determining factor for rates.[27] Hopefully more states follow suit soon. I would encourage you to shop around and always try to find the best rate, which may come from a provider that doesn't consider your desire to avoid debt, and therefore set yourself up as well as possible for the long-term, as a negative attribute! Even if you do end up having to pay slightly more for your insurance as one of the few without a credit score, you have to ask yourself if the cost and risk of credit is really worth the small savings in insurance rates.

You need a credit score to secure a job or a security clearance – both false! These are also myths that have grown legs in our society. First off, employers don't see your credit score, rather a modified version of your credit report.[28] So, if not your score, what is it that employers are looking for? According to a nerdwallet.com article, "credit-check-based rejections are typically the result of bad credit - not a lack of credit."[29] They couldn't find an example of someone losing out on a job because they had no credit history. The article goes on to report, "When employers look at applicants' credit histories, they're usually looking for red flags, like collections or current outstanding judgments." Would it really make sense for an employer to turn down a well-qualified new hire because they chose to avoid debt, instead choosing their own long-term financial success? If such an employer did exist, would you really want to work for a company that valued your use of debt and being a slave to payments over a desire to build wealth long-term?

You need a credit score to purchase a house – false! First off, the credit score is of no consideration for someone purchasing a home with cash. As crazy as that concept may seem, it is a growing trend amongst financially savvy millennials that see any debt as drag versus added thrust to their lives. Second, for the vast majority that take out mortgages for the purchase of their homes, it is still possible to purchase. Nerdwallet.com recently reported that "plenty of lenders out there are more flexible about working with people who have nontraditional credit histories."[30] Many smaller banks and credit unions still offer manual underwriting, which results in a deeper look into the borrower's employment and payment histories. Have you had secure employment for at least a couple of years? Have you made your utility payments in full and on-time for an extended period? Due to the deeper investigation, the process can require more time and work on the borrower's part. But you can still purchase a house without a credit score! And is this level of scrutiny really a bad thing? Were all lenders required to do this level of homework before handing out loans, would we have greatly reduced or even avoided the 2008 housing market crash? You be the judge.

Our relationship and beliefs with credit scores has got to change. Until then, you will likely continue to see a high credit score as a sign of winning. It's really a sign of overextending yourself in the past, allowing others to use your income to build wealth, not you!

In 1947, Chuck Yeager became the first pilot to break the sound barrier. Many naysayers believed that his aircraft would disintegrate at the speed of sound, Mach 1. Not only did that not happen, but it was essentially uneventful. There have been multiple times that I got to exceed Mach 2 in the F-16, over 1500 miles per hour... and it's still uneventful. Most wouldn't even know without their airspeed instrument showing it. But the myths first had to be dispelled.

Don't allow cultural myths to hold you back from your potential. What may be considered a fear today is likely to seem uneventful when you look back. Breaking through the barriers of cultural myths will allow you to reach new heights. If you find yourself struggling, go back to the first question of the Decide section. *Are my current ways working, putting me on a path towards financial freedom?* If the answer is still no, then you have to ask yourself if believing in these myths could be part of the problem. Also, could changing your opinions on investing, debt and credit scores put you on a path that brings you further away from your goals than the one you are on right now? If not, what do you have to lose by embracing new ways?

Almost every aircraft mishap report talks about a chain of events, breaking down contributing factors and causal factors. Very rarely is it one factor, but rather a multitude of factors. Our belief in most or all of these cultural myths certainly adds to our financial demise. But the myths are contributing factors, not the root causes. What's the difference? Contributing factors influence the likelihood and severity of the end result but eliminating them doesn't guarantee that the effect is ultimately avoided. Our use of debt, for example, is not causal in and of itself but rather a symptom of a greater problem. While it's important to open our eyes to truth and debunk myths, we have to get to the root to change our behaviors with money for good.

*"Until we are dealing with the root,
we will never change the fruit."*
- Louie Giglio

15

How did we get here?

After every flight, fighter pilots spend hours deconstructing the entire mission in a process called the debrief. Shortly after landing, the entire flight gathers to discuss the details of the flight. The timing and execution of every radio call, maneuver, formation, weapons shot or drop, fuel usage, as well as the administrative portions of the flight, are picked apart, one by one, second by second. It's not uncommon for the flight of pilots to spend an hour or two debriefing the 20- or 30-minute tactical portion of the flight in great detail. This process of deconstruction takes place after every flight, whether in peacetime training or actual combat.

The purpose of the debrief is twofold. The first goal is to determine whether all objectives for the mission were accomplished. Was the target destroyed or neutralized? Did all members survive and return to fly another day? Was all communication between the flight members clear, concise and correct? The objectives, which are well known by all prior to the flight, are each graded as a yes or no. If all objectives were met, the mission is deemed successful.

The second goal of the debrief is to identify lessons learned. If any of the objectives for the flight were not met, we want to open our eyes to the root cause for the failure and, in turn, the takeaway on what can be fixed to avoid failure to meet similar objectives on future missions. Even if all objectives were met that day, there are always areas that could have been done better – quicker, safer, more efficiently, or more effectively. Learning from past mistakes in an effort to continually improve tomorrow's mission is one of the cornerstones for the success of our military. The same can be said for seeking improvement in any area of our lives, to include our finances. Before we move on to improving, it's critical that we first understand the root causes. Otherwise, just as with attempts to fill a crack in a foundation versus addressing the source, struggles return.

An effective tool to get to the true root cause of an issue is to continue asking, "why?" A popular method used is the "Five Why's." This is different than figuring out the financial "why" that fuels our thrust and discipline. In the Decide section, we covered why we want and need to do better. When asking why in the root cause context, we are looking to uncover why we haven't been doing better up to this point. By continuing to ask why, it brings us to the ultimate root cause versus just scratching the surface. A true root cause, when removed, results in avoidance of an undesired outcome.

The primary obstacles that get in our way of not doing better with our finances, as covered earlier, are a lack of future vision, a lack of belief that better is possible, and a lack of an effective plan. Since most would agree that all three of those obstacles are ultimately something that each of us can control and overcome, we have to understand why most of us are not doing so. Those obstacles are not the root causes. We have to get to the root of why we allow ourselves, as the freest and richest society in the history of mankind, to go right back into bondage and be weighed down with stress.

Having a very low or misguided standard in which we aspire to with our finances is certainly a contributor. A common bar of success that many set for themselves is to accumulate as much as possible while keeping up to date with the monthly payments and not be foreclosed on or forced into bankruptcy. When this bar is held as the standard to meet, two things become true. First, that's about what we are likely to achieve. The likelihood of exceeding any standard that we have set for ourselves is low. The second piece that becomes true with a low standard is that we tend to think we are doing much better than we actually are. With these goals, most are unknowingly aiming for a bar that results in them living paycheck to paycheck, so it's no wonder that while nearly 80% live paycheck to paycheck, over 70% have accepted that they are doing okay.[1] If the standard has been met, it's no surprise that so many find themselves accepting their position. But why do we set such a low bar?

Our natural tendency is to place fault on our circumstances instead of the only thing in our control... ourselves. A common place for blame is our lack of financial education. I agree, our schools could be doing a better job of educating our youth as to how to be more financially literate and better prepared to handle money going into adulthood. Without financial literacy as a foundational part of our education system, we revert to what we observe, which for most is what we see from our parents. We become a natural byproduct of our childhood observations, which, for most, is likely not the best example to follow. While I would agree that an overall lack of financial education is a contributing factor, it is not a root cause. Every single adult in this country has access to books, podcasts, YouTube tutorials, etc., that could provide ample education on how to do better with our finances. But most don't take ownership and advantage of the resources available to them. Also, just because someone receives financial education does not necessarily mean that they will choose to make smart financial decisions. Why is that?

Most know we should have savings for a rainy day and invest for our future selves, but don't. Instead, we prioritize and rationalize getting stuff we can see in the here and now versus what we can't see for tomorrow and beyond. Yes, debts may slow us down, and for some become an addiction, but our use of it is only a symptom. And, yes, our natural weaknesses are exploited by the marketing machine that surrounds us, which provides incredible ease to purchase and pay later. The more convenient the marketplace becomes, the less we feel the pain of spending. But if we remove the conveniences and marketing fueled enticements to spend today and focus only on the short-term, would that directly result in all of us becoming wiser with our finances? While removing some of the marketing temptations would perhaps result in fewer purchases, it would not necessarily make everyone become focused on their long-term financial goals.

Many would place blame on their income level, as I did for too many years, thinking that if I could just make more, then I would finally be comfortable and content. But as long as a household is living above what is considered the poverty level, there are far too many examples of those who have still managed to build long-term wealth, even with below average incomes. Likewise, there are far too many examples of those with well above average incomes still ending up broke to allow us to buy into the income myth. So, if it's not education, marketing, availability of debt or our income levels, why do we allow ourselves to fall prey to prioritizing today when we know that it comes at the expense of tomorrow?

For most of us, the two main root causes for our financial woes are our own struggles with pride and contentment.

We allow our pride to get in the way. Most have a strong desire to show that we have made it, or at least appear that we are doing well, financially. We equate having things to having achieved personal success, and become bent on proving to ourselves, and others, that we have made it. This is especially common for those entering into the workforce, seeing large paychecks for the first time and wanting to prove to ourselves, Mom and Dad, friends and family that we have arrived and found financial success. When we hit adulthood and finally have a job, it comes with a bucket of money to spend, any way we want. The newfound freedom experienced by the greatest increase of income most of us will ever experience in our lives is exhilarating. We feel as if we have broken away from any chains that were holding us down from our wants during childhood. There is also an unrealistic expectation to pick right back up where we became accustomed to in terms of standard of living. The demand that we put on ourselves is often amplified for those that grew up without much, creating a burning desire to have more in adulthood. For those who grew up with wealth, the pressure to achieve the same level of success for themselves is real.

An innate part of our pride is a burning desire to achieve significance. We all desire significance, seeking meaning and purpose in our lives. We want to matter and live lives that matter. Increasingly, our country has turned to material depth to define our success. Despite being more connected electronically, many have become much more disconnected relationally. Those that don't feel a sense of purpose and significance in their lives, relationships and occupations have an even greater likelihood of trying to fill their bucket with more stuff to prove to themselves and to others that they have made it and are living lives of achievement.

The temptation to have things and achieve significance is further fueled by our comparison to others, which starts at an early age and has been amplified through the world of social media. Our friends and neighbors are doing the same thing, which makes it like an endless loop of keeping up with the Joneses. As we get more stuff, the Joneses get more stuff, which convinces us that we need and should have more stuff. Somebody always has more or the next newer thing than we do, making this desire to keep up an insatiable drive. That is the unending loop that we find ourselves in. We want to impress others and prove that we have made it, ultimately drawing our happiness from our comparisons to others. What's ironic is that our attempts to show our wealth and affluence actually sabotage our ability to actually do it!

Our insecurities and fears, masked as pride, also hurt us when it comes to reaching out for help. We want to maintain control and convince our hard-headed selves that we've still got this. When the loop of buying stuff starts to hurt and becomes difficult to manage, most of us don't seek help to escape the loop until we reach a breaking point. After all, seeking help would mean that I overextended myself, which means that I haven't done as well as I came across. That puts me in a lonely and awkward spot because what's my problem, everyone else is doing just fine! No, they're not. They are no different and likely worse off than you. The greater it "looks" like they have found financial success, the greater the possibility that they are broke, not only with no or little savings, but up to their eyeballs in debt. But we don't see that. None of us wear a nametag with our net worth listed in big bold letters and most certainly don't share their financial struggles. Our personal finances are held very private and are typically not discussed. So, we fall for appearances, and as we should know, appearances can be deceiving! We allow ourselves to be deceived, entering a vicious cycle of trying to keep up and provide our families with the same nice things and nice vacations as the other families.

Overcoming pride and reaching out is especially difficult for many men, who feel responsible for adequately providing the stuff, experiences and overall happiness levels for their families. Those serving their country in the military or as first responders carry an extra burden in this regard. No room for showing any chinks in the armor on the job, and that carries over into our personal lives as well. Admitting troubles would be admitting that we're human, and have flaws, which is the opposite of the persona that we fill while on the job.

The second most common root cause is a lack of contentment. Regardless of how we stack up and come across to others, most truly believe that having that next greatest car, house, vacation, whatever "it" may be, will bring the comfort and long-lost happiness that we have so desperately desired. When we bring in our first large purchase...a new car for many, it may feel good and what we equate to success, but the high slowly fades. Instead of realizing early on in adulthood that no amount of stuff or nicer things will ultimately bring long-term happiness, most of us, myself included, assume that the target was just wrong. The new car was okay, but it's really going to be the nice vacations that do it for me. So, we aim our sights on filling our bucket with great vacations. Don't get me wrong, vacations are great, and can certainly feel good in the moment and even provide some great memories. But even the amount of happiness gained from world travels fades with time.

New cars were nice to have, nice vacations were enjoyed, albeit costly to sustain. Now if I could only buy that nice house, then I will have finally found the ultimate source of my long-term happiness and contentment. The problem, of course, is that when we finally achieve that next greatest level, whatever it may be, it may scratch the itch for the short term but it's not long until we are wanting more. The newer nicer car or next bigger house was great, but if we could work ourselves into a slightly bigger house, then life would be awesome and I will be perfectly happy there, for good. So, we sacrifice ourselves at work, go into more debt, and convince ourselves that this next jump up will be it. As just about anyone that has achieved that perceived pinnacle, it's NEVER enough to completely fill our cup.

Our contentment also ties back to our comparisons with others. If we aren't feeling content with what we have, we have a tendency to look to others for what appears to be making them content. And we don't have to look very far. Not only are we surrounded by others and their stuff in our neighborhoods, but we see the very best sides of others and their stuff through our social media accounts. Amazing vacations, houses, cars - you name it, we see it, nonstop, and convince ourselves that if others look content then that must be what we need too. In an effort to scratch the contentment itch, things previously considered wants become needs. Feelings of "I need..." or "the kids need..." becomes our mantra on our unending quest to achieve contentment.

Our pursuit of more stuff is insatiable. We have greater access to nicer, newer stuff than the vast majority of the world. And that's exactly what many of us aim to do... get more stuff. We even run out of room for our stuff in our homes, attic spaces and garages, driving many to go out and get even more space for their stuff in a storage unit. We now have over 2.3 BILLION square feet of storage space in this country.[2] That's nearly enough for every single American household to have nearly twenty square feet of storage space. That's A LOT of storage space. And it doesn't come cheap either, often costing renters $100+ per month. Despite having more stuff and paying dearly to store it, most of it just sits and goes unused, collecting dust while draining our ability to use the same dollars for long-term growth.

An added challenge and contributing factor is that we are literally surrounded by industries appealing to our weaknesses. We are bombarded by advertisers, all looking to convince us that their service or product will bring us our long-sought after contentment. Their job, which many marketers are fantastic at accomplishing, is to make us feel that instead of a want, or something we deserve, they are selling us something that we absolutely need and cannot live without. But how often have we fallen for that appeal, only to regret the purchase months, weeks or even just days later?

Our fears associated with a low credit score deliver us right into the hands of credit agencies, banks and the credit card industry. Their use of fear as a marketing tactic is absolutely brilliant, as it also simultaneously exploits our biggest weakness, a desire for more stuff!

A sense of entitlement is also a contributing factor to our struggle with contentment. We often feel due for things that have been earned, with a strong case of "deservitis," after putting in long hours at work or going through a life changing event. Our level of entitlement often traces back to our childhoods. Those given much from their parents are likely to carry the same feeling of being due things into adulthood. If we remove any feelings of entitlement, that in itself does not guarantee fulfillment and contentment. It can amplify our struggles, however.

When we can't afford more stuff, we either go far into debt, turn our focus to raising our income as a solution to buy more stuff, or both. I chased a higher income for many years for that exact reason. If I make more, I can take nicer vacations, buy nicer things, have a bigger house, and ultimately, find contentment and happiness. I was chasing an unending dream for more. But would it really bring more happiness?

There was a study done a few years back that looked at the correlation between higher incomes and increased happiness. The takeaway was that the "knee in the curve" is a salary of around $75,000. "No matter how much more than $75,000 people make, they don't report any greater degree of happiness," Time reported, citing a study from Princeton University.[3] But how could that possibly be? Having more income allows us the opportunity to buy and do more – how could our level of happiness not continue to go up as our income rises above this level?

The really unfortunate part is that by the time most of us achieve that long awaited higher income level, that we so desperately wanted, and then realize that it didn't bring the expected increase in overall happiness and contentment, we are much further down the road, full of regrets. Regrets of lost time with family. Regrets of wasted income. Regrets of lost opportunity to save and invest for the long-term. All of the stuff that we thought would bring contentment actually ended up having the opposite effect, bringing debt and discontent. It's a tough lesson to learn on our own, made even tougher by the fact that we can't buy back time, our most precious commodity in terms of our finances.

Struggles with contentment don't necessarily mean that we are being selfish and looking out just for ourselves. In fact, for many with families, it's more about providing a great life for them. We want to provide well for our loved ones, ideally even better than what our parents did for us growing up. This is especially true for those that didn't have much in their childhoods. We saw other kids that seemingly had everything and although we couldn't enjoy that feeling as a kid, we can try for our own kids. Since it looked like those kids with more than us got to experience more happiness, we aim to provide that for our kids. Our families may be perfectly provided for without having a lot of nice things or nice vacations, but we want our kids to have what others have and have and experience more than we did.

The fault in this is twofold. First, those kids that we thought had everything growing up, and were therefore happy, were probably not nearly as happy or content as we think they were. Many likely had parents that they saw very little of, or were part of broken families, and deep down would have traded most of the things and experiences for closer relationships and more quality time with family. The second downside is that by being a great provider of all of our kids' wants, we are likely teaching them that they CAN have everything, which is not setting them up for success in adulthood. This becomes a vicious cycle, raising our kids to expect to have what they want for themselves and their own kids once adults. By the time we start to see that more stuff really doesn't buy happiness, the seed has already been planted with our kids and the cycle continues into their adulthood. In the end, we are left with generations of broke adults, chasing an ideal and standard that has no end. Meanwhile, the retiring generation is full of regrets of not doing a better job preparing themselves for their retirement years.

We are masters at justifying the purchase of wants. "I deserve or my family deserves…" Often strong wants even become needs, upgrading to "I need or my family needs." The more we have, the less we appreciate, which fuels the fire and accelerates the downward spiral on a quest for contentment.

I will share two quick examples from my own life, from a pursuit of stuff. The first was a shiny new sportscar as a young adult. If I'm honest with myself, it was as much to impress others as it was about my own enjoyment. Don't get me wrong, it was an awesome feeling when I first had it, fun to drive and surely impressive to those around me (or maybe not). After getting married and deciding to go with something more family friendly, along with a much lower insurance premium, I decided to sell it just a few years later. The car had already lost half of its value! Being a glutton for punishment, I couldn't help calculating the amount that I had lost by driving that sportscar as a young 20-something. Had I instead invested that amount that was lost in three short years, it would have been nearly enough to purchase a house, with cash, twenty years later when I retired from the military. Was three years of driving a sweet ride worth that loss of opportunity cost to me? Not even close.

The second example occurred just before the financial light bulb finally went off. With moving around every couple of years, I convinced myself, and my wife, that we should buy a vacation home. Not a time share, but an actual second home. It would be for the kids really... providing them a place to call home despite the many military moves around the world. An added benefit would be having the house available in retirement. It was in a great location, on a lake and not far from a major city in the northeast. Not only would this be a great thing for our family, but it would also be a great investment that would appreciate as well. Win-win! So, we went through with it, and proceeded to use it for about six weeks every summer. Don't get me wrong, the times we spent there were amazing, and I don't regret the great family memories. But did we really have to purchase a house that we could only use for a fraction of the year? We could have made the same awesome memories in the same area by just renting a nice lake house for those same weeks every summer. Except that would have cost us a fraction of the amount than what we spent by owning! That purchase proved to be a painful, yet powerful lesson driven by multiple root causes... my own pride and contentment, as well as my family's, rationalizing with our kids' happiness to seal the deal.

If we want to change our ways long-term, for the purposes of achieving our "why," we absolutely have to get past the symptoms and to the real root of our behaviors. Otherwise, we will be destined to fall right back into the same ways that have brought us to where we are today. We need to identify what we have allowed to have a hold on us. If it's more stuff, is it for our own pride or are we trying to fill an insatiable contentment bucket? Ask yourself, what is the driving force behind my spending and chase of more stuff? Am I willing to seek wisdom from others, or is my ego getting in the way? Be honest with yourself as to whether your pride and struggles with contentment are getting in your way of achieving your goals. Recognizing that they are the roots is half the battle, bringing us wisdom beyond our years that very few discover until time has passed and the climb to achieving wealth becomes unattainable. And remember that any feelings that you are alone in this battle are simply not reality, recalling that most households in this country are struggling, living from one paycheck to the next.

Take some time to really examine what things and experiences have brought you true long-term contentment. If you are a young adult, talk to some older family members and see what wisdom they may have to share on the topic. This doesn't mean that you shouldn't buy or experience things, but instead may need to become more selective in which are truly worth the cost and lost opportunity in other areas. Perhaps after giving it some thought and gaining wisdom from others, it's really only one or two areas that you deem worth it instead of ten. There will always be a new shiny object that we will convince ourselves is a need if we don't get our arms around the contentment issue. If you don't identify and cure the contentment issue, it will be increasingly difficult to ever get ahead and achieve your goals. Once again, the best answer is going back to your "why," and deciding whether each desired object or experience is bringing you closer to or farther from achieving the desired end result. If the answer is farther away, then you may need to choose more selectively, given what's at stake.

Applied knowledge is power. That is never more true than when it comes to learning about ourselves and what fuels our fire. Very few achieve long-term wealth, projecting themselves into a position to achieve their goals of prosperity and generosity, without first overcoming their own shortfalls. The great news is that while our environment can influence our behaviors, the true root causes of our financial paths are ultimately within our own control. If you truly desire to DO BETTER, you have to identify and change the roots, which means changing the person in the mirror!

D
O
BELIEVE
E
T
T
E
R

"Whether you think you can, or think you can't, you're right!"
- Henry Ford

16

The Power of Belief

Everything that you have ever accomplished, and remain proud of accomplishing to this day, happened in large part because you had purpose, your "why," then decided to make it a reality because you believed it to be possible. If we don't believe, we don't achieve.

When I look back over my time in the Air Force, there are a few professional events that stand out. Soloing a powered aircraft at 18 as a cadet. Leading packages of 30+ aircraft as a mission commander in air combat as a Captain. Having the humbling honor of leading a fired-up group of TACPs in ground combat. Briefing the Chief of Staff of the Air Force on F-35 testing as a young Major. Flying the three different service variants of the F-35 as an initial cadre pilot. All stood out as being special opportunities for this kid from a small farm town, and I will always remain grateful for each and every one.

I have zero misconceptions that any of those accomplishments were a result of just being that good. But as opportunities presented themselves, often due to favorable timing and forces way beyond my own capability, I would have never pulled any of those off had I not believed they were possible. And trust me when I say that with each of those events, I had my share of doubts and many thoughts of doing an about face and turning down the opportunity because my belief wavered. That's normal though, after all we are human. I'm not telling you that should have no doubts. That would only be possible if you were a robot, which none of us are. No matter how confident someone appears, they have doubts in their abilities from time to time. But you have to believe that building wealth is possible for you, more so than you believe that it's not.

So how do we build a belief that something is possible? Seeing the example of others that have gone before us is a huge bonus. I wasn't the first to ever solo an airplane, not the first F-16 combat mission commander, not the first to brief the Chief. Nor was I the first to fly any of the three F-35 variants. All of those had already been accomplished. Had any of those not been done by others, that would have required a whole different level of confidence and belief. Chuck Yeager being the first to break the speed of sound, for example. Talk about some guts. But that's not what we are looking at with doing better with our finances. There are over ten million millionaires in our country, 80-90% of whom started with nothing, no different than most of us.[1,2]

If others before you have done it, many times over, why not you?

The influence of others that you allow to speak into your life and sway your belief is also huge. Throughout all of my career, I have always had the benefit of parents that believed and supported my dreams, and, after getting married in my early 20s, a wife that was my biggest supporter. I also had the enormous benefit of leaders that believed in me which boosted my confidence. Whether it be an instructor pilot, a squadron commander, or a multitude of other Air Force leaders, their support and encouragement had a powerful impact on my belief that overcoming challenges were possible. Who are you allowing to speak into your life and sway your belief?

One of the problems we run into with our finances is that we don't talk about them very much, if at all, with others besides our spouses. Also, most of those around us don't believe that wealth is possible for everyone in this country, so even if we do talk with others, it's unlikely that they are filling us up with confidence. When provided the opportunity to speak with servicemembers on military installations, or with groups of veterans or first responders, I often start off with a survey. One of the questions is in regard to their belief as to whether building wealth, of at least a million dollars by typical retirement age of 65, is possible. The results have been surprisingly consistent. Overall, 65% say that they don't believe that level of wealth is likely for them. Two out of every three, the majority of whom are in their 20s, don't believe. You can probably guess what one of my primary goals is when speaking... helping them believe that wealth is not only possible, but 100% doable.

Many of you reading, just like most that I coach, are probably thinking... "that's great for them, but what about me? My situation is different." I believe in each and every one of you reading this book. How could I say that if I don't even know the specifics of your situation? Because I have coached you. Over the years, I have coached many just like you, and seen it all. No matter what the starting point, I have seen singles and couples turn it around and get on a solid track to building wealth. But they had to first believe and, for many, hear it was possible from someone else. You have far greater potential, and are capable of much further results, than what you may give yourself credit for! Most of us are our own biggest obstacle... don't limit yourself like that. Don't fall for your own mythology, for anything is possible for anyone, if you believe!

** CAUTION **

Failing to truly believe that you are in charge of your own financial destiny, and that wealth is 100% possible for you, will very likely limit your long-term effectiveness, regardless of any other financial principles that you learn.

Sometimes, despite desperately wanting to believe, we just can't see a way out on our own. When we lose sight and can't see the other side, it's hard to convince ourselves that taking action to fix our circumstance will pay off in the long run. If you are struggling to see a way out, feeling defeated by your circumstance, I would encourage you to search YouTube for debt-free screams and find a family that you can associate with. Seeing the examples of others that have gone before us can be incredibly powerful, restoring our hope and belief that better is possible. If you can find someone else that was where you are today, and was able to work themselves out and back on track, then why can't you do the same?

"It doesn't matter where you came from,
it matters where you are going!"
- Condoleezza Rice

17

Line In the Sky

One of the most difficult aspects of flying through clouds or at night is overcoming the lies that you tell yourself. Without a horizon to reference, a line in the sky, we have a tendency to rely on our equilibrium. Without getting too far down in the weeds, we get our sense of balance from fluids inside our ears. These fluids tend to work okay as long as a pilot flies straight and level. But when a turn is held for an extended time, your ears start to sense that the turn is your new straight and level. When that happens, and the pilot then comes out of the turn, even though they may be going straight again, the ears now tell the brain that they are in a turn going the opposite direction. When this happens and our senses start lying to us, it can have catastrophic results. For this reason, aircraft must have reliable instruments to be safely flown in the weather or at night. One of the primary instruments is an attitude indicator, which provides an accurate line in the sky in the cockpit. All pilots know that in order to survive, they have to disregard the bad info that their ears are sending their brains and rely fully on their instruments.

The information that our brain gets from our senses regarding wealth is often a lie as well. In this case it's not the fluids in our ears, but rather what our ears are hearing. Sources all around us are constantly feeding us bad information, not based upon facts and truths, but rather misconceptions and blatant lies. We hear from others that wealth comes from winning the lottery, or inheritance, or from having a high income, or from get-rich quick schemes, or is reserved only for those that came from wealth. When we hear this type of information, it's easy to fall for it and start to convince ourselves that those paths are the only way to build wealth. Many of us also use those same pieces of information to justify to ourselves why we will always struggle with money. If we don't win the lottery, or receive an inheritance, or have a six-figure job, or pick a lucky stock that hits it big, all of which most in our country don't, then we use that as an excuse and it goes into our "box of buts."

Have you caught yourself believing one or more of these paths is necessary to build wealth? I sure did. For many years, I was convinced that a high income was the solution. I wasn't playing the lottery, expecting an inheritance, or playing around with the stock market, so that left salary as the solution. Sure, I knew that there was value in investing, but since I didn't earn a high income, I had convinced myself that I couldn't do it. The fact that we were spending like it was going out of style wasn't the problem at all. The obstacle standing in my way of achieving financial independence was salary. And since I couldn't increase my salary, other than with incremental promotion cycles, that belief fit well with my justification of not investing, complementing my "yeah, but" really well.

What are you telling yourself regarding the source of wealth? If you're like most in this country, you have likely fallen for one or more of these false horizons. In fact, in a recent study, nearly three out of every four millennials believed that millionaires in this country had inherited their wealth.[1] Is that really the case? Not even close. In reality, the same study found that only 3% of millionaires had received an inheritance over $1M. While nearly 75% thought that's where the wealth came from, in reality it was found to be only 3%! Not only is that not in the same ballpark, but it's essentially the complete opposite of truth. Just like a pilot thinking they are in a right turn while actually going left, in the opposite direction.

In order to start believing that we can do better with our finances and ultimately achieve financial independence, we have got to have an accurate financial line in the sky. A horizon line that provides truth based upon fact, versus falsehoods that we perceive as truth. Fortunately, there have been many studies on those that have built and successfully managed wealth. One of the first break through studies on wealth was conducted by Thomas Stanley and William Danko, documented in the release of their book, *The Millionaire Next Door*, in 1996. The authors really burst the bubbles of many of our misconceptions of where wealth comes from and how the wealthy live. Since then, several books and studies have been written on the topic, highlighting the truths behind wealth that we can learn valuable lessons from.

Before highlighting some of the findings revealed in these studies, let's pause for a minute. Most of these books and studies have focused on millionaires, meaning those that have a financial net worth of at least one million dollars. I would like to highlight that there is nothing magical or pivotal about having a million dollars. All too often I see or hear of those that achieved this desired level of wealth and then find themselves at a loss, thinking "now what?" and not nearly as satisfied and content as expected. This often leads to increasing the goal. If $1M didn't bring contentment, surely $2M will! But it doesn't. Setting your sights on a certain amount of money, strictly for the purposes of achieving that dollar figure, will always be a moving line and one that will never satisfy on its own.

Remember that we aren't chasing a number just to reach the number, but rather setting our aim on goals that will help us to achieve our "whys"...to provide for our family, provide a comfortable life without the burden of daily financial stress, put us in a position where we can give generously if we choose, and in a position to retire with dignity. A healthy achievement of wealth is all about having a healthy and noble "why," not about us being able to call ourselves a millionaire.

With that said, a one million dollar or more financial net worth, the definition of making someone a millionaire, is often used for studies. While I do not recommend becoming focused on setting that number as your goal simply to be able say that you are a millionaire, we can still learn from those that have achieved and held wealth, thereby in a position to meet their personal goals.

What can we learn from these studies to bolster our belief that better is in fact possible for each and every one of us? First, several of the major studies find that the vast majority of millionaires are first generation. Danko and Stanley's study reported that the percentage of those that did not come from wealth represented more than 80%.[2] Not only did most not come from wealthy families, but many are not even born here. Research shows that immigrants, meaning those not born in America, are four times more likely to become a millionaire in this country.[3] One plausible explanation of this finding is the fact that many who come to this country give up everything they have known for the opportunity that is available in the U.S. They made a decision, have a strong "why," goals and commitment level, often have counter-cultural views on the "benefits" of debt, and definitely believe that life here will be better. In other words, they have uncommon levels of thrust! Not only is better financial opportunity possible for those that arrive later in life, but also for anyone born here in America.

In his latest book, *Everyday Millionaires*, Chris Hogan reported the results of his team interviewing over 10,000 millionaires, representing one of the largest studies of millionaires ever completed in our country. It's a great read, which I highly recommend for anyone looking to be further motivated by the many inspirational stories of everyday folks who have achieved financial independence. There is nothing common about what these people have done with the same average incomes that most of us in this country are blessed to have. The book is chockful of eye-opening findings. Here are a few very interesting takeaways from their study on millionaires[4]:

- 8 out of 10 came from families at or below middle-class income level
- 79% received zero inheritance
- 1 of every 3 never had a $100K or greater annual household income
- 69% did not average $100K or more in household income per year over course of their career
- The top three occupations of millionaires in the study: accountants, engineers and schoolteachers

That's right, the majority were not high-income earners as most may think. Many that I ask guess that doctors, lawyers and top executives top the list. But that was not the case in this very extensive study. The bottom line is that wealth, for most, doesn't come from where we would typically think that it would. The takeaway? If everyday folks can do it, why not you? Which "yeah, buts" do you have left?

The last point to highlight is what you may believe about those with wealth. Have you built up a belief that wealthy individuals are all greedy jerks? While that can be a common misconception, there are lots of great things that many in these studies choose to do with the wealth that they have built up over decades of disciplined saving. Many are extremely generous and have philanthropic ideals. Of course, as always there are exceptions, but I would contend that many with an inward focus are likely to have always had that attitude. The opposite is also true. Those who choose to be incredibly generous with their wealth are likely to have had that spirit all along. Money, in and of itself, is not inherently good or bad. The holder gets to choose between doing something positive or negative. Wealth often accentuates the attributes that we already have, good or bad.

By and large, your ability to do better financially relies upon your decisions and levels of discipline and proactive approach. Same goes for how wealth is used – the choice is yours!

"When everything seems to be going against you,
remember that the airplane takes off against the wind, not with it."
- Henry Ford

18

Overcome

The most common anchor that I see sabotage one's belief that better is possible is something from their past or present that has convinced them otherwise and is holding them back. While I have experienced my fair share of financial stress and frustrations, I haven't personally experienced bankruptcy, foreclosure or any other catastrophic financial events. How could I understand if I haven't been there myself? Because I have been there in other areas of my life, right there where you are, with the same kind of doubt and discouraging past that has sunk my belief in doing better.

You heard many of the accomplishments that I was blessed to have experienced during my Air Force career. You may have thought, "good for you" or "yeah, it's easy when everything just falls into your lap." And some of those opportunities felt like they did fall in my lap. But I have also experienced my share of adversity.

After years of goal setting, hard work and occasional minor setbacks, I finally achieved my childhood dream by becoming a CMR (combat mission-ready) F-16 pilot at my first assignment in 1998. After learning to fly the jet at Luke Air Force Base, in Arizona, I was assigned to Kunsan Airbase in South Korea for my first operational tour. Towards the end of what I considered a fairly successful year long assignment, my wife flew over to join me for my last couple of weeks in country. We had plans to travel down to Australia, then visit family in the States, enroute to our next assignment in Germany. On August 11, 1999, I picked up my wife at the nearby airport, then had to hustle back to the squadron for a flight that afternoon. It was going to be good one that I didn't want to miss, with an opportunity to drop live bombs at one of the nearby training ranges. Getting to drop live weapons is an opportunity that happens few and far between, so I was really looking forward to it.

I was #4, flying the fourth aircraft in a flight of four. I was, by far, the youngest and least experienced of the four pilots on the flight, with two of the pilots being leaders of the wing and graduates of the Air Force Weapons School (think the Air Force's version of Top Gun). The flight went uneventfully, and unfortunately, we were unable to expend our live weapons due to some popup restrictions near the range after getting airborne. So, we flexed to a backup mission and then headed back to base with our live bombs still hanging under our wings. As we got back to the base, we split up into two sets of two aircraft. My element lead, #3 in the flight, passed me the lead of our 2-ship, as he had to burn down some extra gas before landing. I accepted the lead of our formation and proceeded to fly back to our home base with him strung back a couple of miles behind me. Much to my regret, I proceeded to fly too directly to the base, at way too high of an airspeed, which was my habit pattern from flying a different type of approach. But today, due to having live bombs on our wings, we were directed to fly a straight-in full-stop approach. By the time I realized the mistake that I was much too steep and fast to fly a straight-in, it required focused effort to slow down and get down to the proper glidepath. What I should have done was gone around and set it back up for another approach. But I didn't. I continued proceeding too steep and too fast, convinced that I could salvage the approach.

With my focus on slowing down and fixing my steep glidepath, I completely missed the fact that I was gaining on the other two jets in our formation that had gone ahead of us to land. To make matters worse, my radio call to tower happened at the same time as their radio call, so I completely missed the fact that I was gaining on them quickly. What happened next has been seared into my mind since. Out of the corner of my eye, I picked up one of their aircraft just below and to the side of my jet. Quickly realizing that I was about to impact another aircraft, I put in full control inputs to turn and climb away. Unfortunately, my last-ditch effort wasn't enough. My right wing impacted the #2 aircraft's left wing, shearing the live bomb off from under my right wing. As I quickly tried to process what just happened, I saw a fire break out on his left wing, followed by his canopy separating from the jet, and then watched in disbelief as the ejection seat took him out of his jet. I continued to climb my jet away from the ground, just a few hundred feet below, as I watched #2's jet, now without a pilot in the seat, impact the ground and explode into a fireball not far from the end of the runway. With my heart feeling like it was about to pound out of my chest, trying to understand what had just led to the destruction of a $30M+ aircraft, I circled back around and landed my damaged aircraft. After landing, my thoughts immediately turned to the pilot that had ejected. Did he make it out safely? Did his parachute have time to open given how low he ejected over the bay just south of the runway? What if I just killed him? Millions of thoughts flooded my mind as I powered my jet down and watched countless emergency vehicles scream down the taxiway towards the crash site.

After waiting for what seemed like an eternity, I received word back that the pilot was alive and ok. Thank you, God! The weeks that followed were intense to say the least. Two different types of safety boards convened, as is normal protocol for any high dollar military mishap. The pilot that I had collided with was well and quickly cleared back to fly. For obvious reasons, I was held from further flying until the boards convened. My leadership could have decided to take my wings, but, thankfully, they did not. I was a young Lieutenant that had made a costly mistake, and they decided to give me another chance. My commanders also attributed their giving me a second shot to the fact that I had no made excuses or placed blame on others, but rather taken ownership for what had gone wrong. Being given another chance and seeing the return on owning mistakes served as valuable lessons that stuck with me for the rest of my career.

So, I got back up into the air and, shortly after, headed out to our next assignment in Germany. My confidence had definitely been shaken, but I didn't have time to deal with that, or so I thought. I had a new squadron to report to and all that kept going through my mind was the impression many of my new squadron mates were now going to have of me, and how I was going to overcome that.

The new assignment in Germany went well initially, with each day slowly putting more distance between the present and that horrific event. While I would like to say that was the end of the story and my career had no more major hiccups, unfortunately I cannot. Just a few months after reporting to my new squadron at Spangdahlem Airbase, Germany, I was finishing up my local checkout and flying a local night mission. As we headed back to base to land, we were told that there were reports of some minor wind shear on final. That essentially means that the winds weren't consistent, varying in direction. Our flight pressed on, with a plan to simply carry some extra airspeed on final to overcome any of the varying winds. I was the second aircraft of our flight of four to line up for landing. #1 was able to land successfully. So, I continued along on final, carrying a few extra knots of airspeed, as we say as pilots, "for Mom and the kids."

As I came across the runway and prepared to touchdown, I encountered what felt like a stall, with the left wing of my jet quickly dropping out of the sky towards the runway not far below. Thankfully my reaction was quick – pushing the power back up to full afterburner, quickly accelerating and going back around. Although not quite as intense as the incident in Korea, here I was once again flying with my heart about to pound out of my chest. Fortunately, I was able to make it back around and have an uneventful landing. As I pulled back into the run station, I asked the crewchief to take a close look at my left wing, concerned that it may have impacted the runway. I'm sure he was pretty surprised by the request, as scraping a wing on the ground is not what you would call a common occurrence! He reported back that in fact I had scraped my wing and there was damage to the underside of the left-wing weapon station. I couldn't believe what was happening...first the mishap in Korea and now this!?

179 days after the accident in Korea, I came a fraction of a second away from another near catastrophic event. I had never come as close to being killed in an aircraft accident, other than the mid-air collision six months before. Yet here I was, now in my second operational assignment, still a young Lieutenant, with two events under my wing that most are fortunate enough to never experience over an entire career.

That second incident rattled me even more than the first. This time, now with a newborn on the way, I decided I was done. Despite putting in years of work through high school, at the Academy, through pilot training, F-16 training, and now into my second tour, I was done. I no longer believed in my flying abilities and had zero interest in ever flying another airplane ever again. I made the decision to turn in my wings to my squadron commander, telling him that I was finished flying. Despite giving up the dream, my will to fly had been broken and I felt confident that this was the right decision for me and my family. Flying wasn't worth it to me, and I figured I could just move over to a non-flying job, which there are many of in the Air Force, and still serve out my time that I still owed the Air Force.

Fortunately, the Air Force, which had just spent several million dollars getting me trained up as a fighter pilot, wasn't so quick on closing that door for good. After taking some time off, contemplating my future, our flight doc, "Voodoo" Nelson, brought me in to his office to see how I was doing. I shared more details on both mishaps, and my decision to quit flying, but he had another idea. Whether I ever flew again or not, he wanted me to make sure that I was back on top of my game for myself, for my wife, for our unborn child, and, lastly, for the Air Force. He convinced me that talking through the events with a doc back in San Antonio, Texas, was in my best interest. He even worked it out so my pregnant wife could come with me, as this had all impacted her quite a bit as well. I figured if nothing else it was a chance to get away, with my wife by my side, from the constant reminders of the events at the squadron.

Long story short, my wife and I spent a week talking with an amazing individual. Along with Doc Voodoo, Dr. John Patterson will always have my utmost gratitude and admiration. Collectively, these two gentlemen got me back on the step, not only as a pilot, but as a contributing member of society, as a husband and, shortly thereafter, as a father. Soon after, my wife and I were back in Germany, and, after some flights in the simulator, I got back up in the air in an F-16. My confidence didn't come back all at once, but slowly, flight after flight, I regained the belief in my abilities, even surpassing where I had been before the two mishaps.

For many years, I often questioned why those two events had to happen. Over time, I started to see that they had made me even stronger than I would have been had they not occurred. I will remain eternally grateful that neither myself nor any others were killed during those incidents. I don't think I will ever get to the point that I can honestly say that I wouldn't trade that trying period of my life if I could go back. But now, years later, I can actually say that those experiences made me stronger and inspired me to do better. Once I believed again and had my hope restored, I decided to use those events to push me to be as good as I could possibly be.

Those two near-death aviation mishaps were not the last of the challenges that I would face while in the service. Several combat deployments, both in the air and with ground forces, presented new challenges to work through. Beyond my own experiences, losing many friends over the years, all in aviation accidents on training flights, served as a constant reminder of the risk associated with fighter operations. One of those lost, who had, upon my request, taken my place on a night flight presented the greatest struggle of my career. But despite the ensuing struggles, I'm still here, just as you are, and know that I've still got work left to do.

Working through challenges, disappointments and loss will never be easy. That would require one to be inhuman. But making it through those first two aircraft mishaps greatly strengthened my ability to make it through future challenges. They helped me arrive at a few key realizations. The first was that we are only meant to carry so much on our own, which is very often less than we convince ourselves of. I had also learned the value, and absolute necessity of, dealing with challenges by facing them head-on. The docs had helped me become more comfortable talking about struggles with others rather than keeping them bottled up inside left to fester. Most importantly, those initial experiences had taught me to lean on my faith, which was certainly strengthened as a result.

I definitely do not have all the answers and know that I am not done growing, nor will I ever be. I realize those experiences strengthened me. Not only that, they gave me the opportunity to strengthen and encourage others. Had I not experienced each of those painful events, I can honestly say that I would likely not have achieved many of the accomplishments that came after and would be less equipped to understand and identify with the adversity that many others face.

Are you feeling hopeless regarding your financial outlook, as if any financial hole you may stand in today is inescapable? Just as Doc Voodoo and Doc Patterson did for me, I am here today as your personal finance instructor pilot to tell you that better is possible. You can overcome your present circumstance regardless of where you are and where you have been and still come out on top. You do not have to allow any setbacks or failures to define you and become a permanent condition. Whatever it is you may be facing, regardless of how steep the odds, your situation is not fixed. It can be changed with your decisions and effort. You can use the pain of the past to serve as a catalyst for changing tomorrow for the better. Yes, you've got a story to tell, but also have a story yet to be written and told. Only one person gets to decide which direction any past struggles will take you – the one in the mirror. It's you versus you.

If you are convinced that your present circumstance will never pass, I would challenge you to think back on some of the other adversities that you have overcome in your life. While other circumstances likely felt as if they would never pass and would always define you, my bet is that as you look back today that part of your life likely feels like much shorter now in hindsight. And if it was big enough to define who you are today, those situations likely molded you for the better in the long run. Most importantly, you overcame them, just as you will overcome whatever you face today.

You are far stronger than you may give yourself credit. Don't allow yourself and your disbelief that better is possible to stand in your path any longer. Many others have been right where you are today and not only made it out but rose back to the top, fully realizing all of their potential. Restoring your vision for the future, eliminating whatever is dragging you down, whether internally or externally, and believing in yourself is everything to your thrust. The stronger you believe, the greater your thrust. Do not allow any event to define you or what you are capable of. Instead, use it to fuel your fire and kick the power into full afterburner! Get back up and keep on getting up. You have to decide, will those events be your story, or are you going to rise above them and rewrite your own story?

There is no doubt that <u>you can overcome</u>…. but to do so you absolutely must believe!

Believing that you can do better is a make or break step to generating, and maintaining, your thrust. You can decide you are ready to commit to new ways, decide your why, and have your eyes opened to truths. But if you do not believe that better is possible for you and in your ability to ultimately achieve your why, regardless of where you find yourself today, it just won't happen. Your engine will flameout and soon be back to generating zero thrust.

Our belief in ourselves can either be extremely powerful, or very crippling. The best intentions and plans in the world are often sabotaged by a negative attitude...that voice in the back of our head that tells us we can't do something. Many of us carry around our own personal "box of buts," as in excuses we use to convince ourselves why we can't do something. If we allow it, that box becomes an anchor. On the other hand, someone that truly believes they can reach great heights in any part of their lives is a force to be reckoned with. Do you believe that better and achieving your financial why is possible?

Deciding, opening your eyes and believing give you the thrust needed to taxi out of the chocks, takeoff, and, very importantly, stay airborne! Now that we have the left-hand working, and can push up the throttle, we need to switch to the right hand and learn control of the stick. The control stick provides a plane with its ability to climb and turn to a new vector. Being "all thrust and no vector," as new pilots who are all go but no direction are referred to, would have us flying in circles. Education gives us our flight plan, focusing us on the "what" and the "how" to reach our "why." We have looked at what doesn't work. Now we need to look at wise and proven principles that work for everyone that commits to them.

* A Note to our Combat Veterans and First Responders:

Many are facing battles that no one else can see. This is especially prevalent within our communities of guardians who willingly put their life on the line for others and endure traumatic events on a regular basis. Our servicemembers and first responders often put the needs of others before their own… after all, it's what their occupations are founded upon. These professions demand extreme levels of reliability and call us to be superhuman. But at the end of the day, we are all still human and have limits to what we can take and handle on our own.

If you have experienced traumatic events, please don't allow any perceived stigma of seeking improved mental health and wellness to prevent you from dealing with them. There is help available to walk with you, see you through any struggle that you may be facing, and guide you back to become even stronger through post-traumatic growth. If you or loved ones have recognized that you haven't been yourself, get yourself past the stigma of talking about it and talk to someone. True courage is having the guts to recognize and own your struggles, deal with them using available professionals, grow from them and get back on top. Where you go from here is up to you.

Also, recognize that financial wellness goes hand in hand with our mental and physical wellness. Taking charge of your finances will put you on a more solid financial footing, and in a better position to deal with challenges when they arise in the future.

Remember, while you may be bent from time to time, you will not be broken. Seek out the help that is <u>always</u> available and standing by to help!

D
O
B
EDUCATE
E
T
T
E
R

19

The Experts

A handful of instructor pilots fly and teach all of the other less experienced fighter pilots in a fighter squadron. These IPs, who represent 10-20% of the squadron, teach pilots to become an MR wingman for the unit's assigned mission, years later to become a flight lead, and then long-term to become the next set of instructor pilots. It's the continuous cycle of growth, experience and knowledge in a squadron. This construct is similar to how many of us grew up in a family. The kids are the wingmen, the parents the flight leads and the grandparents the instructor pilots, sharing their years of experience and gained wisdom. The instructor pilots have lots of great lessons learned to share.

Learning from our experience alone, with the associated bumps and bruises, is a tough way to learn. We can't afford to have a revolving cycle of pilots trying their own version of tactics, learning as they go, refining, and ultimately figuring out what works best. That would be a really inefficient, not to mention dangerous, way of doing business. So, where do instructor pilots learn as they progress through their flying career, other than from older instructor pilots? The go-to tactical expert in each fighter squadron is the weapons officer. Every pilot, including the instructor pilots, knows that if they have a question on the best tactics, there is no better source than the weapons officer. What's makes these pilots the go-to, and the desired source of improved knowledge and effectiveness? To become a Weapons Officer in the Air Force, or Top Gun in the Navy, a pilot is sent away to a unique special flight training program. The purpose of this incredibly intense program, six months in duration for the Air Force, is to make a small group of select instructor pilots even far better than they were. They are taught the latest and greatest threats, as well as the proven tactics that have been recently tested and validated.

Those that pass this intense test ultimately graduate and return to their home station to become their squadron's weapons officer for the next two to three years. The rest of the squadron pilots, looking to become the absolute best that they can, bring their questions to be answered by the weapons officer. They look to gain knowledge and wisdom from these proven tacticians and battlefield leaders, the go-to experts of the mission.

In the Open Eyes section, we learned what doesn't work. Adhering to the financial myths of our culture will result in us becoming and staying broke. Regardless of how much income you bring in, if you follow habits that make people broke, you will also eventually find yourself broke. Fortunately, the opposite is also true. Regardless of income, if we follow the habits of others that also started with nothing and built wealth, we will do the same. Having taken the time to build up the thrust to do better, the next step is becoming educated on how to actually do better.

As with any area of life that we want to improve in, whether it be our marriage, with our kiddos, in the workplace, getting into better shape, or becoming the best first responder or servicemember we can be, we need to look to the wisdom of experts for guidance.

While most of us recognize this in just about every other area of our lives, many are led astray when it comes to our finances. We tend to listen to others that appear to have a valid point, especially if it looks to have brought them the financial success that we would like for ourselves. So, we aim to emulate those who look the part of financial success, well dressed and living in nice houses and driving nice cars, for advice. While that seems like a completely common-sense approach, when it comes to our finances it is almost always a completely backwards approach. Those that appear to have wealth are very often in massive amounts of debt.

Here are a few examples from recent experiences with clients that I have coached. Two looked the part of the wealth that we are fed on TV and social media, driving really nice expensive cars, living in amazing homes, and fueled by great incomes, one a doctor and another a business executive. But each of their net worth statements told a different story. Despite consistently making between $200-300K for the past 5-10 years, with the lifestyle to show for it, one had a very low net worth, and the other actually had a negative net worth. Despite the amazing income that they were bringing in, they weren't consistently investing, and didn't see a way to afford doing so. Both had reached out for coaching after recognizing how crazy it was that they could not find money to consistently save and invest. When you make that kind of money yet struggle to save, it is no small task to swallow your pride and reach out for help, but each turned out to be very glad that they did.

I also had two other clients in the same time period, one a schoolteacher and another an aircraft mechanic. Both lived very modest lifestyles, making $50-70K per year, drove older used cars, but each had over a million dollars between their various investments. Millionaires, while making a fraction of the salaries of the doctor and executive! I can just about guarantee you that if I had asked 100 random folks that didn't know any of these four clients which two of these four individuals were millionaires, nearly every single one would have answered that it was the two with the high incomes, not those that looked and lived like everyday folks.

So, if we can't necessarily heed the advice of those that appear to be financially successful, who should we look to follow? Since most of those with actual wealth are much less likely to talk about it or show it, our best source of knowledge is studies that have been done on millionaires. That will be our focus. We need to study and learn from those that started with nothing, like most of us do, yet have built wealth with modest incomes and then held onto their wealth long-term, instead of squandering it like the many lottery winners that end up broke within a couple of years of winning.

If we want to build wealth and, in turn, achieve our goals and our "why," we need to emulate those that have done it, not just talked about doing it and certainly not those that look like they have done it but have not. Most fighter pilots will boast that they are the world's best fighter pilot, but when push comes to shove all of us know that the true oracle of tactical knowledge and effectiveness is the weapons officer. We seek out those that have walked the walk and graduated a most grueling program. It can be no different with our finances. We are surrounded by so called "experts" that always seem to have a theory and trick up their sleeve to help us all get rich quick. These are not the droids you seek!

I have lost count as to how many times I have had folks come up to talk with me after a group speaking engagement, mostly with servicemembers and first responders, and very quietly relay that they, too, are a millionaire. They don't do it to gloat or boast out of pride, and usually tell me so, but rather to validate the proven principles of those that successfully build wealth and achieve their unique goals of prosperity and generosity.

We have to learn the principles, all very simple to understand but requiring discipline to do, that are not theories, but actually proven by millions to generate millions! Be very careful who you take guidance and wisdom from. Just as with the many myths that were exposed in the Open Eyes section, if wealth building looks or sounds too good to be true, it nearly always is! Learn from those that have actually done it and sustained it before you, then fight the good fight and do the same for you and your household!

20

Scaling Mt. Wealth

In the Decide section, we talked about the why, the what and the how. Without the why, the what and how really don't matter much, as we won't do them anyway. Now that you have focused on and ignited your drive by identifying your "why," we need to visit the "what" and then dive into the "how." In the Open Eyes section, we looked at investing from the perspective of power lost each year that we delay...what not to do. In this chapter, we will look at it through a different lens...what we need to do from here on out to achieve financial goals. So, while we are discussing a similar topic, challenge yourself to look at it from a winning perspective versus a losing one.

The general premise to the "what" of meeting your financial "why" is wealth-building. How can I say that without even knowing what your why and goals are? Because I don't have to know your unique situation. No matter what it may be, I know what it is likely not. I will take a wild guess and presume that your "why" is not financial insecurity, with more stress in your life. I will also go out on a ledge and guess that one of your "whys" is to be in a position to comfortably provide for your family, achieve financial independence one day, and not <u>have to</u> continue to work until the day you pass. Choosing to continue working is a completely different story, but I have yet to meet anyone that would willingly choose to <u>have to</u> work into their 70s or 80s. If, by chance, you are fine with the thought of working into old age, I would still contend that this section applies, as you may not have the choice. Six out of every ten Americans end up not having a choice in the matter, due to sickness, injury, loss of employment, or needing to care for a loved own.[1] I am also confident in the fact that no matter what your long-term goals in retirement may be, whether traveling, volunteering, being super generous in your giving, whatever, that having wealth would put you in a stronger position to do so than without.

Regardless of what your goals and "why" may be, building wealth will put you in that position sooner and provides you with options. Options equal freedom. So, we are going to press on under the assumption that no matter which options you would like for goals of prosperity or generosity, that you are onboard with building wealth.

For those who have built wealth on their own, without an inheritance accounting for a majority of it (which is the overwhelming majority of millionaires in the US), there is one key to their wealth building. This is going to be mind-blowing...wait for it....

Consistent investing over a long period of time, taking advantage of the magic of compounding interest with an investment profile that spreads out risk by covering different asset classes.

There it is folks, that is the source of wealth for most of our millionaires. Crazy, right?

For many more than not, wealth is not about striking it rich, having the luck of stumbling upon the next up and coming company's stock, an inheritance, or even being a high-income earner. Can those things happen and result in wealth? Absolutely. But do the facts tell us that this is how most build wealth in America? That would be a big negative, ghostrider.

Let's go back to some of the statistics from recent studies on millionaires.[2]

- Top two factors to wealth-building, as reported by millionaires: discipline and <u>consistent</u> saving, both ranked much higher than having a high income
- 79% achieved millionaire status thru employer sponsored retirement plans
- 7 out of 10 saved more than 10% of their income throughout their working years

Scaling a mountain that represents the wealth required to achieve our goals and why can either be very easy or very difficult, depending upon three primary factors: how many years we have, the interest rate that we can consistently achieve (dependent upon the investments we choose and the amount of time we are in them, with longer typical being better) and the amount that we consistently invest each month. Let's take a look at each of those factors with a snowball analogy.

Since compounding interest has the same effect as rolling a snowball, the longer we roll the snowball, the larger it will get. One rotation of a snowball, like one year's time of investing, picks up a little bit of snow when we just start out. But as the snowball gets bigger, the same full rotation picks up a lot more snow each time the ball is rolled. As long as we keep the money in a solid investment, and keep rolling the ball, it will continue to get bigger with each rotation. Just the same, most years our investment will continue to grow, even if we had to stop putting money into it for a short time.

If we use an example of a single $100 invested into a solid investment that had a nominal compound annual growth rate of 8%, the table below shows us how that single $100 would snowball due to compounding interest. The first year we would make $8, but the second year we would make interest on the original $100 as well as on the $8 in interest made the first year, for a total of $8.64 in interest. Doesn't seem like much of a difference, right? But over years and years, the effect becomes insane. Looking at the example, by the end of nine years, the $100 will have doubled and become $200. The amount of interest earned in the ninth year would be $15, totaling $100 in interest over the nine-year period. That effect basically keeps doubling every nine years, for a total of five times in this example of 45 years.

Years Initial $100 Invested	Amount of Interest Earned in Past Year*	Amount of Total Interest Earned*	Total Value of Investment
After 1 year	$8	$8	$108
After 9 years	$15	$100	$200
After 18 years	$30	$300	$400
After 27 years	$59	$700	$800
After 36 years	$118	$1500	$1600
After 45 years	$236	$3100	$3200

* Assumes a compound annual growth rate of 8% (figures rounded)

Power of Compounding Interest ($100 invested)

The longer your dollars stay invested, the more snow the snowball picks up every year. The first year the ball picked up $8 in snow, but after rolling over and over, the ball picks up $236 in snow the 45th year. The effect turns your $100 into $3200, which means that only just over three percent of the $3200 is actually money that you put in (the $100 snowball you started with), and almost 97% of that is from the snow you picked up.

The important factor here is the number of years that the investment is in, with each year growing the snowball bigger and bigger. Someone starting at 20 years old will have the same effect at 65 as someone starting at 30 years old will have by the time they turn 75. 45 years is 45 years. The sooner we start that clock going, the sooner the result is achieved. That said, if a parent invested $100 on the day that a child was born, assuming the same 8% annual growth rate, it would turn into $3200 by the time that child, now an adult, turned 45 years old. (While 45 years aligns with an average number of working years in our country, that's not to say that someone will need 45 years before they can achieve financial independence. In fact, many achieve this status much younger.)

Since $3200 won't last us very long in retirement, we need to take this example of the power of time to the next level. To illustrate the power of starting early, we can compare it to scaling a mountain peak. The later that I wait to start climbing, the steeper of an incline that I have to climb to reach the same peak by a certain age, making it much more difficult to achieve the same result than if I had started much earlier. Every year we delay starting investing, even if only a small amount, we make reaching our goals increasingly difficult, and likely unachievable. Take a look at the example below.

Monthly Savings Rate Required for $1M by Age 65

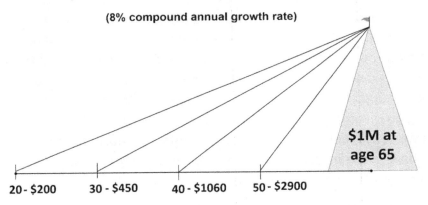

(8% compound annual growth rate)

$1M at age 65

20- $200   30 - $450   40 - $1060   50 - $2900

When we give ourselves 45 years, it only takes $200 per month to achieve $1 million. If we delay 10 years and give ourselves only 35 years, it then takes over double the amount each month to achieve the same result than if we had given ourselves 45 years. We are effectively still walking towards the peak (65 years old in this case), but don't start to climb uphill until getting closer, which makes our required climb steeper and therefore more difficult to ascend. That effect gets worse and worse each year, as we lose nearly 8% of power each year that we delay the start of our investing. Waiting 20 years later, thereby only giving ourselves 25 years of compounding, results in needing over 5 times the monthly amount ($1060 instead of $200 monthly). How many people do you know that saw their income increased tenfold from their early 20s to their early 40s? I certainly didn't see that! And even if you did, wouldn't you rather the investment require much less of your own money by starting early? The investor that gave themselves 45 years only had to put in $108K, or 11% of the $1 million. Waiting until 40 in this example would require the investor put in $318K of their own money, or 32% of the $1 million, and the one who waited until 50 has to put in $522K, meaning over half of the $1 million had to be their own money! Personally, I like the idea of achieving the same end result but only having to put in $108K of my income instead of $522K... don't you? Again, those no longer in their early 20s cannot travel back in time. The takeaway is that the sooner we start, the more effective we can be going forward.

The second factor impacting how quickly our investments grow, and one that is 100% within our own control, is the amount of our own money that we continue to add to the investments. Using the snowball example, this is the snow that we pick up and add to the snowball ourselves, in addition to the snow that the ball picks up by rolling on the ground. This should come as no surprise, but the more that we consistently add to our investments, the more that we not only have in the investment, but also the more that we can take advantage of compounding interest.

The third factor to how quickly our investments grow is the interest rate that is achieved. Almost no investment in the world gets the same return year after year, so in our examples we use a compound annual growth rate, which is different, and more accurate, than an average growth rate. The interest rate that you achieve long-term also has a significant impact. Using the snowball analogy, think of the interest rate as the amount of snow on the ground. The deeper the snow that I roll the snowball through, the more that it picks up each time I roll it over. If we use an example of 2% compared to 8%, many would think that the impact in the long run would be four times as much. But it's much more than that. Take a look at this example of saving $100 per month from age 20 to age 65 (45 years) comparing these two example interest rates.

Interest Rate	Value of $100 per month after 45 years*
2%	$88,000
8%	$501,000

Comparison of Interest Rate Power ($100 per month at 2% and 8%)

Although an 8% interest rate is four times larger than a 2% interest rate, the effect is much larger due to the compounding effect. In this example, the result is nearly six times! The takeaway is that interest rate matters a great deal.

So, what interest rate can you reasonably expect to make? As with the typical fighter pilot answer to most tactical questions... it depends. The interest rate primarily depends upon what investments you have your money invested in, and for how long you keep them in. Speaking very generically, most diversified investments, such as mutual funds that spread your money across many companies unlike an individual stock, the longer that you keep your money in the investment, the greater the compound annual growth rate becomes.

Three really important points to make here regarding interest rate. First, you will notice that I don't use the term "average interest rate," instead using "compound annual growth rate" or CAGR. These two are different and only the CAGR is truly representative of long-term performance, not simply taking an average. For example, if you were to invest $100 and the first year it went down -20%, you would have $80. If the second year it went up +20%, you might think your average interest rate is 0% (-20 + 20 / 2 = 0). While you would be right on the term "average," it would not accurately reflect reality, as an investment worth $80 that goes up +20% is now worth $96, not $100. Using the CAGR takes this into account and is therefore a more accurate tool.

Second, you have probably noticed that I use 8% for most of the examples throughout this book. Some of you may think you could easily do better than 8% with your investments over the long-term, while others may think that this is too high of an assumption. So, where did I come up with that and why do I use 8%? A company called Standard & Poor's tracks the performance of 500 companies in our country, generally 500 of the largest publicly traded companies. These are the heavy hitters in the U.S., companies like Apple, Amazon, Home Depot, and Target for example, that when combined account for around 75% of the value of the total stock market. The tracking of these 500 companies is called an S&P 500 index.

Many advisors would likely agree that the S&P 500 is a fairly accurate representation of the overall pulse of the stock market in our country. Given their large combined footprint, as those 500 companies go, so goes the overall market. If you were to look at the performance of the S&P 500 over the past 40 years (1 Jan 1979 to 31 Dec 2018), you would find that the CAGR of this particular index was 11.56%.[3] So why don't I use a higher percentage than 8%? Great question. We certainly could use that for our examples, but it leaves out one important variable: inflation. Due to the rising cost of products and services, typically 2-3% per year on average, the value of a dollar today is higher than the value the same dollar will hold next year and every year after that. So even if the S&P 500 repeated the same performance for the next 40 years, with a CAGR of 11.56%, examples using that number would be misleading since inflation would not be taken into account. If we use the same S&P 500 index for the past forty years, this time accounting for inflation, our "True CAGR" would drop down to 7.96%.[4] That's why I have chosen to use 8% for the examples, so that the results can be looked at in today's dollars. If we account for inflation, then you can get a better feel for how much your investments would be tomorrow from where you stand today.

Let's look at a quick example. If you invested $100 today and it made 11%, next year you would have $111. But if inflation was 3%, each dollar would only be worth 97% of what a dollar today would be worth. That means that your $111 would be like having around $108 today ($111 x 97%). Taking inflation into consideration when it comes to your interest rate can enable you to better connect with for exactly how far that future amount would go.

The third point on interest rates, and a really important one to keep in the back of your mind, is that the stock market goes up and down, and <u>nobody</u> knows exactly what tomorrow is going to bring. That said, just because the S&P 500 had a true CAGR of nearly 8% for the past forty years, there is no guarantee that it will do the same over the next forty years. The only fact that we have to go off of when it comes to expected investment returns is past performance. The good news is that the S&P 500 has done well, over the long-term, since its beginnings as the Composite Index in the early 1900s. Historically, performance over a shorter period is at times much higher and other times much lower, but generally around 8% once you get outside 30 years. That's another great reason to start investing early. Not only does doing so allow you to take advantage of more of the snowballing effect, but historically it also takes more of the market's ups and downs out of the equation.

The graph below shows the performance of the S&P 500, after accounting for inflation, over the past forty years. The three lines show the best, worst and average performance of all five to thirty year periods of time from the beginning of 1979 to the end of 2018. For example, the first five-year period covered January 1979 thru December 1983, then the next from 1980 thru 1984, and so on.

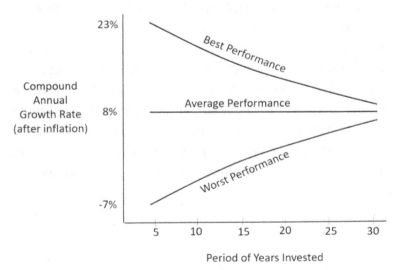

Variation in S&P 500 Performance Over 40 Years (Jan 1979 – Dec 2018)[5,6]

So, what exactly are we looking at here? The point of this graph is to show the variations in performance of the S&P 500, which represents the bulk of our market, and the fact that the ups and downs dampened out over time. While the average performance after inflation generally remained flat for all periods, right near 8%, there was a lot of variation in performance, especially in the shorter time periods. The five-year periods varied greatly, with a delta between the best and worst periods of over 30%. As the number of years invested increases, the variation got less, down to a delta of 10% for the twenty-year periods and less than 2% for the thirty-year periods. The historical takeaway? The earlier you get in, and the longer you stay in, the higher the odds that you will build wealth!

> *Important side note: In addition to staying in investing for a longer period of time, there are also other investing strategies that can be used to dampen the ups and downs, such as diversifying between multiple classes of assets. We aren't going to get into all of these options in great detail but will tackle how to get the best advice for you and your goals.*

Consistent investing, over a long-term, is the key to building wealth for most that have achieved and held onto it in this country. If this comes as no surprise as your ticket to building wealth, I'm glad. Most of you reading, assuming you believed wealth was possible for you, likely already knew that investing to take advantage of compounding interest, started early and maintained consistently, is your best shot at building wealth. Yet most of us aren't doing it. We need to look at the key tenets that allowed those who have done it to do so consistently, month in and month out, over their working lifetimes.

21

The Four Pillars

You should now have confidence that consistent investing and taking advantage of compounding interest has been the most effective vector of those before us, and therefore the most likely and best path for your own wealth building. My guess is that many of you already knew that or at least had a hunch that it was the best way to build wealth. Yet, most of us don't actually do it <u>consistently</u>. That said, next we need to get educated on the critical enablers that put us in the best position to actually do just that.

There are four basic pillars that put us in a position to consistently invest, thereby putting ourselves on a nearly guaranteed path to wealth building. Just as with the consistent investing principles, none of the four pillars are difficult to understand or comprehend. Actually doing them, however, is another story. The more closely that you adopt these four pillars, the faster they will become steadfast habits, and the faster you will be in a position to consistently invest, which equates to you building wealth.

The first pillar is to consistently live below your means. Simply put, if we always spend all of the income that we bring in every month, we will never be in a position to consistently invest and build wealth. This pillar requires spending less than you make each month. Don't do as I did for many years and push this off until the next pay raise or promotion. That didn't work for me and is unlikely to work for you. Starting today, you have to commit to spending less than the income your household brings in, this month and every month going forward.

Living below your means is all about creating a gap between what you earn and what you spend, thereby allowing you to consistently invest. The larger the difference between earning and spending, the more you will have to add to your investment snowball. We can enlarge that gap by one of two ways. The first is raising our income while keeping spending levels consistent. Whether it be by seeking out growth or new opportunities within your primary career field, or implementing side hustles for additional streams of income, increasing income can be a huge help in growing the margin available to scale Mt. Wealth. The other option to grow your gap between earnings and spending is to reduce how much you are spending. This comes down to knowing where your money is going and then prioritizing what and where it gets spent on. While adopting an extreme level of frugality works for some, for most that I coach it does not. Instead, I would suggest adopting selective frugality, smartly choosing the areas that you cut while embracing others that you truly deem worth it. The ideal way to grow your gap is to continue to seek improvements in both areas, income and spending.

The second pillar is to get out of debt. For all the reasons that we hit on in the Open Eyes section, remember that debt is like having a leak in your fuel tank, your income. If we are going to be able to do what we need to do each month, we have got to have full access to our monthly income. In order to get rid of debt we must first stop using debt. You must develop a visceral reaction to debt, likening it to the thought of being robbed at gunpoint, which is exactly what you are doing to your future self when you remain anchored to the chains of debt. You need to reach a point where the thought of taking on debt makes your stomach turn. And it should, because you work too hard to have your dollars making banks and credit cards companies wealthy with hours upon hours of your time spent at work.

Without adopting this mentality toward debt, you will remain likely to go right back into debt. And we all know, it's impossible to dig ourselves out of hole if we keep digging the hole deeper. So, the three keys to this pillar are to 1. stop using debt, today, 2. get focused on getting completely rid of any debt that you may have right now, and then 3. never going back into debt...ever!

The third pillar that is absolutely critical to building wealth is having an emergency fund. Life throws us curveballs, often when we least expect it. No matter how well you think you can see things coming, none of us have a crystal ball that gives us the ability to see something like a water heater going out, a major component breaking on our vehicle, a job loss, injury or the passing of a family member across the country. If we are not prepared with some money set aside when these events surprise us, it is very likely that we will go right back into debt. If we are serious about getting out of debt, which all of us certainly should be, the emergency fund is what prevents us from ever going back in. Even while we are digging ourselves out of the hole of debt, we need a pad between us and life's curveballs.

For most Americans, myself included for many years, their emergency fund is their credit card. Nearly 2 out of 3 Americans are unable to cover a $1000 emergency without using debt as a "fix."[1] But isn't that exactly what it's there for, anyway? The credit card really isn't a fix. In fact, it makes an already difficult situation even worse. Not only do I have to deal with life's curveball, which can be stressful enough, but now I also have to worry about taking on an extra debt. By not having an emergency fund, we are basically hoping for the best, rolling the dice that Murphy will skip our house and move on to the next. But emergencies happen to ALL of us. They are not a matter of if, but when. When it comes to being prepared for whatever life may throw our way, hope is not an adequate plan!

Deciding to skip over having an emergency fund is one of the top mistakes that I see from many that I coach. When my wife and I first started to get our financial act in check, I was guilty of this mistake as well. As a military member, I convinced myself that I had great job security and therefore could do without an emergency fund. I also had a credit card and could take a loan from my Thrift Savings Plan (federal retirement plan similar to a 401K) to buffer any emergencies. But I was fooling myself. Even with solid job security, life's incoming artillery shells still rain down from time to time. I quickly realized that having a credit card, which may or may not have enough room on it to even cover the emergency, was not an adequate plan. Also, whether it be a 401K loan or a loan against the equity in your home, which is another common "plan," I came to the realization that I didn't own those things in order to borrow against them. Retirement investments are not there for emergencies, they are there for retirement, hence the name! Also, borrowing against our houses with a home equity loan turns unsecured debts into secured debts, thereby adding risk of losing our home if things turn for the worse.

An example comes to mind from the flying world. How would it feel to think that the commercial plane that you were flying on had planned to use every last drop of fuel on your flight across the country, just enough to make it to the arrival gate? That would be a horrible plan, right? Instead, on all flights, including every flight I have ever flown over my career, the pilot carries an extra pad conveniently called 'emergency fuel.' Every pilot knows that no matter how good they are, there are lots of things out of their control. The winds being stronger than expected, a runway being closed due to another plane's emergency, or the weather deteriorating worse than the weatherman forecasted to name a few. The reason for carrying extra gas is to avoid a catastrophe if the plane were to run out of fuel. The same can be said for our finances. There are things that are out our control and having an emergency fund helps us avoid having a bad day turn much worse by not being prepared for it. This extra step of preparation turns most emergencies into an inconvenience.

Another added benefit of having an adequate emergency fund is peace of mind. For the majority of attendees polled at our speaking events, dealing with popup expenses is their top financial stress. Other studies have found similar results, citing that for many, the financial aspect of dealing with emergencies is more stressful than the actual emergency itself! Life just doesn't have to be this way. We can avoid the day to day worry of "what's going to happen next?" as well as handling the cost when emergencies do happen by simply having an emergency fund. If any of your "whys" had to do with reducing financial stress in your life, take a minute to think about how having $10,000 or more in a separate account, strictly as a pad for life's emergencies, would feel and what it would do for your overall outlook and stress level. This one key component to your finances can have dramatic results.

The fourth and final pillar to consistent long-term investing is consistent giving. I'm sure, as I did, you are probably wondering how in the world giving money away helps us to have more money. Unlike the other three pillars, which made good logical sense, this fourth pillar defies logic. Stay with me here for a minute. This pillar ties directly back to one of the primary root causes for our financial situations, contentment. Remember, if we don't deal with the roots, no matter what other pillars we put in place, we are very likely to go right back to where we started.

So how does giving money away help with contentment? When we give to a cause that we believe in and support, whether it be a local charity or church, a national nonprofit, friends or family, etc., it makes us feel grateful for all that we have. When we have gratitude, we can't help but to feel more content with our position in life and all that we have. Gratitude and contentment go hand in hand. If you haven't experienced this, I would challenge you to try it for yourself. If giving to others or a worthy cause doesn't do something inside of you, it may be because you are only seeing it as money lost or having even less to tackle your own financial mess. If you decide that you need to get your own head above water first, that's entirely your call. However, if you do decide to delay giving, I would challenge you to come back to this pillar once you feel you are able to do so. Again, don't miss the fact that to do better long-term, you will need to keep contentment in check and consistent giving is often a very successful way of doing just that.

If we look back to studies of those that have built and maintained wealth, we find that 70% set some of their income aside every month to give to others.[2] You may say, "sure, I would do that too if I was a millionaire." That is a common misconception. It's not something that wealthy do because they now have wealth, rather something that many of them have always done which helped them build wealth. As much as we think the new latest and greatest gadget is going to bring us long-term happiness, we all have examples of things we thought were going to do it for us, but then quickly faded and turned into regret. Think of a time when you have given to someone else or a great cause that you support. Do you look back at that and ever regret giving? Very seldom do I hear of regrets with giving, whether it be with our time, treasures or talents. It goes back to how we are wired. As Sir Winston Churchill once said, "You make a living by what you earn – you make a life by what you give."[3]

Living below your means, getting out and staying out of debt, having a solid emergency fund and consistent giving represent the "what" we need to do. Other than the giving pillar, these probably don't come as much of a surprise. Yet most of us haven't been doing what we know we should. Implementing these four pillars in our own lives is the proven way to enable a consistent level of investing. The ability to build each pillar in our own financial lives all goes back to our "why," which represents what's at stake if we don't do these things. The last component that we need to look at is the "how."

22

Building Your Pillars

With a strong "why" and commitment to a new way as your thrust, and a solid understanding of what you will need to do to build wealth, we now need to get into the "how." This is where the rubber meets the road and separates those that want to do better from those that will do better. In the fighter community we identify a fired up young pilot as having "all thrust and no vector." Granted, I would take this person, whether in flying or with finances, over the opposite case of "all vector and no thrust" any day of the week, as thrust is the critical component that most Americans are missing. But once I have someone that is fired up, has ignited their afterburner and is ready to get to work, we need to move on to phase two, giving them a vector. Otherwise we will stay as effective as a holiday balloon that is untied and let loose, flying in aimless circles around us until it eventually runs out of thrust.

Not only does having a solid vector, or plan, put us on track to achieve our goals, but it also increases our thrust. Just by virtue of having a solid, executable plan that allows us to see the path laid out in front of us, we get even further fired up. A plan shines light on the path forward, which raises our confidence and increases our belief that better is actually doable. In addition, a clear and executable plan continues to build our thrust as we successfully take steps forward. Each time we make progress on the plan, bringing us closer to the next goal, the thrust continues to build. So, the effect of having a solid vector is not just critical to arriving at our desired destination, but also to sustaining and increasing our thrust along the way. It's similar to our investments starting to grow and compound. With each step forward, and hurdle crossed, our confidence and belief that we can do better continues to compound.

So how do we go about doing what we know we need to do?

Let's start with getting out of debt and building an emergency fund. The first step to getting out of debt that we already hit on is vowing to not use debt any longer. You have to ask yourself, and answer 100% honestly, whether you can truly trust yourself with a credit card. Look back at your use of them over the past few years. Have they gotten out of hand and has there <u>ever</u> been months that you haven't paid off the balance in full? If you look back and have struggled with paying them off, or not paid off the full balance for even one month, I would contend that you have proven to yourself that you really can't trust yourself with them going forward. That was a tough realization that I had to admit for myself. As much I would have liked to say that I would handle credit cards differently going forward, experience had proven otherwise.

I also came to the realization that credit cards weren't helping me to build wealth, but rather helping others build wealth with my income. My default fighting position held strong, telling me that I "needed" the credit card for popup emergencies. But why would I need a credit card if I had an emergency fund? The points? As much as I researched, I could not find any studies of millionaires that attributed their ability to build and maintain wealth to their credit card points. Ultimately, my wife and I decided that we would be best off and set ourselves up for meeting our long-term goals most effectively, if we got rid of our credit cards altogether. So that is exactly what we did. Was there some apprehension with that decision? Absolutely! The thought of needing a credit card had been so ingrained over time that it was tough to see how we could survive without it. Going against the grain was not an easy step, but we did it. We cut up every last credit card and vowed them off for good. Have we regretted that decision for one day since? Absolutely not! Knowing that we would never carry credit card debt again was, and has continued to be, incredibly freeing.

Another option instead of credit cards is to use a checking account with cashback for each purchase with your debit card. While this may not seem as lucrative as miles or points earned with credit cards, it can easily result in two to three hundred dollars of cash each year (as it has for our household). Couldn't you purchase an airline ticket every year with that method as well? And cash doesn't have any restrictions, unlike the points and miles of most cards, which explains why a third of them end up going unused.[1]

If I still haven't convinced you to cut them up, what's holding you back? As Zig Ziglar says, we need a "checkup from the neck up to avoid stinkin' thinkin."[2] Feel as if you "need" your card for security despite having an emergency fund in place? Convinced that you truly spend no differently with your credit card than with cash? Believe that the points will be the factor that puts you over the top? Think you have to keep the card in order to maintain your credit score, which enables you to go back into debt? Truly believe that your cards are bringing you closer to achieving your "why" and, in turn, will prove to be a blessing to your household's long-term financial success? What exactly is it that is preventing you from letting them go?

If you remain steadfast in the belief that credit cards are advantageous to your financial journey, I would challenge you to walk the walk and tie any credit card directly to your checking account. There are services available now that make your credit card become more like a debit card, deducting any charges from your checking account. Again, I would argue against the notion that points or miles are truly worth any credit card and could not be convinced that they outweigh the peace of mind that comes with knowing that credit card debt will never happen again. But for those that I can't convince and believe that miles and points are really a key element of their wealth-building, at least start with this step. It will force you to actually think about whether you have the money in your account, right now, for any purchase you are considering. Also, set a reminder on your calendar for six months from now to take another look – have I paid any interest? Even if the answer is no, has charging to a credit card altered my spending in any way, or do I honestly believe that I would have made all of the same purchases had I been using a debit card? You can deceive others but not yourself, so answer honestly as to whether keeping a credit card is worth the risk and is ultimately bringing you closer or further from achieving your long-term goals.

Once you have sworn off debt and made the right moves to prevent it, we can then turn our focus to paying off the debt that we have today. We talked about the importance of having an emergency fund as well, so which should come first? Or is it be best to payoff debt and build up an emergency fund simultaneously?

Having a clear, simple and executable plan to pay off debt and build an emergency fund is make or break. If we try to do too much at once, we will see less progress and therefore be much less effective. For those reasons, I am a huge proponent of every client starting off by first focusing on three critical steps. As with most of our efforts in life, we are most effective when we focus on one thing at a time. For my wife and I, as well as hundreds of clients that I have had the privilege of guiding, I can attest to the fact that focusing on one step at a time, one debt at a time, is hands down the best way to tackle building an emergency fund and paying off your debt. So, what is the order for most effectively accomplishing this?

1. Save $1000 for a starter emergency fund, as quickly as possible.
2. Payoff all debts (other than the house) in order of smallest balance to largest (regardless of interest rate).
3. Build up fully funded emergency fund to cover 3 to 6 months of living expenses.

For those familiar with radio host Dave Ramsey, these are the same as the first three of what he calls Baby Steps.[3] I believe in these steps, 100%. They worked for my household and as a financial coach I have seen them work for those that embrace them, without fail. I also believe in following the order of the steps. Just like when a pilot is trying to strain against g-forces, if they strain the required parts of their body in the wrong order, the results are not effective, and can actually make things worse. Stick to the order of these steps...they work, every time.

Let's explore each, as these are critical to escaping debt and building financial security, both very common short-term goals.

Step #1, build a starter emergency fund of $1000. As we highlighted earlier, we can't get out of debt if we keep going back into debt. That is why a starter emergency fund is the first critical step. We need that small pad between us and life's curveballs, so we don't get the wind knocked out of us when an emergency happens.

Another critical component of the emergency fund is where it is kept. It must be kept in a separate account! Whether it be a separate savings account or money market account, your emergency funds have to be kept separate from your day to day checking account, otherwise it will get tapped into. For many, the temptation to get into their emergency fund is too great if held at the same bank as their checking account, so a good solution would be to open an account at a different bank. You still want to have access to your emergency fund at a moment's notice, but also out of sight and out of mind to prevent you from touching it for non-emergencies. You have to adopt the mindset that this money is ONLY there for true emergencies. Not for a TV going on sale, vacation funds, or even a wealth building investment. Your emergency fund is an investment, but not the kind that grows. It's an investment in your peace of mind, avoiding going back into debt and for your long-term ability to maintain consistent investing in other accounts.

Another common input that I get regarding this first step is the desire to have a higher amount in an emergency fund before tackling debts. The point of the starter emergency fund is to provide some protection, but also motivation to get your debts paid off as quickly as possible in order to then build your emergency fund up to a higher level. That said, if you are dead set against dropping your savings all the way down to $1000, then pick a minimum number that you could be comfortable with, perhaps $2000 or one month of expenses. Bottom line, don't let your disagreement with the amount of $1000 get in your way. Millions of people have achieved success by sticking to the letter of the law with these steps, my wife and I included. So, if you find yourself questioning them, go back to the very first decision you made in the Decide section...is your way working as well as you would like it to? If not, I recommend going all in on a new and proven way.

Once you have the starter emergency fund setup in a separate account, it is time for step #2 - to start knocking out your debts, one at a time, with the debt snowball method. That doesn't mean that you stop paying on any of your debts and only focus on one. You need to keep paying the bare minimum owed on each and every debt... cars, credit cards, student loans, personal loans, etc. We do not want to fall behind on any debt, so always paying the minimums across the board is critical.

Then, with any extra funds that you can scrounge up, focus on attacking one debt at a time. As each debt gets fully paid off, you then apply its minimum payment to your extra funds to then attack the next debt. This method provides a larger amount to attack each subsequent debt as you go along, erasing one at a time. So which debt should you pick to focus on? Our logical side would tell us to focus on the debt with the highest interest rate first. In theory, that would be the most mathematically efficient way to pay off debt. But we have to remember that math is not the problem. If math were the primary concern, would we use credit cards in the first place? Remember that math is not the issue, and our use of credit is only the symptom. Our spending is the issue and building momentum as we pay off debt is the best thing we can do to actually see it to the end and pay it all off. If we attack one of our highest debt balances first, with the highest interest rate, but don't see quick progress towards paying it off, our momentum fitters out and most don't end up paying off their debts in the long run. Building momentum by seeing progress is absolutely critical!

Instead of prioritizing debts by interest rate, the debt snowball method has us paying them off in the order of smallest balance to largest balance. This helps us see progress, which leads us to believe that this paying off debt thing may actually be possible, which makes us a force to be reckoned with! In order to create your debt snowball plan of attack, you will need to find out the balances to every single debt that you owe, other than the mortgage on your home. In the Open Eyes section, you should have already figured out the balances for all of your debts as you calculated your current financial standing and net worth. Now, all that you will need to do is to write out your debts in order of smallest balance to largest balance. Don't forget about your cell phones if you are paying on them as part of your cell phone bill – those are debts, too!

The beauty of the debt snowball method is not only building your own momentum by getting small wins fast, but also building momentum with paying off your debts. Again, each time you pay off a debt, that minimum payment goes away and can be applied to attacking the next debt on your list. In my experience, both personally and for clients as a seasoned financial coach, the debt snowball is THE way to pay off your debts.

While many would assume that paying them off in order of highest to lowest interest rate would result in becoming debt-free much sooner and save significant amounts in the long run, it is probably much less than you think. Writer Rob Berger recently provided a telling example for Forbes magazine.[4] He compared the payoff timeline and amount spent on interest between two techniques, the debt snowball and the debt avalanche (paying off debts in order of the highest to lowest interest rate). Tackling the payoff of six consumer debts, with interest rates ranging from 6.5 to 18%, all debts were paid off in 52 months with a total interest charge of $7,784 when using the debt avalanche. When instead choosing to use the debt snowball technique, paying in order of smallest to largest debt balance, all debts were paid in the exact same amount of time, 52 months. The total cost of interest in this case was $8,007. No savings in time and only $223 saved in interest. But comparing these two techniques from only the perspective of time and total interest misses a critical aspect. Which technique is the most effective, most likely to get you across the finish line?

Several studies have been done in recent years that have independently verified the debt snowball as being the most effective technique for those looking to pay off their debts. A 2012 study by the Kellogg School of Management at Northwestern University found that those using the debt snowball technique were more likely to stay motivated, sticking with the payoff of their debt, and therefore more likely to shed their debt completely.[5] In 2016, a study at the Questrom School of Business at Boston University (BU) found similar results, reporting that "people are more motivated to get out of debt not only by concentrating on one account but also beginning with the smallest."[6] That said, with any perceived benefits in terms of time and interest saved being essentially negligible in the big picture of things, is there really any comparison between the debt snowball and other techniques? What matters most is that you actually payoff all your debts! Again, the debt snowball is the way to go. For those who want to debate this method, I would ask you to revisit your first decision regarding whether your way has been working for you. If not, try something new and PROVEN!

Clients often ask whether they should go the route of consolidating their debts. In general, I am not a fan of debt consolidation for a few reasons. First and foremost, many that go down this path feel as though they have made progress and chocked up a financial win. In reality, they have played the shell game and not actually reduced debt. Consolidating debts is treating the symptom, not the root cause. More often than not, those that utilize consolidation end up incurring additional new debts shortly thereafter. Also, consolidating often ends up costing borrowers more in the long run. Even if the overall interest rate is lowered, which is not a guarantee, many end up paying more over the duration after extending their payback timeline. Again, it all goes back to asking what will be most effective in the long run? The BU study referenced above answered this question as well, adding that "findings would argue against pooling debts into a single larger one."[7] Your best bet, proven by multiple studies, is to get intense about tackling debts, one at a time, using the snowball method. It's all about building your momentum by achieving quick wins. When you see progress, you will believe, and when you believe, you will achieve!

A quick note regarding debt payoff. If you are not able to make all of your minimum payments on your debts, after meeting needs, here are a few suggestions. First, take a hard look at whether you are only paying for needs or if wants are sneaking away with some of your income. Next, if you are truly living on bare bones spending and still cannot pay all of your minimums on your debts, what items could you sell and what additional income can you round up for the short term? Picking up a part-time job for a short time can be a huge help with getting your arms around your minimums. I have seen many folks go out and pickup extra income for a short term to help them build a starter emergency fund and payoff the first few debts of their snowball. What are you willing to sacrifice for the short-term to set yourself better for the long-term? Only you can answer that question. In the interim, a third option, for a very short duration, is using a pro rata method with your debts. You can search to find out more details, but it is essentially paying less than your minimum payment to your debtors to keep them at bay for a short period of time while you look to secure more income and chop expenses.

Each time you successfully pay off a debt, or every other debt if knocking them out in short order, consider celebrating the occasion with a small reward. Of course, I want to see you continue to build momentum and keep paying off debts until none remain, but it's also important to celebrate progress throughout the process. The point is certainly not to go further into debt...which should have already been sworn off...but to enjoy a meal out or some fun, within reason. Ideally something that you really enjoy but have decided to give up while working these three steps. Taking time to celebrate progress helps us stay fired up and provides something to look forward to as we work through the steps. Getting into debt takes very little effort but getting out often takes a concerted effort and a good deal of discipline. If a small celebration helps you to stay focused and motivated, and the celebratory meal or event is within reason, then I'm all for it and would encourage you to do so. This is also a great time to revisit your "why" and reflect on the fact that you will be capable of doing more of what you enjoy once you get your financial house back on solid ground.

Once you have finished Step #2, having paid off all your non-mortgage debt, it is time to move on to Step #3 and build up your emergency fund to cover 3 to 6 months of expenses. This step should ensure that you will never have to go back into debt again, putting you in a position to weather even a 3 to 6-month job loss and still be able to provide for your family's needs. So, which should you aim for, 3 or 6 months? The answer really comes down to the amount of security you need and want. If you live on a single income and it has any potential for job loss, I would recommend leaning towards the 6-month side. Even if you have a two-income household with very stable jobs but would like the peace of mind of having six months of income, then aim towards six months. No matter how stable you believe your income to be, do not go any less than a three-month emergency fund.

Remember, it's not just about covering a potential job loss. It's also there to cover life's curveballs that have nothing to do with your job – medical emergency, water heater or air conditioner goes out at the house, needing to buy a last-minute plane ticket to fly across the country to attend a funeral, etc. The more months of expenses that you can cover, the more security you have bought for yourself. That said, for most I do not recommend having more than six months of expenses tied up, as that leads to having less that you could be investing and growing wealth with. One exception to this would be going into long-term retirement without active job income coming in. For that case, I recommend retirees have a 12-18-month emergency fund to help weather any financial storms or market drops that may occur to prevent having to tap into investments at a time when their values have significantly dropped.

Once you have zeroed out all your debts, other than your home, and decide on whether it will be 3, 4, 5- or 6-month emergency fund, that becomes your focus as step three.

You may have noticed that to this point there has been no mention of investing or saving, other than for the emergency fund. Don't we want to start investing as soon as possible since we know each year is less powerful than the last? Yes, we do want to get you to a point where you can consistently invest. However, I recommend pausing your investing until complete with step three for a few reasons, with a couple of caveats. First, we are most effective when we solely focus on these three steps, one at a time. If you invest at the same time, that would give you less to knock out the three steps, thereby taking you longer. You need to complete these three steps as quickly as you possibly can, so I recommend every last dollar you can scrounge together to focus solely on steps one through three.

But wouldn't that result in less time and associated power of compounding interest? After all, our investing snowball (not to be confused with the debt snowball) isn't gaining any ground if its sitting still. In theory, that is correct. But we have to take a step back and remember why we are getting out of debt in the first place – so we are in a stronger position to consistently invest long-term, and thereby more effectively build wealth. While I don't want to see you delay investing any longer than needed, I do want to see you get in a stronger position where you can invest more, both in the amount and in your consistency.

What about if you get a match? You certainly don't want to give that up... after all, it's free money, right? I would still recommend that you suspend investing, even if it means giving up the match. If delaying investing for a short period of time puts you in a position to build better long-term wealth, then that's what we want to do. Not only does focusing on the debt payoff and emergency fund first put you in a stronger position, but it will also move along faster when investing is paused. Remember, it's all about focus, building momentum. The greater the amount and intensity that can be thrown at taking each debt down in sequence, the more effective you will find yourself becoming. You can also use the loss of employer match to add to your thrust, firing you up to get these three steps completed as quickly as possible.

Still not buying it? Here's an example to prove the value of delaying, even if it means giving up your employer's match... for a short time! Let's say your employer offers a match of up to 5%. For easy numbers, we will assume that 5% of your pay equates to $200 per month. So, if you invested 5% of your pay, plus the employer match, you would be putting away a total of 10%, which in this example would be $400 per month. If we did that every month for a five-year period, using an interest rate of 8%, your total investment would be valued at $30,412. Not bad for only putting in $12,000 of your own dollars ($200 x 60 months).

Now let's compare that to pausing your investing completely, for two years, losing the associated employer match for those two years as well. Instead of investing, you decide to focus on attacking steps one through three with a vengeance. After tightening the belt on your spending and busting it for 24 months in full afterburner mode, you are now completely debt free, other than your house, and have a 3-6-month emergency fund in a separate savings or money market account. Now, because you are debt-free and have opened up full access to your income, you are able to start investing 15% of your income each and every month. When you start, the employer match kicks back in at 5%, bringing your total investing up to 20%. That would be double the total invested amount, $800 per month in our example. After not investing for two years, even giving up the match, how much would you have at the end of the five-year period? Again using an 8% interest rate, you would have a total of $33,658 in your investment. That's right, even though you gave up the match for two years in order to focus on paying off debt and building your emergency fund, it would result in $3,246 more than if you had kept investing at the lower rate and taken five years to pay off your debt.

This method of pausing on any investing allows you to focus on one thing at a time, which ultimately results in seeing more movement on your emergency fund and erasing debts. When you see more movement, the result is greater momentum, which, in turn, gives you a higher likelihood of continuing to crush debts and become debt-free. Most importantly, this method puts you into a stronger overall financial position which translates into a better ability to build wealth. Another point to highlight is that there is no guarantee of earning 8% during those three to five years you may take to pay off debt if you weren't to pause investing. However, the interest earned by paying off debt has a guaranteed rate of return, with no risk!

I had mentioned a couple of caveats to the technique of pausing your investing. The first comes down to having a high level of commitment with focused intensity to rid debt from your life and build your emergency fund as fast as you possibly can. If you are kinda sorta in, with weak intensity, I would not recommend pausing your investments. If you fall into this category, you are probably better off just continuing to invest and getting your match, because you are unlikely to pay off debts within a couple of years. So, if you didn't give yourself at least an 8 or 9 out of 10 when you decided your commitment level, you may not want to pause investments. That said, you may want to revisit your "why" and whether your current ways are putting you on a path to achieve your goals or not. A weak "why" is typically the primary reason for a weak commitment level.

The second caveat to pausing your investing is if you cannot possibly become debt free and secure a full emergency fund within two years. If you become as intense and committed as possible, cutting expenses to the bare bone and working multiple jobs to maximize income, yet still cannot get your debts paid off within two years, you may want to consider investing up to at least the match. But before you accept this route as the only viable option for your situation, take a close look at every other option available to you to pay off the debt even sooner than you think. What can you sacrifice in the short term and how much can you tighten the belt to get you out of debt sooner? No eating out? Second or third job? No vacations? Remember, these sacrifices are not forever, just for a short part of your life in order to put you back on a path to reach your goals and build wealth for your "why."

When my wife and I got intense about paying off debt and building our emergency fund, we adopted a full-afterburner mentality, a 10+. Anything that wasn't a true need to keep the lights and water on and food on the table was shut down for the short term. We knew that the tighter we made the monthly budget, the sooner we could press through this period of our lives and then pick up a much better lifestyle with lower stress and more effectiveness in every area. We even decided to sell one of our cars and lived with just one car for a few months. It made things fairly inconvenient, for American standards, but at the same time also motivated us to bust through the debt. The sooner we could erase the over $60K of non-mortgage debt, the sooner we could regain control of our income and start enjoying life much more comfortably, as well as set ourselves up for the future.

Our debts consisted of cell phones, credit cards, car loans and a loan from our retirement account used for a house deposit. Yup, like I had mentioned in the very first chapter, we were fairly normal with balancing debts and focusing on "affording" the monthly payments. But then we stopped being normal with our finances, and months later it brought us to a place that we had never been in our adult lives – completely debt-free with a 3-6-month emergency fund. For the first time in many years, we got to experience a whole new level of financial freedom! We felt as if the wheel chocks had finally been removed and we were no longer hamsters in a wheel. Sending in that last payment to officially obliterate every cent of our non-mortgage debt resulted in indescribable relief, as if we could actually feel our family's financial outlook morphing right before our eyes. Soon after, keeping the peddle to the metal while building a full emergency fund, came another wave of relief and security, knowing that we would NEVER have to rely on credit cards or go into bondage again. And we had given ourselves a great raise, ready to attack our future goals.

These are all feelings that I have seen many experience since, and now want you to experience...and it's certainly one that you can, if you decide to!

23

Stand, In the Door

Once you have efficiently and methodically taken down your debts and built up a solid emergency fund, life is good. Before you do anything else, I would recommend rewarding yourself. Nothing too crazy, and of course paid for in cash, since you are now determined to vow off debt for good (right?), but it's really important to breathe it in and pat yourself on the back. For most, you will now find yourself in a much more secure financial position than likely ever before in your adult life. Whether it be a small vacation, an item you have been eyeing for awhile, or just a really nice dinner out, take time to reward yourself. You have earned it!

So, what do you do with this newfound income, an average of 15-25% of take-home income for those I coach, now that you have no debt payments? In addition to loosening the spending up a bit, within reason, it is now time to get serious about investing in our future. How much and into what should we invest? The answer to that question ultimately comes down to answering a few follow-on questions...what are my goals, how much time do I have to reach them, and what level of risk am I willing to accept? If, for example, your goal is to achieve financial independence by age 60, how many years does that give you, and what kind of money do you expect to need to achieve the quality of life in retirement that you desire? I recommend thinking in today's dollars and then using an investment rate that accounts for inflation. Let's say, for example, that your goal is to have your home paid off and a passive income of $50,000 per year, in today's dollars, starting at age 60, and you are 28 right now. We'll get to the house next, but first let's look at how much you would need to draw $50K per year from your investments, and how much you would need to save from now until then to build that amount.

In order to draw an income from investments for the rest of your life, increasing withdrawals for inflation and never running out, a conservative multiplier is 33 times the annual amount (which equates to drawing 3% out each year). With the example being $50K, that would equate to having $1.65M ($50K x 33). So, what would you need to save to achieve $1.65M in 32 years (from 28 to 60)? The answer depends upon what to assume you will see for an interest rate over those years. If we use 7.3%, the real CAGR of the S&P 500 over the past 30 years, it would require a total monthly investment of approximately $1100 per month. If we used a more conservative 6% compound annual growth rate, it would require a monthly investment of around $1400. Sounds like a steep amount, but again, you don't have any debt payments other than a mortgage at this point, so you can likely afford the investment. And remember that the sooner you start, the less it takes. Had we been using a 22-year old in our example instead, the monthly amount required would be half! Another option is to subtract the amount of the match that you are getting. For example, if your employer match accounted for $400 per month, then you could subtract that from the amount that you would need to save of your own dollars.

Those with high confidence of receiving a pension for life may choose to take that into account when making their calculations. For example, if you have high confidence that you will receive an income of $30,000 per year from a pension, you could subtract that amount from your total desired income. A few notes of caution. First, remember that no pension is guaranteed until it has been fully qualified for. Even then, all pensions come with some level of risk of drying up. Next, be aware that most pensions stop, or have payments greatly reduced, when the employee passes away. That said, if counting on pension income, have a robust plan in the event that the pension income goes away for a surviving spouse. Lastly, I do not recommend including any expected Social Security income into your equation unless you are already very close to retirement age. Current estimates have Social Security's reserves being depleted by 2035, which will likely result in greatly reduced payouts.[1]

Our previous example was for someone wanting to retire at age 60. In that case, it would likely work out well to do all of your long-term investing in retirement accounts, which have a tax advantage but typically can't be touched without penalty until age 59 ½. If, however, your goal was to achieve financial independence earlier, at age 50 for example, then it would not be a great plan to have all of your investments tied up in retirement accounts that wouldn't be accessible without penalty between ages 50 to 59 ½. I would always recommend that at least a portion of your investing be within a retirement account shelter in order to ensure that you are setup for the long-term and are taking advantage of the associated tax benefits that retirement accounts offer. For those looking to achieve financial independence before 59 ½ through their investing, consider also building a portion of your investments in regular taxable investment accounts that will provide you access without penalty prior to reaching 59 ½.

The earlier you start, the greater the percentage of income you invest, and the less that you believe you could comfortably live off of in terms of annual income, the sooner you can reach financial independence. Many of those that subscribe to the FIRE movement (Financial Independence, Retire Early), aim to reach financial independence in their 40's or sooner. Limiting lifestyle in order to sock away as much as 40-50% of their monthly income puts them on the path. Also, accepting a lower annual income in retirement equates to needing less in investments. For example, if you decided that you could comfortably live on $30K per year, versus $50K per year, that would mean that you need a nest egg of $1.0M versus $1.65M ($30K x 33). That all said, there is no cookie-cutter approach on the path to financial independence. It all comes down to your goals and "why."

If you don't have clear enough goals and objectives to do that level of analysis, recommend you reattack. The earlier you know your number, the amount needed to provide the passive income for your desired standard of living, the better. If not now, when? If all else fails, I would recommend that you invest at least 15% of your income into one or more tax-advantaged retirement account (401K, TSP, IRA, etc.). That way, you will likely start building a good amount for retirement and be in far better shape than most once in your 60s.

One of the obstacles with investing is that there are literally thousands of different options. Retirement or non-retirement accounts? Actively managed mutual funds or passively managed index funds? Roth or traditional retirement accounts? Investments focused on large or small companies? Investments on American or overseas companies? High, medium or low risk? The end result for many of us is that we get intimidated by all of the choices available and then end up on the worst path possible - not investing at all!

Another obstacle is the perceived volatility of investing in the stock market. This is especially pronounced for those that felt an impact from the market drop in 2008 and 2009. While there certainly are ups and downs, we have got to remind ourselves that we are in this for the long haul. First off, remember that no money is lost during a market drop unless the investor cashes out. Had those that pulled out of the market during drops in 2001 and 2008 just held on for a year or two, they would have seen their investments return right back to their value before the drops. If you have less than five years, there is likely a good argument to be made to stay out of the market. However, when you are committed to staying invested for at least five years, the odds of coming out on top become exceedingly high, historically. If we look at all rolling five-year periods over the past forty years, from 1978 to 2017, the S&P 500 had a positive rate of return nearly 90% of the time. If we extend our scope to all seven-year periods, that number exceeds 97%.[2] Those are great odds! Every market downturn in history has been followed by an upturn. Yet due to skepticism of the market, many decide to remain on the sidelines.

You are wise to be cautious, as there are a lot of bad investments out there. So, what can you do? If you do not feel 100% confident in choosing your own investments, I recommend reaching out for professional assistance. Once you get to a position where you can invest consistently, seek out an expert. That's exactly what most millionaires have done, with studies showing at least 2 out of every 3 get help from an investment professional.[3] Unfortunately, just like there are poor investments, there are many investment advisors out there that do not have your best interests in mind. So how can you go about finding an advisor that will listen to you and your goals, then put you on the best possible path with diversified investments to achieve those specific goals? I would strongly recommend that you seek out a "fee-only registered investment advisor." Not fee-based, but fee-only. That means that the advisor is a pure fiduciary – someone that is legally held to acting in your best interests.

Most advisors are also brokers, which means that they are making money off of you and your investments, as well as money in the form of commissions for the investments that they invest your money in. If an advisor is not a pure fiduciary, how do you know, with 100% confidence, that he or she is not being swayed by what is best for them versus best for you? By the fact that they seem like nice folks? Most advisors have a conflict of interest, and are held to a suitability standard, versus a best-interest standard. That means that as long as they are investing your money in something that is deemed generally suitable for your age group, which is a very wide and ambiguous measure, then they are perfectly legal in doing so. But a fee-only fiduciary is held to a higher standard. Recommendations must be in your best interest, meaning the best for achieving your objectives.

So how do you go about finding a trustworthy advisor that will have no conflicts and only serve your best interests? The National Association of Personal Financial Advisors (NAPFA) is an organization that requires advisors to adhere to the absolute highest fiduciary standard. All advisors in this organization must be fee-only fiduciaries, and they also have some of the strictest continuing education requirements of any group of advisors out there. To find an advisor in your area, you can plug your zip code into the NAPFA website, at napfa.org, and get a list of fee-only advisors in your area. Take some time to sit down with at least two, preferably three of them, which should cost nothing, to see which one you connect with the best. Do they ask you about your goals right off the bat? They certainly should. How do they get paid and what are their fees? Do they think they can pick actively managed mutual funds and beat the market? This is a feat that very few can actually do, consistently, over a long-term of time.

More and more of the most successful investors are now recommending a passive investment style, utilizing low-cost index funds, which generally incur much lower expense ratios and taxes. Unlike active mutual funds, which include the active trading of company stocks, index funds are considered passive, simply following an index, such as the S&P 500. While active funds are marketed as beating the market, very few actually do over the short-term. In fact, 95% of actively managed funds failed to beat the market benchmark over the past three year period.[4] The same can be said over the long-term, with 96% not beating the market over a 15-year span.[5] In addition, active funds generally have much higher expense fees associated with them, often as much as 20 times higher than index funds. That said, if your advisor is of the mindset that he or she can beat the market by choosing active funds, ask them to prove it, subtracting out any fees to make it a true comparison.

Other than the performance of your investments and expense fees, it's important to keep in mind the greatest threat to the growth of your long-term investments – the investor! The first way that most investors sabotage themselves over the long-term is by making the mistake of not automating their investments each month. When we require an action to send money into our investments each month, there will invariably be many months that another use of those dollars pops-up. For many, that becomes the case for more months than not. We have to take our emotions and decision-making out of the loop in order to stay disciplined and on track. Regardless of the investment vehicle that you choose, set up automatic monthly payments each month!

The second way that we shoot ourselves in the foot is by reacting to market swings. While most would agree that riding out the market for the long term is the best thing they can do, very few pull it off when left to their own devices. When the market drops and the associated media coverage is all doom and gloom, very few investors have the discipline to stay the course. Besides helping you pick investments that meet your best interests, being a voice of reason during times of market turmoil is the greatest benefit gained from working with an advisor. An experienced fee-only advisor will provide their best value added to you during the storm, reassuring investors to stay the course and not pull out early. That said, even if you feel qualified to choose the best investment vehicles to meet your goals, I would still recommend having a professional in your corner unless you are absolutely certain that you will remain fully committed to staying in the market no matter what level of fear the day's news may invoke. Do not become your own worst enemy by reacting to sensationalized media blips and falling into the trap of trying to time the market.

Diving into investing can feel very similar to skydiving. As part of my military training, I had the opportunity to earn my parachutist wings, which required five solo jumps from a perfectly good airplane. After several days of intensive ground training, about 15 of us loaded up onto an Air Force jump plane, a Twin-Otter. We took off into the sky and proceeded to circle up to a few thousand feet above the ground. Once we arrived at the proper altitude, the instructor opened up a door in the side of the plane and then called us up, one by one, pointing and yelled, "stand, in the door!" Looking out of that door and seeing the ground thousands of feet below was one of the most terrifying experiences in my life. And to think I had voluntarily signed up for this experience! Somehow, I built up the courage to propel myself out of that door, freefall for ten seconds, which seemed like an eternity, and then opened my chute and floated down to the landing zone. I successfully completed the course after jumping a total of five times. It was a huge confidence builder, but would I ever want to do that again? Probably not.

There were two in our group that went up to the door of the airplane, looked down, and then elected to sit back down. The risks were too high, and fear resulted in inaction. For many that I coach, investing invokes a similar level of fear as jumping from a plane. Too many options, too many risks, too many things that can go wrong, so I will sit back down. While in the end nothing was really lost by those that chose to back out and not jump, the same cannot be said about those that choose to stay out of investing. By staying out of the market, they are essentially giving up their best opportunity at building wealth and ultimately realizing their long-term goals.

Do not let your fear of the stock market keep you on the sidelines. Doing so will likely be the decision that prevents you from your best wealth-building tool – the awesome power of compounding interest. Could you just avoid the market altogether and save your own million dollars? You could, but most won't, as it would require 5-10 times the amount of savings as taking advantage of the market's compounding interest.

After getting on track for your own goals of financial independence, you may also choose to consider investing for your children's education. That is a choice up to you, collectively with your spouse if married. If you do elect to do so, I recommend doing this <u>after</u> you have gotten securely on track for your own retirement. It may seem odd to prioritize yourself over your kids' education, but there is no doubt that you will want to retire someday or be forced to earlier than anticipated as many are. Your kids, on the other hand, may or may not choose to go to college, may or may not get scholarships or join the military, and may or may not actually finish college. If you don't set yourself up for retirement, no one else is going to be there to bail you out. Secure your retirement needs first, then look into opportunities to save for your kids, if you choose to do so. Educational savings accounts (ESAs) and state 529 plans that allow you to retain control are viable options and another topic that your fee-only financial advisor is equipped to help walk you through.

Once you have secured your financial goals, and are putting money aside for your kids' educations, what if you still have money left each month? You may choose to build some more wants into the monthly plan, which there is nothing wrong with, as long as you don't go back into debt or jeopardize your long-term investing. Another great option is to start paying down extra towards the principal loan balance on your house. Having a paid off house, and truly becoming 100% debt-free, is where you want to be long-term. Don't discount the power of sending even a few hundred extra dollars towards the principal on your home mortgage each month.

I often get, "but why would I want to pay off my house early? I don't plan to stay in it." It doesn't matter how long you plan to stay. If and when you move, you would then have the ability to roll any equity into the next house and get it paid off that much sooner. Another one is "wouldn't I be better investing the money and getting a higher interest rate?" That thought process leaves risk out of the equation. The market may exceed the rate of your mortgage, but it also may not. Paying off your home is a guaranteed rate of whatever your mortgage is. "What about the tax advantage of having a mortgage?" Most in this country don't even itemize on their taxes due to the high level of the standard deduction, so there is no tax write-off for mortgage interest if you don't itemize. Even if you could itemize deductions on your taxes, would it really make sense to pay the bank $1 in interest to get only $.20 back on your taxes? Follow the lead of the millionaires in this country. The majority of them do not average annual incomes over $100K over their working years yet successfully pay off their homes in just over ten years.[6]

Think of paying your house off this way... if your house was paid off today, first off, how freeing would that feel? Soak that one in for a minute. Second, is there any chance that you would go and take out a loan against your fully paid for house, putting yourself back into the bondage of debt, in order to invest it or get a supposed tax benefit? Most would likely answer this question with a resounding "no." If you wouldn't do that later, why would you do it now? Third, how strongly could you build wealth and give if you didn't have a house payment? Lastly, if you have qualified for a pension, as some military members and many first responders do, the payoff of your home may be the difference maker in terms of how quickly you can achieve financial independence. You will definitely want to bring any pension income into consideration when developing your plan. For those with very high confidence of a pension, maintaining a minimum of 10% going into long-term investing should be considered. 15%, at minimum, for those without pension income.

Again, it all goes back to your goals, and what steps get you where you want to be the soonest. There is no cookie-cutter approach because no two people are exactly the same. Where you stand today, the destination that you want to get to, and how quickly you are looking to get there is different for each of us. Put together a plan, unique to your goals and objectives, and get advice from an expert who is committed to serving your best interests. Remember that choosing to remain on the flightdeck versus taking off and investing in the market will cripple your ability to achieve your goals and realize your "why." You can't win the air campaign from the chocks – you have to takeoff and get engaged in the fight!

** CAUTION **

Failing to invest and capitalize on long-term compounding interest is likely to limit your achievement of long-term goals.

24

Department of Defense

All of our nation's armed military branches fall under the Department of Defense. We are not a conquering nation, intent on expanding our territories. Instead, the primary focus of our military forces is to defend our nation, our citizens and the freedoms inherent to being a citizen of the United States.

This focus on a strong defense carries down into each of the branches, all the way down to each and every unit and its individual members. The same goes for our first responders, with protecting and defending their bread and butter. If we do not establish and maintain a solid focus on having a strong defense, first and foremost, all other efforts are weakened from the start of any operation. For each of these professions of defenders, each and every member is well aware that tomorrow's mission is inherently compromised if man or machines are not available. In turn, any necessary offensive capability is strengthened by first having a strong defense.

The area of personal finance abides by the same principle. If one's focus is solely on building wealth, without securing a strong defense, all offensive progress can easily and quickly be erased in the blink of an eye. One major medical emergency, an injury that prevents income from being made, an automobile accident, a job loss, or, worst case, the loss of a provider can quickly result in financial ruin for a household. As an example, medical emergencies, and the associated bills that accompany them, account for the leading cause of bankruptcy in this country.[1]

We have already covered one critical layer of your defensive plan – the emergency fund. It represents your first line of defense between you and life's curveballs, and the importance of securing this portion of your financial plan cannot be overstated!

As frustrating as high insurance premiums can be as a drain to our monthly income, we absolutely must maintain the proper coverages for a very good reason – to limit risk to our households. That's all insurance is, paying a monthly premium to offset risk from our wallet to an insurance carrier in the event of an unforeseen emergency.

Although several types of insurance are absolutely foundational to having a strong financial defense, the waters can get murky, as there are lots of insurances available out there. Each and every one of us ultimately have to make a decision as to which coverages are best for our household. We have to keep in mind that every dollar sent to insurance premiums is a dollar that we cannot attack debt with, build an emergency fund with, or invest and build wealth with. That said, this is an area that has to be carefully considered, balancing the need to have a strong defense against being over-insured, which can cripple our offensive systems.

So which types of insurances are foundational to having a strong defense?

The first is medical insurance. No matter how healthy you and your family members may have enjoyed being in the past, none of us having a crystal ball to see what tomorrow will hold. Given my experience with clients over the years, I know, with absolute certainty, that young families are not immune to medical emergencies. In fact, it is younger and healthier families that I have seen roll the dice and not carry medical insurance, given the high cost, that seem to get bitten the worst, quickly finding themselves in over their heads with medical debts that they didn't see coming. Again, medical expenses are the number one cause of bankruptcy filings in this country!

There are a ton of different medical insurance options available, so you will definitely have to do your homework and weigh the risks versus rewards. If a decision to accept any risk is taken, I would recommend that it be in terms of the deductible, not whether or not to carry medical insurance. If you take the risk of a high deductible, given a healthy family history, and guess wrong, at least that loss should be manageable, whereas having no medical insurance can quickly result in an unrecoverable situation. High deductible plans may also have the benefit of a tax-free Health Savings Account (HSA). For those without solid options available through an employer, another avenue to consider may be participating in a group plan. Regardless of which option you choose, medical insurance is absolutely foundational to having a strong financial defense!

Another critical type of insurance to carry is an adequate auto insurance policy. Many states require insurance coverage now, but even in those that do not, you should take extreme caution before choosing to forego auto insurance. First, given the rising cost of medical care, injuries caused by an accident can quickly add up. You may also want to reconsider using the same standard as previous generations, 100K/300K/100K. With that type of coverage, the liability of injuries caused to others is limited to $100K per person, which doesn't take much to exceed due to today's rising medical care costs. Second, having strong liability insurance coverage can protect you against litigation, especially as we become more and more of a litigious society, with many jumping at the option to sue someone found at fault for everything they've got. Consider having a higher level of liability coverage to protect yourself. Third, you have to consider the impact of the loss of your own vehicle, through comprehensive coverage. What impact would a loss of vehicle, potentially one that you still owe money on, have on your household?

I highly recommend shopping around to compare rates, to include various levels of deductible sharing. Once you have an emergency fund in place, your ability to accept a higher deductible, and therefore enjoy lower rates, may be much better than before when you had no emergency fund. Do some math and see how much higher deductibles will bring down your monthly or annual premiums. Then ask yourself, given your driving history and financial standing, which deductible has the best risk versus reward tradeoff?

Homeowners insurance, or renters' insurance for those renting, is also a critical need. The loss of a home without proper coverage would of course be devastating to one's financial future. Many make the mistake of not updating their homeowner's policy as the value of their home goes up due to market appreciation. Having extended replacement cost coverage can help with rising values and labor costs, as well as refreshing your home value with your insurance agent on an annual basis. Even for those that do not own their homes, but rather rent, having renter's insurance that protects your belongings is often overlooked. Renters' insurance is typically available at a very low cost and provides valuable protection in the event of loss of your clothing, furniture and other items of value.

Another often overlooked insurance is long-term disability coverage. While many in their younger years may consider this coverage unnecessary, the decision to not have it can crush any financial plans. The fact is that one in four in this country have a disabling event at some point in their working years, before anticipated retirement, often at a much younger age than when many believe themselves to be at risk.[2] A disability which prevents income generation can be devastating, especially for those supporting families with single incomes. Imagine being injured at 30 years old and not being able to earn income for the rest of your life? Nearly 50% of all home foreclosures and bankruptcies are attributed to disability.[3] Many incorrectly assume that they are covered by their employers, but often are not. Check with your employer and if not already covered, or covered only for on the job injuries, strongly consider securing long-term disability coverage by shopping around on your own. Most long-term disability policies can be chosen to kick in after 90 or 180 days, as you choose. Again, once you have secured your 3 to 6 months of expenses in an emergency fund, you should already be covered for the near-term, so it's the long-term coverage that should concern you.

The last critical type of insurance for anyone who supports others with their income is life insurance. The point of life insurance is to replace lost income for family members that rely upon it. A relatively standard measure used for determining an amount needed is 10-12 times each income earner's annual salary. For example, for someone making $50K per year and supporting a spouse and/or kids, 10-12 times would equate to $500-600K of life insurance coverage. Other points to consider are the value of any investments, which can reduce the amount of coverage needed, potentially choosing to add an outstanding mortgage balance to the total amount of coverage, and the type of life insurance to buy.

In my opinion, there is only one type of life insurance that makes sense for those committed to doing better with their finances and building long-term wealth – term life insurance. Universal and whole-life policies have become popular over the last twenty or so years. They are sold as a combination of an investment, holding a cash value, and death benefit. While that may be true, it comes at a steep price. Universal/whole life insurance often comes with a monthly premium that is over ten times that for the same amount of term life coverage. This massive increase in premium is typically justified by the fact that these policies are also an investment, holding a cash value, and keep the premium set for the insured's lifetime. Both of those are technically true but have holes in them. Regarding the insurance also being an investment with a cash value, when you calculate all of the upfront fees with these policies, the cash value ends up being a fraction of what a separately held investment would result in. The other hole, which to me represents the largest, is that any cash value of these policies is typically surrendered upon the insured individual's death.

For example, if you paid $100 per month from age 25 to 65 for a $100K policy, you would have put in $48,000, which is likely $44,000 or more than the cost for the same amount of coverage with a term-life policy. Let's say the cash value had built up to $60K after paying into it for 40 years and all required fees paid (an extremely poor return compared to the market by the way). If the insured were to pass away at 65, the beneficiaries would still get the $250K death benefit, but not the death benefit plus the cash value of $310K. So let me get this straight, I pay 10 times the monthly amount, but if I die before I cash out the policy, which likely grew at a fraction of what it would have in a solid separate investment, I would still only get the death benefit of $250K? That's correct!

The second "benefit" of whole life or universal life insurance policies is often said to be the fact that the monthly premium won't go up over time. Sure, there is always the chance that the premium would go up after the years of coverage selected with a term policy. Would those increases have justified paying 10 times or more for all of those 20 or more years? Likely not. The other piece to keep in mind is that fact that if you consistently invest and build wealth, at some point shouldn't your investments make you self-insured? Yes, a term insurance policy secured at 70 years old is going to be a lot more per month than it was at 30 years old. But if I get out of debt, protect myself from going back into debt with an emergency fund, and then consistently and smartly invest, shouldn't investments help me to become self-insured to take care of my loved ones by the time I'm in my late 60s or 70s? That's the plan, right? If you abide by the principles you have learned, you are very likely to build wealth over the decades to come. Keep that in mind when being sold whole or universal life policies, which by the way pay much higher commissions to those selling them when compared to term policies!

As an example, a friend of mine and his wife took out very small whole life policies, with death benefits of just $60K and $75K respectively, soon after getting married. After paying a combined

$117 per month for over 23 years, today their total cash value is $42K. Over $32K is what they have paid in themselves, which means that their "investment" has made just $9K. Had they gone with term policies, which would have likely been only a few dollars per month each, and instead invested the difference in the market at 8%, they would have had nearly $80,000 today. Instead, the rate that they achieved was a measly 2%, which means that their dollars didn't even keep up with inflation. Some call that a good investment?

Regardless of which type and amount of life insurance coverage you decide to get, recommend securing the policies on your own, outside of work. If your employer is going to provide you extra coverage for free, that's great. But you do not want your life insurance needs tied up at your workplace. If you change jobs or lose a job, and leave that employer, life insurance coverage is typically lost, which puts your family at great risk in the event of your passing. At a minimum, choose to supplement the coverage from your employer with an outside policy. Using an insurance broker that shops around to get you the best available premium can save you a lot of time and money. At the end of the day, none of us know when our time here will be up. If you have family that is dependent upon your income, don't make the mistake of delaying to put life insurance coverage in place, which in turn puts your loved ones at risk.

In addition to having your insurance coverages in place, there are several other critical components of having a strong defense. One of these is protecting yourself against fraud and identity theft. The era of convenience and online purchasing has also brought about increases in fraudulent activity and stolen identities. If you haven't experienced either of these yourself, you likely know a close friend of family member who has. While there is no one-stop action that can protect you from these events, there are some smart moves you can take to greatly lower your risk.

Monitoring your credit report is an important action to take at least once, if not several times, throughout the year. Your credit report is different than your credit score, showing activity with creditors. Even if you have vowed off debt, that doesn't prevent others from applying for and taking out debt in your name, fraudulently. Each of us are allowed free access to our credit reports each year, from each of the three primary credit reporting agencies: Experian, Equifax and TransUnion. The only approved method, backed by the federal government, is through the website **annualcreditreport.com**. Federal law allows you to get a free copy of your credit report every 12 months from each of the three credit reporting companies. That said, you could either get all three at the same time each year or spread them out and get one from each of the three agencies every four months. If you notice any activity that has occurred in your name that was not initiated by you, the site has directions regarding the actions you will need to take to report and then clear up the fraudulent activity.

Another great defensive measure is to freeze your credit. Once in effect, this should prevent someone pretending to be you to be approved for credit in your name. Although a freeze does not prevent fraudulent charges to an already existing account that you have open, the purpose is to make it much more difficult for criminals to open up new credit accounts in your name. Up until recently, there was a fee for every time you froze and "thawed" your credit with each agency, but this is now free. You will have to go to the websites of each of the three credit bureaus mentioned above and elect to place a freeze on your account. It would also be a good idea to freeze the credit of your entire family, including minors, as anyone with a social security number is susceptible to having their identity stolen. Once frozen, you will have a pin number that can be used to thaw your credit in the unlikely event that you chose to go out and take out a loan in the future. Be sure to keep the pin numbers stored in a safe place. An added benefit to freezing your credit, aside from safeguarding against fraud, is that it adds another layer of action required on your part in the event that you make the decision to go back into debt. Perhaps having to thaw your credit will cause you to rethink going back into the hole with new debt!

A solid line of defense against fraudulent activity comes from carrying identity theft protection. Unlike simply monitoring your identity and letting you know when suspicious activity is detected, identity theft protection takes it much further. In the event that your identity is stolen, this service also provides recovery assistance. An identity breach often requires hundreds of hours spent trying to clear your name. Having a service that does the recovery legwork for you can save you many hours and be worth its weight in gold in the unfortunate event that your identity is stolen. If you opt for this service, utilizing a reputable company found online, you will want to sign up for it before you freeze your credit so the service can gain the necessary access to your credit files.

One last critical defensive measure is to have a will. Approximately 70% of American adults have not put together a will, detailing their final wishes upon death.[4] This is another defensive measure that's really more for your loved ones. Dying without a will leaves quite a mess for those that you leave behind and allows the courts to make decisions on your behalf. Forcing your estate into probate court can not only delay the settling of your affairs for months or even years, but also rob your estate of many dollars due to court costs. Your passing is going to be difficult enough for your family members but dying without a will can make an already very tough situation much worse. You and your spouse need to have a will, and potentially a trust if you have minor children, that are specific to the state you reside in, as rules can change from state to state. Most, or even all, of this can now be accomplished online, so there is really no excuse. If you care about your family, which I'm sure you do, and want to avoid the court deciding your wishes, take an action to get this done!

** CAUTION **

Failing to build a solid defense, for yourself and your loved ones, can sabotage all other progress made with finances.

25

Tac Admin

After getting a jet fired up and checking the basic mechanical functions, the next phase of ground operations entails getting the combat systems setup. With each tactical system and weapon allowing many different options, setting up the systems most effectively to support the mission at hand is a critical step. This phase is referred to as the tac admin. While this is administrative in nature, incorporating the proper settings often means the difference between either success or failure of the tactical mission.

There are several big-ticket financial decisions that will play a large part in the success of your financial mission. The top three areas that households typically expend the most resources on are vehicles, college education and homes. While small purchases like eating out or buying a latte every day can certainly add up over months and years, they often pale in comparison to these primary expenses. That said, it is absolutely critical that we get them right. As with many areas of our spending, there is a lot of misleading info regarding the best path to follow. We need an accurate standard that provides us with the tac admin for most effectively setting ourselves up for mission execution.

Car Buying

We have highlighted the crazy amount that is lost in value with new cars... as much as 60% in the first four to five years. Vehicles are one of the top items that I see keeping clients from building wealth. The arguments that buying new is justified due to warranty, repairs and reliability just don't add up. But most of us need vehicles as part of our everyday lives, so what's the smartest way to purchase these depreciating and income-draining necessities?

The first key is to purchase a vehicle that you can afford...with cash! Instead of taking out a loan, consider saving up and paying with cash. That doesn't mean that you need to save ten or twenty thousand dollars before you can buy a car. How quickly could you save up $2000-3000 for an entry level vehicle? And then how quickly could you do the same thing and upgrade to a $5000 car? Just ten months of saving $300 each month will result in $3000 of savings. Then work your way up. But isn't saving $300 a month the same as having a $300 car payment, without the car? No, it's not! First, instead of owing someone else the $300 and being focused in the rearview mirror, you are paying yourself the $300 and looking forward, not to mention reducing stress and risk. The money that you are saving to upgrade in vehicle is also sitting in your account and can therefore be used for something else that life throws at you if needed. Most importantly, saving and paying cash for a car ensures that you are staying within your means versus depleting your income with things purchased in the past.

The next question is how much of a car should you work up to? What's the most that you should spend on a car? The most important thing to remember is that cars go down in value, and therefore are taking you away from building wealth and achieving your goals. But they are also necessary for most of us. One rule of thumb is to limit your vehicle value to $1/10^{th}$ of your annual gross income. That would ensure that no more than 1 out of every ten hours that you work are tied up into an item that is losing money versus gaining value and wealth. Regardless of how much you make each year, my recommendation would be to go with a car with a value of no more than $10,000-12,000. Today, that likely equates to a car that is around four years old, which is when most cars begin to lose much less value each year. Interestingly, four years is also the average vehicle age for our country's millionaires.[1]

Ultimately, you have to decide if your car is a necessary tool, that takes you from point A to point B, or a status symbol? And which is more important, driving a new car or achieving your financial goals? Even if you feel as if you can afford a monthly auto payment, it comes at a great cost to your future as well as your risk and stress level of carrying a payment. Yes, you may need a car, but for most of us, the level of car we purchase is well beyond need and much more of a want. At the end of the day, what is most important to you and what are you putting at stake with your financial future by driving a newer car? You get to decide.

Graduating College Debt-Free

Earning a marketable college degree can serve as a great steppingstone into many careers, when part of a specific plan. Fortunately, it is also possible to graduate debt-free, as many do each year.

Scholarships are certainly a viable option, with many dollars available to students willing to put in the time and effort to apply for many during their later years of high school. But even without scholarships, graduating debt-free is within reach for those with a plan. The primary determining factor is which college is chosen. Starting out at a local community college for a couple of years to knock out core requirements is a much more affordable option, costing as little as one-tenth in tuition.[2] Also, choosing an in-state school, or one that a student can qualify for in-state tuition with, can make a huge difference in tuition. Many choosing to go to out-of-state colleges end up paying up to three times more in tuition to obtain the same degree! Working through college, which, again, studies have actually shown to result in higher GPAs for most students, also teaches time management skills and invokes a partial or full ownership of their college expenses.

Another very important and even more basic consideration is the path that the degree is leading towards. Far too many with student loan debt went to college because they thought that was the best thing for them, even though there was no clear plan as to what career was the ultimate goal. This decision process leads many to pursue unmarketable degree fields, while at the same time racking up thousands in student loan debt. College degrees need to be viewed as a means to an end. If there is no goal in sight, perhaps entering into the workforce for a few years is a better option than diving right into college without a plan.

College is not for everyone, nor does every career field require a college degree. For those that choose to pursue a degree based upon requirements for jobs they are ultimately pursuing, graduating college debt-free is doable. For more on how this can be done, I recommend checking out *The Graduate Survival Guide*, written by Anthony ONeal and Rachel Cruze.

Another excellent option, for those enticed by the opportunity to answer the call to serve our nation, is through the military. The tuition assistance and GI Bill, earned after just a few years of serving, provide another fantastic opportunity to achieve a college education without the use of debt. Without question, I would never recommend that being the sole reason for one joining the military. But for those dedicated to preserving the freedoms that we enjoy in our nation, voluntarily putting their lives on the line for others, the earned education benefit is a great perk. (To those currently serving: recommend visiting your installation's education office to ensure that you are aware of all of the education benefits available to you.)

Entering into the trades is another great option that many are overlooking due to a focus on college degrees for all. Our country is seeing a shortage of those in the trades, which there will always be a demand for. These can also pay extremely well and make for a very lucrative career!

We have to get past the mentality that every high school graduate needs to go to college. That is simply not the case and is perpetuating the student loan crisis. If you or your child don't have a plan, there are other great options available besides going into college and racking up extreme levels of student loan debt. For those with a plan, for which a degree is a necessary step, the goal needs to be graduating debt-free and not putting yourself in a hole from the start.

Home Purchases

For most Americans, the largest purchase that we ever make in our lifetime will be a home. How can we avoid making regrettable mistakes with home buys in the future? There are four keys to smart home purchasing.

The first is sticking with renting if our situation dictates. If there is a moderate to high chance of moving any sooner than three years, the odds of losing money from a home purchase goes up significantly. The purchase and sale of a home is expensive in and of itself...closing costs, realtor fees, furniture and appliance needs, etc., not to mention the cost of required upkeep. In addition to your timeline, the market of the location should also be a major consideration. Purchasing in a stale or small market brings the risk of not being able to sell when it's time to go, whether by choice or for military members when they receive new orders. Also, be cautious of purchasing in an area that is highly dependent on one company or one military installation. In the event that company shuts down or the base is closed, the market is likely to crash in that area, regardless of what is going on in the rest of the state or country.

Don't rush into a purchase in these situations. Instead, look to rent until your confidence in these negative factors changes. There is absolutely nothing wrong with renting for a season of your life until you find yourself in the right situation with adequate preparation.

The second key is having a large down payment. Not only does every dollar of down payment lower our monthly mortgage payment, and overall debt load, but also protects us in the event of a market downturn. None of us can predict if and when the housing market in our area will go up or down in the coming years. While, in general, homes have appreciated over the long-term in our country, the short-term is a wild card, ultimately a roll of the dice. When we put down a sizeable down payment, it greatly reduces the risk of being stuck with a house that we can't get rid of and find ourselves underwater on. Ideally, the down payment should be at least 20% of the home purchase price. Putting 20% down also avoids having to pay private mortgage insurance (PMI), which can add hundreds of dollars to your monthly payment. At a very minimum, if you are very confident that you will be in the house for five or more years, I would recommend putting down at least 10% for a house down payment.

If you qualify for a loan that requires very little or even no down payment, such as a VA or FHA loan, this doesn't change the facts or give you a pass. If it's too good to be true, it probably is! Don't make the mistake of automatically assuming that these options are your best solution, because more than likely they are not. Unless you are disabled, VA loans come at a steep cost in the form a funding fee, often thousands of lost dollars. FHA loans come with added fees that often make them more costly in the end. And remember that even aside from fees, buying without at least a 10% down payment puts you at high risk of finding yourself stuck with no options down the road. There is no free lunch. When loans make it relatively easy to qualify and purchase a home with very little or even zero dollars down, they often spell long-term disaster to our finances.

After determining that your situation makes good sense to buy, and you have built up an adequate down payment, the third key to smart home purchasing is the decision to use a 15-year mortgage versus a 30-year. While a 30-year is the go-to home loan for our country, we have to remember that nearly 80% are living paycheck to paycheck, so doing what is normal is going to get you normal results. Will a 15-year mortgage result in a higher monthly payment for the same home? Yes. Therefore, will a 15-year mortgage equate to buying less of a house than you could "afford" with a 30-year mortgage? Absolutely. But there's a catch, as there always is with anything that appears to allow us to have more. While the lower monthly payment of a 30-year gives you the ability to have more in the here and now, it's going to make you pay the price for it over the long-term. On average, a 30-year will equate to paying about double in interest to the bank over the life of the loan as compared to a 15-year.

Let's take a look at an example using a $250,000 home mortgage, using current average interest rates – 4.5% for a 30-year and 4.25% for a 15-year.

	30-year Mortgage	15-year Mortgage
Monthly Loan Payment	$1267	$1881
Total Paid Over Life of Loan	$456K	$339K
Total Interest Paid	$206K	$89K

* Numbers rounded

Comparing Cost of Interest Between 30-Year and 15-Year Mortgage

With the 30-year option, you would end up paying the lender over $200K in interest, nearly as much as you paid for the house itself! The 15-year loan would have saved you $117K in interest. That's a difference of nearly two full years of income for the median household in this country! Think about that. Two years of work and income lost, making your bank very wealthy with your hard-earned money.

Another benefit of the 15-year over the 30 is how much of your monthly payment goes towards paying off the loan each month due to the amortization of the loan payback. Let's say you bought the same house and ended up deciding to sell and move after five years. How much of your payments would have actually gone towards paying off the house over that five-year period of time?

	30-year Mortgage	15-year Mortgage
Balance After 5 Years	$228K	$184K
Amount Paid In 5 Years	$76K	$113K
Amount Paid to Loan Balance	$22K	$66K
Percentage of Payments to Loan	29%	58%

* Numbers rounded

Comparing Loan Payoff Progress Between 30-Year and 15-Year Mortgage

With a 15-year mortgage, 58% of your payments went towards the principal of the home loan. Let's compare that to the 30-year option. Of all of the house payments you made for the five years, only 29% of them went towards paying the house off. 71% of your hard-earned income sent off for mortgage payments went to the bank in interest. Said another way, for every ten dollars you paid the bank, seven went into their pocket. It's no wonder banks are doing so well yet most households are broke!

Having bought our first house with a 30-year loan, I can tell you that it was very demoralizing to watch so little of our payments actually go towards paying off the house each month. Compare that to our first 15-year mortgage, when we saw over half of our very first payment go towards our loan balance. Still a lot of money, but at least we could see some traction and movement with each monthly payment.

Not surprisingly, I get a lot of questions from clients that I coach after recommending 15-year mortgages over 30-year. One is whether you can get a 30 and send in the extra amount each month to pay it off like a 15. The mathematical answer is yes, you could absolutely do that. The question is, will you? I have NEVER seen a client, myself included, pay off a 30-year loan like a 15-year loan every single month. When things come up, there is a month here and a month there that we find other uses of the money for. I would venture to guess that only a very small percentage of our population would be disciplined enough to pay the extra amount towards the 30-year to make it into a 15-year. So, the odds are not in our favor. The other question you have to ask is if that is your intent, why not get the 15-year and lock in a lower interest rate from the start?

Another common question is "wouldn't it be better to invest the difference given the low interest rate of the mortgage?" In theory, if you could consistently make 8% investing, which would be better than the 4-5% you would pay the bank, that would make sense, mathematically. But we aren't robots and the world isn't perfect. Very few invest every dime of the "savings" from a lower 30-year mortgage payment. Even if you were to do that, consistently, every single month, it leaves out other important factors. Remember all of the downsides of debt that we talked about earlier? One big one is risk. The longer that you keep yourself in debt, the longer you stay at risk, and enslaved by payments to others.

In addition to eliminating your exposure to risk and providing a guaranteed rate of return, there is also the value of emotional peace that having no payments would bring. How good would it feel to have a paid-off home? It's really difficult to put a value on that amazing feeling of knowing that you owe nothing to anyone.

The last question that I often get on the 30 versus 15 is whether that makes sense if a buyer doesn't plan to stay in the house forever. Almost none of us will stay in the same house for our entire life. But that doesn't change the facts one bit. If you pay down more of the loan each month, you will in turn have more equity in the house. That means that whenever you do sell, you will take more cash out of the sale and therefore have more to put down on the next house that you purchase.

What if you already own a home with a 30-year mortgage? Does is make sense to refinance to get a lower interest rate? More often than not, unless interest rates have fallen considerably (1% or more), it is likely not worth the expense. Refinancing is not cheap, resulting in thousands of dollars in closing costs. Also, with discipline to pay the extra amount each month, you can still payoff your 30-year mortgage just like a 15-year with no dollars lost to closing fees.

The fourth and final key to smart home purchasing, and likely the most important to overall financial health, is not becoming house poor with more of a monthly payment than you can comfortably afford. Although you can likely get approved for a house payment of 40% or more of your monthly take home income, is that really in your best interest? Recall that most take on payments that are too high in comparison to their income, ending up house poor and then running up debt to continue to live the lifestyle they desire. So, if not 40%, what's a good rule of thumb? As a coach, I recommend that your goal should be to not exceed 25% of your take home pay each month on your house payment. That includes homeowner's insurance and property tax. Sticking to no more than 25% will ensure that you do not become house poor, and instead have the ability to continue to meet your needs, wants, invest and give without having to choose or go into debt to do so. Nearly every client that I have ever met that has a home payment that is greater than 30% ends up in debt. Aim for 25% or less as your objective, and 30% as your max threshold. If you decide to rent to save up a house down payment or due to your current situation, aim to have your rent at 20% or less of your monthly take home. That will allow you to save a down payment faster and become a homeowner sooner.

You can use a simple rule of thumb to get you in the ballpark on the level of home you can afford to purchase without going house poor. If you multiply your household's total take home monthly income by 35, that will give you a rough idea of a home you could safely purchase with a 20% down payment. In addition to that amount of down payment, this multiplier is based upon a 15-year fixed rate mortgage at an interest rate of 4.5% and an average level of property tax and homeowner's insurance. For example, if you were to calculate your total monthly take home income to be $6,000, multiplying by 35 would give you $210,000. After bringing a down payment of 20%, which would be $42,000 in this case, your mortgaged amount would be $168,000. For a 15-year loan at a 4.5%

interest rate, that would result in a loan payment of $1285 and, on average, monthly property tax and homeowner's insurance payments totaling $245, for a total mortgage payment of $1530 per month. If taxes and insurance were paid each month into escrow, it would likely result in a slightly higher payment, around $1570 per month, which would still equate to about 26% of take home pay.

Again, a multiplier of 35 is based upon the three assumptions of a 4.5% interest rate for a 15-year loan, 20% down and an average national rate for property tax and insurance. To get a more accurate multiplier for your specific circumstance, you can add to or subtract from your multiplier for these three factors using the adjustments listed in Appendix D. Once adjusted, you will have a very accurate number to use to narrow your home search within a safe range for your household income.

The most common question that I get on targeting 25% and the multiplier of 35 rule of thumb is "what if I can't buy in my area at those percentages?" Where you live doesn't change the facts on what makes good financial sense. If you cannot afford to rent or buy at these percentages, my first challenge would be to keep looking. We often convince ourselves that we "can't" because at the end of the day we don't want to. Get creative and do your research. If the answer is still no, then you have some tough choices to make. If you stay in that area or decide to overextend yourself with higher rent or home payments, you are knowingly putting yourself at risk for building long-term financial wealth.

What if you already own a home and your mortgage is more than 25% of your take-home pay? First off, I would not recommend any drastic moves if your payment is 1-3% higher than the 25% rule of thumb. But if it exceeds 30%, consider changing something in the equation. The best option is to find ways to boost up your income. Is there a promotion that you can compete for? A side hustle that you can pursue, turning one of your passions into secondary income? After exhausting all other opportunities, a last resort may be a change in residence, downgrading to a smaller or less expensive home, or relocating to an area with a lower cost of living. Consider all options on the table, remaining aware that your ability to stay out of debt and on track for financial goals will likely be severely hampered if choosing to maintain a high percentage house payment.

Remember that any questions that we may have as counters to these key principles may be rooted in a desire to buy more house and scratch a contentment itch. We can "what-if" ourselves to death but have to be on guard with justifying what we may want over what is best long-term. We all want to have nice homes, but what we intend to be a great thing for our families can quickly turn into a financial nightmare. Again, if you want to achieve your financial goals and "why" over the long-term, look to embody the habits of those that have gone before us and are where you would like to be, financially. For every millionaire in this country that owns a home worth $1M or more, there are three others that own houses worth $300K or less.[3] In fact, the average millionaire's home in this country is 2600 square feet, not four or five thousand as many may believe.[4]

If you find yourself struggling with these principles, go back to your "why." Is buying a home with a low down payment and lower monthly payment of a 30-year mortgage going to ultimately bring you closer to, or further away from, achieving your long-term why?

D
O
B
E
TEAM & TALK
T
E
R

"Alone we can do so little, together we can do so much."
- *Helen Keller*

26

Mutual Support

In the world of fighter aviation, a good wingman is an invaluable force multiplier. The effect of an aligned formation of two fighters, referred to as a "two-ship," is far greater than the sum of two independently operated aircraft. Mission objectives that would stand little chance of accomplishment individually become highly achievable as a pair. While one aircraft may confidently go up against another single aircraft, most never want to find themselves outnumbered against two threat aircraft. But together, two jets in formation can confidently take on four or even more aircraft, due to the synergy of mutual support.

In addition to better combined lethality, mutual support also results in improved survival. It is very difficult for each pilot to have global awareness around their aircraft. The most challenging sector to scan for threats, and therefore the most vulnerable for attack, is a jet's six o'clock position. Each member of the formation has the all-important job of ensuring no threats approach from behind, called "checking six." All of the great offensive might in the world is no good if it can be brought down by an unobserved threat at our six. A wingman plays a critical role in our survival and, in turn, our overall effectiveness.

Fighter pilots never employ on a combat mission as a single aircraft. At a minimum, they go out as a flight of two, fully aware of the many benefits of operating with mutual support. Although one jet has the lead with the other serving as a wingman, the benefit is mutual. It's not called flight lead support or wingman support for a reason, but rather <u>mutual</u> support. Both pilots mutually serve and protect one another, working in unison to accomplish the mission. They rely upon each other and don't want to let the other down, knowing that they will either win or fail as a team.

In addition to the benefits to effectiveness, survival and overall mission success, there is an added benefit of mutual support – a phenomenal boost in confidence. There have been times where I have become separated from my wingman during combat. It's not a comforting feeling to find yourself seemingly all alone in the middle of enemy territory with no one checking your six. When we lose sight of one another, becoming separated, it's almost as if impending doom can be felt right around the corner. The opposite is true when flying in visual formation with another jet. Being able to look over and see another aircraft in your formation is an incredible confidence booster. Unlike when flying solo, having mutual support makes you not only feel more secure, but indestructible and capable of anything that the enemy may throw your way.

The same can be said of all of the benefits of mutual support for all military and first responder missions. We are most effective when teamed up. Rarely, if ever, is any military combat mission completed by an individual. Likewise, while some first responders may patrol alone, the second any situation develops, backup is called in for mutual support. The same concept exists in most civilian occupations as well. We are nearly always more effective in any job when there is effective teaming, built upon a foundation of trust and adding another set of eyes and perspectives. Having a support structure that you know has your back is more than empowering.... it's liberating, exhilarating and provides an incredible boost, adding lift to your wings and thrust to your drive.

The military team is awe-inspiring. The mission takes many members, all contributing their piece of the puzzle, in order to achieve success on the battlefield. Despite operating at the 'tip of the spear' as a fighter pilot, being the one to deliver ordnance against hostile objectives, I quickly learned that it takes a team of many to get the job done. Those who maintain the aircraft, readying our jets by working around the clock while exposed to the elements, are truly workhorses that every pilot's success and life depends upon. Then there are those that build and load the weapons, those that pack the parachutes and survival kits, those that refuel the jets, those that order and provide parts when the jets break, and those that provide air traffic deconfliction to keep us safe. Security forces protect the base, fire crews respond to emergencies, airfield managers sweep the runway and taxiways for foreign objects. And that's not to mention all of the other support functions on the base that play a key role – command post, communications, hospital staff, family programs, and the list goes on. Each and every member of the team plays a key supporting role, with all aligned through a common purpose of effective mission execution. Without doubt, the team's strength relies upon many mutual parts.

Just as teamwork, trust and communication are critical to the success of flight demonstration teams, fighter squadrons, and every other military and first responder mission, these same principles are a necessity to winning financially. Having a spouse with a common vision, thrust and vector gives our wings greater lift and brings us, collectively, to new heights. If just starting out on a new financial path, trading in our hot air balloon for a jet, having mutual support helps us get airborne and established in our climb.

In addition to serving as a force multiplier, an active and involved spouse often sees things that alone we would have missed. Falling prey to the marketing of a new shiny purchase can be avoided when

206

we have someone checking our six. The power of avoiding bad financial decisions can be immense over the long-term. Teaming adds the benefits of accountability and encouragement.

As much as the importance of teaming may make complete sense, overall, we are failing in this regard with our finances. Money fights and disagreements represent a top cause of divorce in North America.[1] Although it's a great picture of two F-35s, the photo on the front cover shows two aircraft that are misaligned, going in opposite directions, which unfortunately represents most marriages today. The fact that opposites attract often adds fuel to the fire. Many marriages bring together a spender and a saver, one that worries more with one that worries less, a risk-taker with someone that is risk averse, and one that is a planner with the other more of a dreamer. The great news is that neither is completely right or wrong. Both sides of each attribute may have faults but can also have great benefits. The key is finding a healthy balance between the two.

If on two different sheets of music with your spouse when it comes to your finances, take the time to sit down in the evening after the kids go to bed to talk. In order to be more effective, your spouse has to be receptive, which is largely up to you and the way you approach the topic. Don't make the mistake of jumping right in and demanding _what_ needs to change. Start by telling your spouse _why_ it's important for you to get on the same page. Share a vision of what it would mean to not only you, but also to your marriage overall as well as your future together. Paint a picture of what the future could look like if you were to get aligned and on a plan for your income. Sell the benefits of doing better, together. What will being aligned mean to your stress level and marriage overall? What will changes that you embrace, together, result in down the road? Share your "why's" and how much it would mean to you to be more organized and effective, emphasizing that you can't, and don't want to, do it without your spouse onboard.

Do your best not to place blame, regardless of what has happened in the past. A history lesson won't prove to be helpful, but rather keeps you anchored in the past and comes with high potential for becoming even more misaligned. Like it or not, you and your spouse both played a part in where you stand today. Getting unified does not happen accidentally. It happens due to deliberate action, unity of effort and mutual support, and it begins with you.

For singles, you don't get a free pass. You are no different, with it being equally important to have someone that you can share your "why" and goals with, that will provide encouragement and hold you accountable to your goals, having a similar effect of adding to your thrust along the way. Challenge yourself to find a solid accountability partner. Just because you are single, it doesn't change the fact that you need a wingman watching your six and serving as a force multiplier in your financial journey.

Who would make a good accountability partner? Probably not your fun friend that drops down the credit card on a whim to live life fully. Instead, seek someone that you have seen do well financially, and not by the traditional cultural standards of driving a nice car or living in a fancy neighborhood. Remember, those looks can be deceiving, and usually are. Perhaps you know someone who reached financial independence at an earlier age or has been able to enjoy a comfortable retirement instead of having to work into their 70s. Maybe you have seen a friend or family member who has different ideas on money than most in our culture, living modestly or perhaps a generous giver. It could be a friend, family member, coworker, or pastor. If no one comes to mind, it may be worth reaching out for a financial coach. Those who are serving, or have honorably served, their nation as a military member or first responder have earned free access to coaches from the nonprofit, Mission Ready Finances.

When we operate as a single ship, we open ourselves up to more mistakes and failures. While I completely missed the impending midair collision that I experienced early in my flying career, I am certain that it would have been avoided had I still been flying with another pilot alongside my jet. The odds of both of us miscalculating the situation like I did are almost zero. Another pilot would have seen what I was missing that day...a misguided path and an impending disaster. A situation that can overwhelm or overtake one of us, is often easily handled when there is another set of eyes.

Don't allow yourself to make the mistake of flying solo with your finances. We are better when together. Always have a wingman that acts as a force multiplier and is checking your six. The power that an aligned couple, or a single with a strong accountability partner, can have doesn't just make you twice as good as your strengths added together. It will make you many times stronger, and ultimately much more effective in achieving your goals and, in turn, fully realizing your "why."

"A house divided against itself cannot stand."
- Abraham Lincoln

27

C3 Comm

One element of a fighter squadron, or any military unit for that matter, that I find truly amazing is the fact that so many individuals from such varied backgrounds can be in lock step working towards common objectives. Born and raised in all fifty states, with diverse backgrounds, ethnicities and upbringings, somehow all are able to come together as a cohesive unit and execute extremely complex missions with very little variation. Many missions have an even wider group of cultural backgrounds, teaming American units with those from other ally countries, like in the picture above.

How in the world can that be possible, appearing so seamless?

Communication is everything and can either be the catalyst for a very successful mission or the downfall and ultimate failure of a mission. If we are not communicating effectively, any complex mission has little chance of succeeding. In fact, just about every mission failure ties back to some level of miscommunication or a breakdown due to lack of proper communication. With this fact well known, every tactical flight mission, whether in training or combat, has an objective of 'C3 Comm' – clear, concise and correct communication. Information that is passed in a confusing or rambling way can quickly have the opposite effect – halting a mission or, even worse, resulting in one that ends catastrophically. The third C, correct, is also an obvious one but challenging, nonetheless. If incorrect information is communicated, serving as misinformation, it's often worse than passing no information at all.

So, what is the basis of solid communication?

A common baseline of communication begins with training. After going through two or more years of flight training, pilots are taught to speak the same language. A long list of common terms is taught, practiced for what seems like thousands of times to the point where it is ingrained and second nature.

The second important piece of C3 comms are standards. When a particular word is used, it has to hold the same meaning and drive an expected action. When a word or phrase is used, the resultant action has to align for both pilots. I learned a clear example of this when I first flew with pilots from the Marine Corps. In the Air Force, porpoising your aircraft up and down tells the other pilot to spread apart into a tactical formation. In the Department of the Navy, however, the same maneuver communicates to the other pilot to take the complete opposite action and reform into close formation. While both services' teach that porpoising alters the formation, the standard is much different, even among pilots of the same country.

Just as with overall mutual support, being on the same page and effectively communicating with our finances is equally critical. If not aligned with communication and standards, our forces are often counter to one another, versus complementary, and we will ultimately drag each other down. It takes excellent communication to ensure that you and your financial wingman get, and stay, aligned.

An excellent way to get on the same page is take financial literacy training, together with your spouse, which forces you to talk. Most of us have never taken a class or had coaching on how to manage money together, as a couple. In addition to getting couples aligned, the right training can offer a better way of handling money. Instead of getting caught up in his way or her way, which are almost always different, an outside perspective can relieve much of the tension and debate as to whose way should be followed. We all picked up different lessons from our parents, which for most of us were likely misinformed as well as different from what our spouse learned.

After years of being somewhat aligned but at times going different directions with our finances due to not communicating well on money, my wife and I took a Financial Peace University class together. It was a nine-week class, meeting one evening per week for about an hour and a half. Taking the training together did wonders in terms of getting us aligned with our finances. If you are looking to get more aligned with your spouse, I highly recommend the class. You can likely find one being offered at a local church, library or community center if you search online. Whether you are engaged to be married, or have been married for decades, there is incredible value to taking this class, or something similar, together as a couple. Think of the marital strain and divorces that could be avoided if taking a financial class together became the standard. Even if we eventually get to a time where financial literacy education becomes more commonplace, there will still be value in taking time out to get on the same page on a topic that is a necessity and touches just about every part of our lives.

Another beneficial exercise for couples improving their communication is for both to take a DISC personality test. The results can be very enlightening, bringing insight into our own personalities as well as how our spouse is wired. This test also shares tips on how we can more effectively understand, appreciate and communicate with a spouse.

Once a better communication baseline is established, the next step is to agree upon household standards. There should be standards for the here and now, like how much do we want to keep in our emergency fund? What constitutes as a legitimate emergency as justification to use those funds? What bounds do we stay within when it comes to spending? Is there an amount that spouses can agree on to not exceed without first discussing with the other spouse? What level of purchase do we agree that we need to sleep on the decision for a night? How much should be set aside in any funds to handle irregular expenses?

Then there are also long-term standards. What's our common vision for the future? What is our "why"? What is it that we can both agree on that we want to avoid down the road? What are our goals and objectives that we can agree upon to make our why a reality? This doesn't mean that if you both have slightly different goals that either of you needs to abandon them for the other. Instead, look to find a balance with give and take from both sides.

Coming to an agreement on these types of questions gives us standards to abide by and know that we are staying aligned with our spouse. It's all about proactively putting in place some guardrails that keep spouses from getting split apart, with one going one direction and another going in the clear opposite direction. A classic example to illustrate the point is a surprise car or vacation purchase. While one spouse may think that it's a great idea to make a large purchase and surprise their wife or husband, the other spouse may have entirely different idea of what constitutes a "great idea." (Not that I would have any experience with that!)

Good comms and agreed upon standards often create an upward spiral for a marriage...the opposite effect of a downward spiral. Tackling finances together as a married couple can help improve communication and grow skills that carry over into other areas of your life together. Any area of a marriage that has strength often carries into other areas, creating unforeseen benefits.

Developing effective communication and improved unity of effort doesn't just happen. Alignment is the result of being deliberate and taking action to get on the same page with your spouse. What actions will you take to instill C3 financial communication? I can guarantee that any time invested into improving communication with your spouse will be time well spent, paving the path for clearer skies and a less turbulent and more effective flight.

*"If you want to soar like an eagle in life,
you can't be flocking with the turkeys."*
- Warren Buffett

28

Birds of a Feather

One of our biggest downfalls with finances is that we tend to mimic those around us. Since most others are doing the same thing, and nearly 80% are living paycheck to paycheck, it's the blind leading the blind. That explains how most of us end up flying our hot air balloons rather than taking to the sky in our financial jet. So, the easy answer is to simply not pay attention to the financial decisions of those around us, right? Ignoring everyone around us other than those who have achieved financial success would likely put almost every one of us in a better financial position, but it's not realistic. By our very nature, we are inclined to be pulled towards, and influenced by, those that surround us. Whether we like it or not, we are wired to emulate those that we spend the most time with.

If we are surrounded by friends, family and co-workers who are financially normal, living only in the here and now versus proactively setting themselves up for a brighter future, then we are more likely to fall back into those same patterns. The downside is that we can't change any of the people around us, but we can change who we choose to be around us. To be clear, I'm not recommending anyone cut ties with friends or family based upon their financial mismanagement. Instead, I recommend bringing some folks into your circle that will have a positive influence on you. The more that we deliberately surround ourselves with like-minded individuals that will support and lift us up, the better odds of success that we have to continue to improve the management of our own finances.

Behavior change is hard enough as it is. If you surround yourself with negative influences, the odds of staying anchored right where you are today go way up. Instead, if you have positive influences that are also working hard to make good changes in their own lives, it serves as a tailwind for your own journey. Change is also contagious, so when we see others being deliberate and forward focused, their example adds a spring to our step, encouraging us to continue pressing on. As Tim Tebow writes in his book, *This Is the Day*, "your battle is more bearable when you have others fighting alongside you."[1]

Like it or not, we become who we surround ourselves with. Stay intentional and choose wisely!

DO BET**TER**

With thrust, vector and alignment with a wingman, it's now time to prepare for our next mission. Every combat operation, both on the ground and in the air, has three essential phases: plan, execute and debrief. All three are equally important, and how well we do each ultimately determines our success, both for the current mission at hand as well as with the overall campaign.

Our financial campaign is to achieve our why. Although executed one day at a time, we would drive ourselves crazy trying to plan, execute and debrief our financial decisions in daily increments. At the other end of the spectrum, we don't want to focus on spans of multiple months or a year at a time, as it would limit our agility and opportunities to learn from our mistakes. Both my wife and I, as well as many clients, have found that planning and executing in monthly increments is the most successful planning strategy. That said, our mission at hand is to plan for, execute and learn from our mistakes, in monthly increments. This is where the final three letters of the DO BET**TER** acronym will be focused.

D
O

B
E
T **T**ASK INCOME
E
R

29

An Assignment for Every Soldier

On every flight of every airplane, pilots first and foremost must have a plan for their fuel. Bad things happen when an aircraft runs out of fuel. There is no pulling over to the side of the road and flagging down a passerby for a ride to the next rest stop. Fuel is life to the successful completion of every flight. Without an extremely intentional plan for our fuel, to safely and effectively complete the mission and make it to our intended destination, we will fail with catastrophic results, both on today's mission and long-term over the campaign.

Each sortie, whether in training or combat, has a very detailed fuel plan. The goal is not to have a bunch left over at the end. There is of course always a reserve that pilots never plan to use, emergency fuel, but the goal with the rest is to use it all for mission accomplishment. Planning to come back with extra fuel may seem like a win, but it typically means that a pilot didn't make the most of the opportunity given to them on that flight. In peacetime, it means that we didn't maximize our opportunity to train and hone our skills. In combat, not planning to maximize effects on every mission results in a campaign that could be drawn out, or worse, that American servicemembers on the ground didn't get all of the support that they could have gotten. Missed opportunities could be another fly over, instilling confidence for those on the ground, or more intelligence gathered, or a show of force that makes the enemy forces question their move. Those opportunities are lost when we don't make maximum use of the fuel that we have for the mission.

While the stakes are not necessarily our physical life or death when having a plan for our income, the fuel of our financial lives, the stakes are nonetheless high. Your income is, hands down, the best tool you have for achieving your goals and, in turn, securing your "why." Your financial life hangs on your ability to stay in control and maximize the effects of your income. As with any situation in life, when we live in reactionary mode, we are not in control, but rather reacting to life. There will always be some level of reactive nature to all parts of our life, as we never know what curveballs life may throw our way on any given day. But there is certainly quite a bit that we can see coming, and therefore can be proactive and completely prepared for.

Not having a proactive plan for monthly income is the top foundational reason that most ultimately fail financially for. The money comes in, we pay our bills and then spend the rest, or even more, and then wonder where it went at the end of the month. Yes, we have some stuff to show for our income, but most really have no clue where their hard-earned income is going each month. We live life driving in the reactive lane versus the proactive lane. While many believe that living reactively equates to freedom, I wouldn't necessarily refer to the stress that living this way often brings as freedom. No matter how freeing we think living on a whim may be, it typically comes with nagging feelings. The fear of running out of money before the end of the month, or not being able to provide for our family, or not being in a position to retire with dignity and a comfortable lifestyle down the road. We may be able to fool ourselves in the moment with the security of the credit card in our wallet, but we can't fool ourselves indefinitely. The voice in the back of our heads grows over time, bringing uncertainty and stress with it. No matter what we may tell ourselves in the moment, we know that there is no free lunch. Mismanagement and lack of planning today WILL result in less security and achievement of our goals tomorrow.

True freedom comes from having a plan and driving in the proactive lane. If we go into the month knowing exactly how much fuel will be available and having a plan for how we will expend it to reach our destination, we are put at ease and back into the driver's seat. Doing so is more freeing than any month without a plan will ever be.

Besides the sense of peace that having a proactive plan brings, it is also foundational to us achieving our financial goals. How often has any major accomplishment in your life to this point just fallen into your lap? Probably not often, and more likely never. Good things come to fruition because we follow a plan. Following a high school curriculum ensures a student checks all of the required squares and culminates with walking across the stage to collect a diploma. Same for college. No student just picks a bunch of random classes for four years and then shows up at graduation to collect a diploma. Same thing in the workplace. Very rarely do promotions fall into our lap just because we showed up every day. You likely completed training, met deadlines, perhaps met quotas, completed continuing education requirements, etc. Staying reactive may work for someone that just wants to collect a check, but not an employee that is fired up to get promotions and climb the ladder. Same thing for our military members and first responders. Those that get promoted and climb in the organization are those that proactively completed requirements and created effects which in turn made them competitive for the promotion.

Financial success is achieved, not found. Each and every one of you reading these pages can achieve financial success, if you become proactive with your income. You work too hard and sacrifice too much to have any of your hard-earned dollars run off. But that's exactly what they do if we haven't given them an assignment. Think of your income as your soldiers. They work for you, not the other way around. You get to give each of them an assignment. Any of them that remain unassigned won't stick around but will run off, leaving you frustrated and wondering where they went. Every dollar of your income needs an assignment, and each can only do one thing. Some will be assigned to keeping a roof over your head, as rent or mortgage. Some will keep you and your family fed, as food in the cabinet and on the table. Others may be assigned to help others as a donation to your church or charity. Others may be used to build your emergency fund or go to paying off the past in the form of extra debt principal. Some of your dollar soldiers go towards retirement where they will multiply in your investment snowball. Some may go to wants this month...eating out or entertainment for example. Others may be assigned to future wants...set aside for our next planned vacation, or upcoming birthday or Christmas presents. There are unlimited options, but each dollar soldier of income can only complete one assignment.

So, if we want to be in charge of our soldiers, and it brings us more peace, less stress and a much higher likelihood of achieving our goals, why don't more of us have a proactive monthly plan for every dollar of our income? The most common answer that I get from clients is that they think it will feel suffocating. We are fed the lie that living on a plan is like a straitjacket. Can't have any fun... all business. But this couldn't be further from the truth.

First off, only you, and your spouse if married, get to decide how many of your soldiers get assigned to fun versus business. No one else is going to dictate your plan...it's YOUR plan, which means that YOU get to choose how many of your soldiers get assigned to each category. Another interesting observation is that having a plan feels the exact opposite as a straitjacket. It takes us from being a passenger to sitting in the driver's seat. It is also very freeing and empowering for most that put a plan together for the first time, making you feel that for the first time you know exactly where your income is going to go.

Having a plan also helps to reduce impulse spending and the regrets that often comes with it. When we spend in accordance with a plan, we are far less likely to carry regrets because the decision was thought out before hand, rather than directed by our emotions in the moment. We can still maintain a semblance of freedom and living in the moment, but instead we are keeping it within the bounds of a pre-determined plan. For example, if you had $200 set aside for monthly entertainment for the month, you would still have the ability to choose how and when you spend those funds. A plan still gives us that ability to live freely in the moment, but within bounds that we will be much less likely to regret later.

A plan for your income also gives you permission to spend in want categories. When you go spend on clothing, entertainment or eating out, it comes with a liberating feeling, knowing that you don't have to worry about how it's going to impact your ability to pay bills or meet other needs. After all, your plan already accounted for those things and these soldiers are for my wants. Think about going out to eat knowing the dollars you are going to spend are part of your plan and will not impact any other parts of your month. How much more would you enjoy that meal? For an even larger example, imagine going on a vacation that you had saved up for, setting aside some of your soldiers every month so you could pay for your holiday trip without reliance on a credit card. How much more would you be able to relax and enjoy the trip, knowing that it was all covered by your proactive plan and soldiers you had corralled in a fund specifically for this very trip? Having done both, I can tell you there is simply no comparison to going on vacation with everything instead going on a card. As much as we try to enjoy that nice dinner or excursion, there is a nagging feeling in the back of our minds knowing that we will have one heck of a bill coming in the mail at the end of the month.

In order to win long-term financially, you must have a plan for every dollar of your income, your fuel, every month. Despite being educated on proven principles and communicating with your spouse or accountability partner, if you don't have a plan for your income, your efforts will come up short. Just as fuel is life to a pilot, your income, and how you choose to handle it each and every month, is the key to you completing your mission and ending up at the destination of your choosing.

Monthly spending plans for income, giving, expenses, saving and investing trips up many of those that I meet with daily as a coach. We will cover the nuts and bolts of putting together a monthly spending plan in depth, to include how to prioritize expenses, to ensure that you successfully establish this foundational part of winning with your finances. Don't let the budgeting concept throw you off your game. How and where you spend your income will be entirely up to you. The focus is all about having a plan, your plan for your income.

30

Beyond Visual Range

In aerial combat, the most successful aviators are those that can neutralize the enemy before they even know you are there. Just as with the age-old concept that those that hold the higher ground hold the upper hand, a fighter pilot that has the advantage beyond visual range, or BVR, holds a much greater advantage and likelihood of becoming victorious.

If there is an air threat, I want to do everything possible to win at range. There are far fewer variables that I must contend with when another jet is 30 or 40 miles away, than when they get within 10 miles. If I can take down a threat before I am seen, that's where I want to be. As soon as I get within visual range of the enemy, I have lost much of the advantage, entering a much more dynamic and dicey realm, and therefore greatly reducing my odds of winning. Also, if I get into a visual dogfight, I become completely focused on the plane that I am in a visual fight with, worried that any small move could put the opposing pilot in a position to take me out with a multitude of weapon options at that range. Not only do I have more to contend with, but I become completely unable to monitor other activity and threats that may be approaching. My overall situational awareness takes a big hit, which means that I become more likely to lose.

Without question, the most effective fighter pilots are those who own the long game. But I can't just launch missiles randomly out towards the horizon, hoping for the best. To be most effective shooting BVR, a well-defined target and precise range is needed.

Winning financially requires that you identify, prepare for and take down as many threats beyond visual range as possible. To do better with your finances, you will need to shift your focus from getting by today, and to what is within visual range, to neutralizing the long-range threats of tomorrow, those that are beyond visual range. If you become aware of a looming financial obstacle, you are much better off to handle that threat now, with time on your side, versus waiting until it's knocking at the front door.

Most Americans, myself included for many years, spend erratically and without much planning. We react to life and expenses, even though we should know that they are on the horizon. Christmas is probably one of the best examples. It should be no surprise that this year Christmas is in December, just like it is every year. Same goes for many other expenses. Without forethought and attacking BVR, our spending tends to look like this throughout the year:

Reacting to expenses as you go often leads to relying on credit to cover the peaks, as they are often too much to cover any given month. Living this way also adds a significant level of stress!

Just as being more effective in aerial combat when BVR, you will be most effective when you accurately define the threat and how far away it is. What expenses do I know are approaching over the horizon, how much will I need to cover the expense, and how far away is it? For example, if I know that my HOA payment is due next January, I also know how far away it is, and how much it's going to be. When I have that level of awareness, I can, and should, prepare.

The goal is to get our spending looking more like this:

Will the line ever get to a point where it's perfectly flat and smooth? Probably not. Life happens and things pop up. But there are many expenses that we should know are on the horizon, and therefore need to prepare for them. HOA fees, holidays, kids' sports, kids' clothing, home upkeep, auto upkeep (registration, oil changes, tires, occasional repairs), auto replacement, vacations, etc. Basically, any expense that you know will be needed in any given year but typically not every month.

In addition to annual bills paid once every year or two, funds work well for expenses that come up several times through the year as well, such as kids' clothing. Many households don't purchase new shoes and clothes for their kiddos every month, but likely make a clothes shopping push before school starts, again when the weather turns cooler in fall or winter, and then again when the weather warms up in the spring. Don't go too crazy with the funds where you setup 52 of them. Figure out an amount that would be too much to handle on any given month... perhaps anything more than $100 or $200, then setup a fund for it. For an extreme example, if your annual HOA bill was $48 once a year, that's probably something most could handle in their monthly spending plan, versus putting aside $4 each month for a year. Draw an expense line in the sand for your household and go from there.

226

The way that we take the chaotic nature out of our spending is by looking ahead and then making preparations each month, whether the expense actually occurs that month or not. What's the best way to build up these funds? Get a separate account for each one? That would be way too cumbersome. Instead, I recommend that every household have three basic accounts with a bank:

1. A primary checking account for month to month income and bills – where you get paid and pay all recurring bills on a monthly basis (rent/mortgage, utility bills, etc.)

2. A secondary checking account for all of the funds that you decide you should have (vacation fund, car repair fund, kids' sports fund, holiday fund, etc.) [We will hit on how to keep these funds combined yet separate in the Execute section.]

3. A savings or money market account strictly for your emergency fund. If you find yourself being tempted or even dipping into this for non-emergencies, consider setting this account up at a different bank to keep it out of sight and out of mind, yet completely accessible when needed to cover an emergency.

Those that keep their focus forward, handling threats BVR by proactively saving for irregular expenses month by month, will achieve much greater success than those that continue to react and try to pay as they go. Doing so will bring a great sense of peace and security and make your monthly spending much more predictable and streamlined. Other than the stress that a reactive mode brings, as well as the reliance on credit, both of which you should be glad to see go, what do you have to lose?

31

At Your Discretion

When a pilot puts together a fuel plan, the first step is to figure out how much they really have to work with. They don't get much of a say for a good portion of the fuel onboard. Some of the fuel has to be spent starting, taxiing and taking off just to get the plane airborne. Some also has to be used for landing and taxiing back to the parking spot. An additional amount has to be used for going back and forth to the assigned airspace. All of these administrative uses of fuel are not optional...they are needs. When subtracted from the overall useable fuel on board (not including dipping into reserves, which is there ONLY for emergencies), it leaves us with how much is at our discretion for completing the assigned mission.

The same process should be followed for putting together your monthly spending plan. The first step in building a monthly plan is figuring out how many soldiers you have to choose an assignment for. Many of them go to "must-do's," required areas that have to be maintained. Others, however, are completely at your discretion.

Let's go step by step through determining how many soldier dollars you have available at your discretion. You can follow along and build your plan by using the "Building My Monthly Spending Plan" table found in Appendix E. This exercise can also be a great start for improving communication with your spouse. I recommend either going through this drill together or, at a minimum, reviewing it together once completed.

Step one: How much useable fuel do I have to work with for the month? Add up all sources of income that you can count on for the month. Use the take home amount for each income source, which is the amount that goes into your checking account after federal and state taxes as well as any required deductions are subtracted. For any income sources that get paid bi-weekly, every other week, add them in twice. This will cover the most conservative case, as most months of the year (ten of the twelve), you will receive two paychecks, not three.

Step two: For those that give a certain portion off the top of their income, a tithe for example, subtract that portion out now. If giving is something that you want to do, but not off the top, then you may choose to hold off as we will be revisiting that category again in the next section.

Step three: Which categories do I need to assign dollars to in order to get by? For this portion, we want to strip away any wants and drill down to strictly needs. As a guide, we will use the components of a house to guide you. Let's start from the top and work our way down. The roof over our heads represents our shelter. In block 3A, annotate your mortgage or rent payment. If you live rent-free with family or friends, you would enter a zero. This is a good opportunity to check the percentage of your income that your shelter represents. Divide your mortgage (including homeowners and property tax escrow) or rent by your total take home income from step one. Are you at 25% or less as recommended?

Moving down from the roof over our heads, next we will tackle the four walls of our structure. The first is food. In block 3B, fill in how much you would NEED to spend on food to keep your household fed. Don't include wants like eating out here. This is just for all members of your family eating three squares a day. What could you get by with if you needed cash for groceries for a week? If you have no idea, you could try using $40-50 per person per week. Then multiply your weekly amount times four, for roughly four weeks in a month, and write that amount in 3B.

The next wall is utilities. Add up the average amount you pay for these, to include electricity, gas, water, trash, and sewer, then put that total into 3C. (Many utility companies offer level-pay options, at no cost, that allow you to pay the same amount throughout the year, which can be helpful for those with bills that vary greatly.)

The third wall is for transportation. If you have any transportation needs, other than insurance or debts for vehicle payments, add them in here. Public transportation and vehicle fuel cover the two primary considerations for most. For fuel, think about how often each vehicle needs to be refueled, and how much each fill-up generally costs you. Then add those amounts up for each vehicle, as well as any public transportation needs, and fill in 3D.

The fourth and final wall is for clothing. What are your average clothing needs per month? Many clients say that they have none, but we all have needs for new socks, shoes, underwear, work shirt replacement, etc. from time to time for example. Any kids you have are growing, so you will need to purchase replacement clothes unless you get hand-me downs from another child, family member or friend. Enter your adult and kids clothing needs, on average, in Block 3E.

Now that we have covered our roof and four walls, we need to calculate the cost of our structure's foundation, our insurance needs. Add up any monthly insurance payments that you consider needs: auto, homeowners (if not already included in mortgage) or renter's, medical, life, long-term disability, identity theft protection, etc. If any of those coverages were already accounted for by being taken out of your paycheck before take home pay, then don't account for them again here in this step. Add up the total monthly premiums for all of your insurance needs and put that amount in Block 3F.

So far, we have covered our bare bones needs. Block 3G covers some other areas that should be considered needs as well: childcare costs, alimony payments, child support payments, home/mobile phones, pets and basic hygiene/hair care. If you consider any of these areas wants, skip them for now.

Step four: Now add up the monthly totals from Sections 2 and 3. This is your total amount needed to cover any giving off the top and basic monthly needs, whether you are debt-free or not. Subtract that total for monthly needs from Section 1, your total take home income, to find your "Total Income Remaining After Meeting Monthly Needs" and annotate in Section 4.

Step five: In addition to regular monthly needs, most of us have irregular needs as well. As discussed in the last chapter, our spending from month to month and year to year will become much smoother if we prepare for big ticket expenses over the horizon.

Step six: The next group of expenses that are must-dos are the required payments on any debts, other than your house which we already covered. In this section, add up all of your <u>minimum</u> debt payments. This includes the required monthly payment for any car loans, credit cards, store cards, student loans, personal loans, medical debts, etc. Add up all of your monthly minimum debt payments, as of today, and enter that amount for Section 6.

Step seven: Subtract the totals from Section 5 and 6, all of your irregular needs and debt minimums, from the total that you were left with in Section 4, your income remaining after meeting monthly needs. This new amount, written into Section 7, is your "Total Discretionary Income Remaining." This amount is "at your discretion," and is what's left for building your emergency fund, paying off debts, saving and investing to achieve goals, additional giving and wants.

The vast majority that I coach are surprised by how big this amount truly at their discretion really is. After covering just our needs and min debt payments, there is a good chance that you have more left than you thought you would, which can feel like getting a raise now that you see it on paper. Unlike your needs and min debt payments, this amount that remains is truly at your discretion.

If you completed these seven steps and came up with a negative number, you are "in the red," which means that at your current income you are unable to cover your basic needs and min debt payments. If this is your situation, I recommend prioritizing by 1. keeping current on your needs, then 2. any secured debt payments (things that can be taken away like a vehicle) then 3. any unsecured debts for things that can't be taken away (credit cards, personal loans, etc.). Consider using a pro rata type payment system for the group of debts that you cannot cover, which may buy you a month or two with your debtors before having a lawsuit filed against you (emphasis on may, as there are no guarantees without coordination with the company who owns the debt). Using that priority will hopefully keep the roof over your head, walls of needed items up, and insurance covered. Once your needs are secure, recommend spending any waking moment either selling things you can live without or finding additional sources of income for a short-term (overtime, second job, etc.). Your focus, first and foremost, needs to be getting back "in the black," where you can cover needs and min debt payments and have some discretionary income remaining.

Now that we have an amount remaining that is at our discretion, we need priorities and a plan for the rest of it as well. Unlike with most of your needs and min debt payments, you get much more say with this remaining amount. So, what's the best use of this discretionary income?

"Nothing worth having comes without a cost."
- Louie Giglio

32

It Depends

There is always more than one way to skin the cat for every tactical mission. For that reason, when asked for the best way to tackle a mission, the most accurate answer that an instructor pilot can give is, "it depends." What are the goals and objectives? What are the threats? How much fuel do we have to work with? What does our team consist of? What are the lessons learned from missions in the past? Which portions of the mission have hard and fast, unnegotiable, requirements? Which portions of the mission are up to our discretion? Only when we take into account all of the answers to these questions can we decide the best way to proceed.

The same answer of "it depends," applies to putting together your monthly spending plan for all of your dollar soldiers left after meeting needs and min debt payments. There are lots of ways to skin the cat, and you will ultimately have to decide what the best way is for you and your household. Many proponents of budgets use percentages for categories. While those can be decent rules of thumb, there is no one size fits all. A single person sharing an apartment with a roommate who commutes an hour to work each way is going to have a drastically different solution for their soldiers' assignments than a family of six with an income earner that works out of the home who is trying to put one of the parents or kids through college. Because there are endless possibilities, I am generally not a fan of using a cookie-cutter approach. Using a generic approach is also part of the reason that budgets get a bad rap – because it feels like someone else is telling you how much you should or should not spend on any given category. Since you get to decide, and no one else, there is a better approach to building your monthly plan.

The first step, before we jump into actual numbers, is to pause and answer a question on priorities. You, together with your spouse if married, have to decide what your priorities are when it comes to the level of lifestyle you need or want to live today, your level of giving, and your balance of enjoying wants for today versus setting yourself up for your needs of tomorrow. This is a great time to revisit your "why" and your goals, as how you prioritize these categories will ultimately impact how quickly you achieve your goals and secure your why. Since each soldier can only be assigned to one area, whether it be needs, wants, investing, or giving, you will need to prioritize. Your financial success hinges on finding a healthy balance of living for today versus saving for tomorrow. Due to the overwhelmingly high percentage of income going to debt payments for most American households, it makes it very difficult to both enjoy some things today and put some away for tomorrow. When forced to choose between today and tomorrow due to debt payments eating away such a high percentage of income, most of us choose living for today. The best answer, however, comes when you no longer have debt and can therefore do both...live well with some wants today and set yourself up for achieving your goals for the future. And, not or...that is the goal.

Take a minute to prioritize the following categories, numbering them 1 through 6. If you are married, I recommend both you and your spouse completing this exercise, separately, then talking over the results and striving to find a compromise for any differences. Again, it's important to revisit and keep in mind your "why" as you complete this exercise. Don't be distracted by what you think is possible for you today, but rather how you would like things to be in order to achieve your goals and "why."

Your Priority (1 thru 6)	Area of spending
	Having more wants or a higher standard of living
	Being in a position to give more
	Building an emergency fund and paying off debts
	Setting yourself up for a comfortable retirement
	Saving for kids' college
	Paying off your house early

Which category did you prioritize at the top? Do the priorities that you assigned put you in the best position to meet your goals and achieve your "why?" If not, are you making the conscious decision to delay achievement of your goals and why, or do you need to reprioritize? Again, I don't want you to have to choose between living in the now OR setting yourself up for tomorrow. But if you are carrying debt payments or are in risk of going further or back into debt by not having an emergency fund, then I recommend you focus on those areas first. My suggestion, as your coach, would be to make your top priority the "building an emergency fund and paying off non-mortgage debts." Regardless of how you prioritized the other areas, giving this your top emphasis puts you in a better position to accomplish the others, whether it be a higher standard of living, increased generosity, more investing for retirement, saving for kids' college or paying off your home early.

All things become more achievable when you first knock out the three steps we covered in the Educate section: build a starter emergency fund, pay off debts using the debt snowball method, and then build up your emergency fund to cover three to six months of expenses. How quickly could these three steps be knocked out if you really challenged yourself? What expenses can be reduced? What items could be sold? Where could extra income be earned? The more you choose to sacrifice for the short-term, the faster you will be able to complete these three steps, and the sooner you will be in a position where you can comfortably live today while also getting on track for your future goals. You CAN enjoy both ends of the spectrum, but only if you get those steps knocked out first. What was your chosen commitment level when you asked yourself, "how committed am I to change and embracing a new and proven way, and what am I willing to sacrifice to achieve my "why?"

Now go back to your discretionary income amount remaining in Appendix E and put together your plan for next month in Section 8, giving every dollar an assignment. While most bills and funds may remain consistent each month, there are typically relatively small but unique expenses that arise from month to month. For that reason, it is important to create a unique plan for each month. Once completed, be sure there is no remaining amount leftover.

For any want, ask yourself, does this category really do it for me and is it worth the number of hours worked each month to pay for it? Seeing the number of hours worked to pay a bill can be eye-opening and help put things into greater perspective and priority. Also, look at the assignment of your soldiers not as deprivation but as optimization, challenging yourself to maximize their effectiveness.

Another valuable exercise, for those on steps 1-3, is to calculate the percentage of your discretionary income going towards building your emergency fund or paying off debts. Does this percentage align with your intensity level, or is there a mismatch? For example, if you chose a commitment level of 9, but are only putting 20% of your discretionary income towards knocking out steps 1 through 3, would your plan really be in alignment with your intent? One rule of thumb is to have this percentage match your chosen intensity level. Using the above example, a commitment level of 9 would equate to 90% of our discretionary income being allocated towards these critical first three steps of building an emergency fund and paying off debt.

Regardless of how you prioritize your discretionary income, one thing that I always recommend is a set amount of splurge or fun money. Even if it's only a small amount per spouse, it's important to be able to reward yourself with something that each of you enjoy from time to time in order to avoid getting burned out by cutting every enjoyable item out of your plan. Whether it be a dinner or movie out together, or separate amounts for each spouse, strongly consider building this category into your plan.

For those that are paid monthly, or twice a month, I recommend using a spending plan that aligns with a calendar month. However, if the majority of your household income comes from a paycheck that arrives weekly or biweekly, I recommend using a 28-day budget, which just about covers the same month-long period but better aligns with your paydays. If this is you, your 28-day budget would start on a payday, then go for 28 days, ending the day before your paycheck arrives four weeks later, regardless of whether the checks in between arrive on a weekly or bi-weekly basis.

For example, let's say the primary income earner for a household gets paid biweekly and their next payday falls on March 23rd. Their next paycheck would arrive two weeks later on April 6th, then the next payday would be on April 20th. That said, a valid 28-day budget period would run from March 23rd through April 19th, ending the day before the third payday. You would start a new 28-day plan beginning on April 20th. Another example would be someone that gets paid weekly, with paydays every Friday falling on May 17th, May 24th, May 31st and June 7th. In that case, the 28-day budget would run from one payday, say May 17th, then for four weeks, ending on June 13th, the day before the fifth payday. In this case, the next 28-day spending plan would begin on June 14th.

This 28-day approach has worked very well for many households that get paid weekly or bi-weekly as it avoids the problem of trying to use a calendar month plan when their paydays don't align well with a calendar month. If you cover all your monthly bills from one of the paydays within this 28-day period, it eventually leads you to getting ahead on your bills by a month by the end of the year.

Another option is adjusting which payday bills are paid by as the 28-day period slides left.

Regardless of whether you use a calendar month or a 28-day period to best align your spending plan, the next step after assigning every dollar of your income is to allocate all of your spending categories to actual paydays. Unless you get all of your income once per month, which is rare for anyone still working, you will have to split up your plan to align with your actual paydays. Individual categories may be split up across several paydays as needed. For example, if you get paid twice per month, on the 1st and 15th, and have $800 planned for groceries, you could cover all of it with the 1st payday, or split it up, $400 on the 1st and $400 on the 15th for example. Prioritize by due date to ensure that every bill is assigned to a payday before it become overdue. If the total of bills due during one pay period exceed the pay amount, you will have to carry some over from the previous payday. See Appendix F for a template that can be used to go through this drill or create something similar.

If one spouse has more of a hand in putting together the monthly plan, which is typical, it is extremely important that both spouses get together to review and agree upon the plan before going final. It cannot be "his plan" or "her plan," but rather must be "our plan," with complete buy-in from both spouses. For the one that builds the plan, insist on inputs from your spouse to increase teaming and agreement. For the spouse that didn't build the plan, take some time to sit down, review and provide your inputs. Just as with every flight, where the wingmen spend time briefing the plan together to ensure all flight members are fully aligned, the effectiveness of your monthly spending plan depends upon it.

Putting a monthly plan together can be overwhelming and somewhat painful at first. But like anything new, it gets much easier with time! Our natural tendency to avoid pain, a primary reason that adjusting our behaviors is so difficult. None of us want to experience struggles with new ways but have to go back to what we decided was at stake. Staying in control of your income demands that you have a plan...each month, staying as intentional and proactive as possible.

DO BETTER

EXECUTE

"Discipline is the pathway to freedom."
- Jocko Willink

33

Fly the Plan

Every single military and first responder mission ultimately comes down to execution. While the development of the plan can certainly be a determining factor to the success or failure, neither is possible without actual doing. Whether for training or combat, either on the ground and in the air, execution is the foundational requirement. After spending over 20 years in the Air Force, hundreds, if not thousands, of memories comes to mind that highlight the importance of implementing the plan through action. But one story, not associated with the typical day-in and day-out missions, often comes to mind on the topic of executing.

Our State Department coordinates with foreign countries to facilitate their purchase of U.S. military hardware, to include fighter jets. The F-16, for example, which is built right here in America, has been exported to over twenty countries, some of which have not always been our allies. More often than not, it is our services' pilots that deliver these brand new or refurbished aircraft across the globe to foreign territories. As you can imagine, an inordinate amount of planning goes into each and every delivery mission, entailing hundreds of turn points, scores of tanker hookups for airborne fuel, weather cell avoidance and stopovers along the way. Speaking from personal experience after flying a handful of these delivery flights, the top two keys to success are knowing the plan, inside and out, and then executing the plan. Each of the delivery flights that I had the opportunity to lead came with their own unique challenges, but one stuck out and serves as a reminder of the importance of plan execution to this day.

After multiple days of 8-10 hour flights crammed into a cockpit with only a few inches of clearance on either side of my shoulders, our flight of F-16s took its final fuel topoff. We split off from the tanker aircraft and prepared to cross into the delivery country, which will remain unnamed. As with other deliveries, despite lots of prior coordination by both our government and the tanker crew, the air traffic controllers on the other end of the radio seemed surprised to hear from us and questioned our intentions. I had seen this before and wasn't super concerned initially. But as we proceeded further inland, we began to receive heightened alerts, escalating to a point where we were told to turn around and immediately exit their airspace.

The thought of turning around crossed my mind for a moment, but I quickly came to the realization that with our tanker now hundreds of miles away, turning around could very well result in our flight not having enough fuel to make it to our planned destination. Given our location, there also weren't a lot of viable alternate runways. A decision had to be made...turn around and risk running out of fuel, or press on, ignoring the demands of the foreign air traffic controller, who was now yelling at us over the radio. Our formation, operating equipment worth well over $100M, awaited my direction.

After once again attempting to explain that these were their own country's aircraft, being delivered by U.S. pilots, I made a command decision for our flight to continue to fly the plan. I won't lie and say that it wasn't an extremely tense situation for about 10-15 minutes, but at the end of the day the best option was to stay on track along our filed route. Eventually, the control agency must have either made or received a long overdue phone call from higher authorities and we were handed off to the next frequency to continue down track. International crisis averted - check.

All plans, whether for military operations or for our finances, are ultimately created for one reason and one reason only: to execute, thereby advancing us in our progress towards the objectives. In fact, that can be said for many more areas than just the plan. All of your decisions to identify your "why" and goals and to commit to a new way, the opening of your eyes and an understanding of your behavior with money, your belief in what's possible for your future, gaining wisdom and a solid understanding of proven financial principles, your teaming with a spouse or accountability partner and the tasking of your monthly income, while all completely necessary and enlightening, are all essentially ineffective if not put into practice through execution.

While writing down your plan on a piece of paper, or loading the numbers into a budgeting program or app, should certainly be considered progress, neither will achieve results. At the end of the day, executing the plan is ultimately what produces effects and separates those with dreams and plans from those that achieve financial security and independence. This is where some may stumble and become anchored, remaining stuck back on the sidelines. Others may be intimidated or distracted by the noise around us and revert to floating along in their hot air balloon, never seeing the results of their education due to a lack of execution. Too often when we learn new principles, even when we find ourselves completely agreeing with them in concept, we never realize our potential to produce change and results due to a crippling decision to not take action and execute.

Of the eight letters of the DO BETTER acronym, none require such levels of action and focused discipline as this 2nd E, Execute.

What will you decide? What level of commitment to your "why" and goals did you give yourself in the Decide section? Will you be in the group that decides that executing is too hard, or convince yourself that your situation is different, allowing your "yeah, but" to overpower your "why?" I hope not. You have traveled too far to go backwards now. But I can't do it for you, nor can anyone else. You have to decide to either succumb to your excuses and the noise of our culture or step up, execute and persevere with grit to do something that you haven't done before in order to achieve results that you haven't seen before. Always remember what's at stake, with execution now the only thing standing between you and it. So, what will it be? Make a command decision to execute the plan. In the words of retired Navy SEAL and co-author of *Extreme Ownership*, Jocko Willink, "**GET AFTER IT!**"

** CAUTION **

Failing to make every effort to execute your monthly plan, regardless of your intentions or the accuracy of the plan, is highly likely to deem your plan ineffective and keep the achievement of your goals out of reach.

34

Lineup Card

After putting together a comprehensive plan and then reviewing it in detail in a briefing with the flight, next comes stepping out to the jet for the mission. With lots of details... times, radio frequencies, GPS coordinates, code words and fuel plans, along with a slew of other tactical information included in the plan, fighter pilots bring a consolidated version of the plan with them in the jet. The lineup card, as it's called, sits velcro'd over their thigh on a kneeboard. These cards hold key information that ensures all pilots in the flight remain on the same sheet, tracking on time and on target.

Executing a spending plan requires carrying a lineup card as well. We need something to help us keep track of where we stand on spending for groceries, gas, eating out, etc. Having the plan sitting at home while we are out and about doesn't do us much good. While carrying around a paper card with our spending plan on it could work, the downsides are that it takes a bunch of effort to keep updated and opens itself up to spouses becoming disconnected as the month rolls on. Fortunately, "there's an app for that," which makes it infinitely easier for singles and couples alike to stay aligned and on target throughout the month.

There are many budgeting apps available, several of which my wife and I and clients have experimented with over the years. There is, however, a clear leader of the pack. And it's free. It's called **EveryDollar (ED)**. The free version is not connected with your bank, requiring you to enter in purchases as you go about your month. For those that prefer the app be tied to a checking account, that feature is available for a price. We use the free version and it works like a champ for us and has for hundreds of clients as well.

I recommend building your monthly spending plan on a desktop at the beginning of the month (at everydollar.com), then using the app on your smart phones to execute. Entering in a purchase made with your debit card literally takes less than 10 seconds. The awesome part is that the other spouse, logged in to the same account across town, can see the new available balance nearly instantaneously. For example, let's say a couple had entered in $200 for a week's worth of groceries. If the first spouse entered $50 for one trip, then $120 for another trip, the other spouse would see that there was only $30 left for that week for groceries. This app does an amazing job keeping both spouses on the same page, without having to update paper copies or share receipts every evening. One of the biggest challenges we had with executing a monthly spending plan was keeping up with where we stood throughout the month. ED solved that problem for us, giving us a great way to stay on track and in alignment throughout the month.

Another great feature of this app is that whatever plan was built in for a given calendar month is automatically regenerated for the next month. Much of the spending that most couples do each month stays consistent or requires just minor tweaks from month to month. Having last month's plan carry over makes it even easier to build the plan for next month.

One additional feature of the app that comes in super handy is the ability to create funds. Unlike the monthly categories, which don't carry over a balance from month to month, the fund balances continue to rollover each month. Once you have put together your list of all of the non-monthly funds you want to proactively save for (holidays, vacations, car upkeep, HOA, etc.), you can create a fund for that category and enter them into the app. Then, when it's time to spend for one of those categories, such as buying a birthday gift using the holiday fund, you would use the debit card tied to that secondary checking account and enter in the expense into the associated fund in ED. Having all of your funds in the secondary checking account avoids the pain of keeping track of separate accounts for each fund as well as the need to transfer funds back to your primary checking account when it comes time to spend fund dollars.

Let's go through a quick example. Say that you and your spouse decided that you would spend a total of $1200 over the year on holidays gifts for all birthdays and Christmas. If you started in January, you would have 12 months before Christmas, which means that you would need $100 per month to go into that fund. In January, you would have $100, then $200 in Feb, and so on. If you had to buy a birthday gift in May, then you would use the account that held your funds and enter in the expense into your holiday fund. The app continues to roll the balance into the next month, adding the designated amount each month ($100 in this example). Setup an auto transfer from your primary checking to your secondary checking for the total amount going to funds each month, per your allocated spending plan, to make the process routine and simplified.

No, we don't get any cut from the app owners, but do highly recommend it. Our ability to execute our monthly plan when using it has improved in a big way. I highly recommend giving it a shot, as do millions of other users. If you find something that works for your household better, then go with that. Whatever tool you use, find one that works and helps you keep on track throughout the month.

35

Flight Controls

Most of our newer modern-day fighters have fly-by-wire flight controls which can override pilot inputs when the jet gets into a dangerous flight condition. The same characteristics that make an aircraft super maneuverable also often result in a jet design that is inherently unstable. As you could probably guess, an unstable aircraft can lead to disaster, potentially putting a pilot in an unrecoverable situation with catastrophic results. To prevent loss of life and aircraft, both very bad things, yet still enjoy the tactical advantages of great maneuverability, these flight computers know when to ignore a pilot's control input. It may sound intimidating to fly in a jet that has computers with this level of control, but it's for a great reason. Sometimes we need controls in place to keep us on track and clear from an undesirable situation.

We all have areas in our spending that tend to get away from us from time to time. It may be groceries, eating out, clothes shopping, spending on hobbies, or stopping for a coffee every morning. The first step is identifying what your top two or three areas for potential overspending may be. Your spouse should do the same thing, as they may very likely have different spending weaknesses. Admitting any areas of weak self-control can be a great start towards beginning to take their power away and increase spending discipline.

Whatever the identified area may be, we need to have controls in place that keep our spending in check per the plan. Unless you and your spouse are very frugal by nature, simply having a target amount or even a category in our budgeting app may not do the trick. We can benefit from flight controls that keep us away from exceeding the limits and on track for our mission.

The best control to curb potential overspending is cash. If, for example, you have planned to only spend $100 on eating out for the month, you could carry cash, or an envelope of cash, in your wallet to be used anytime you eat out. When the cash is gone for the month, no more eating out until next month. Another benefit of cash is that it makes us think twice about purchases more so than plastic cards, especially credit cards. In the eating out example, if we are committed to only using the remaining cash for a meal, odds are high that we will count the cash before ordering and then spend in a way that will maximize the remaining amount. An example of this for our household is date dinners. If my wife and I set aside $100 monthly for date night dinners, we typically choose lower cost establishments that will enable us to go out three or four times versus once. Having a chance to enjoy a date night three or four times a month carries far greater value, for us, than only going once a month for a high-priced meal. That said, there are exceptions and we do enjoy a higher priced meal out some months. I don't share this to imply that either way is wrong or right, but rather to continue to challenge you to think about what brings you true and lasting contentment.

If you are opposed to using cash as a control measure for any reason, another good option that works for many is prepaid debit cards. There are several companies that will provide you with a group of these cards that you can assign to specific categories in your spending plan then setup an automatic recharge from your primary checking account each month. Some companies will even label your cards with your desired category name, which makes it easier to use the right card and avoid confusion between cards. We use prepaid credit cards for a couple of categories that have posed a challenge to our spending over the years. The company we went with charges no fees as long as the card is run as credit, which should be possible with any debit card. The company has an app that shows the charges and balances on each card, which helps us stay aware of how much remains. When the card balance hits zero, then that category is done for the month.

Having these types of controls in place provides a good defense against overspending, but still ultimately requires discipline to stick with not spending any more when the planned amount is used up. At the end of the day, while controls such as these can help, most will always be their own worst enemy. The beauty of the monthly plan is that you get to decide, with your spouse if married, as to what that plan should be. Then your focus has to be on executing the plan and avoiding making financial decisions any time emotions run high. If you change your mind on the amounts, nothing is set in stone and there is always an ability to change the plan for next month.

"If you fail to plan, you are planning to fail."
- Ben Franklin

36

Expect the Unexpected

Unforeseen events can challenge any good flight plan. Very few flights go exactly as planned. While we may have the best intentions and believe that our plan will prevail, there is always potential for the unexpected – a popup threat, different weather, and system malfunctions to name a few. Our intel, weather forecasters and maintainers are great, but never perfect, so there is ALWAYS potential for an unforeseen wrinkle during your fight. For this very reason, every fighter brief includes a portion at the end called "contingencies." While we can't control our environment and therefore don't know when these things may happen, the best we can do is to always be prepared when they do. Having a contingency plan to flex to when things popup in flight makes a world of difference in the end result and ultimately whether the mission is a complete bust or still effective. In the combat flying world, pilots know that preparation and flexibility are key.

Having a contingency financial plan for unexpected changes in conditions, equipment breaks or popup threats to our monthly spending plan is no different, and absolutely critical to our overall effectiveness. Especially during the period of adjustment that most go through when adapting to executing a monthly spending plan, having and sticking to a prebriefed contingency plan is make or break to our ability to roll with the punches and still prevail. The whole point of a contingency plan is to remain as proactive as possible. While we may not know the specific details of what and when things will arise, a solid contingency plan can still serve a great purpose in covering financial curveballs.

The first key element of a contingency plan is to actually expect the unexpected. When we expect popups or changes to our spending plans, we mentally prepare ourselves and are therefore less likely to react in a way that will end up making matters worse.

The second element are the alternate plans. When unexpected expenses popup mid-month, what are our options? The primary go-to solution for most Americans is to break out the credit card. But that just puts us back in debt, which takes us farther from our "why" and goals...so that's out. Another option would be to just spend away with a "figure out later" attitude. That blows apart our plan and keeps us in reactive status, so that's not a good option either. We really have three viable options for contingencies that will keep us on our financial track versus derailing our efforts to do better.

The first option is to push off the expense until next month or later. If the popup is more of a want than a true need, then this is likely the best course of action. For my wife and I, and most others, wants pop up all the time, at least weekly if not daily. If it's not part of our annual funds and doesn't represent a short-lived opportunity (a great sale, concert in town, etc.), then we add it to a running list that we will then consider for next month's plan. What makes this the best option most often is that it allows us to look at it from a different perspective. What may seem like a need or a really important want in the here and now often seems much less important by the time the list is revisited at the end of the month.

Most things that go on our list end up getting scratched off the list when revisited weeks later.

The second option when an unexpected expense pops up that is deemed a need or a want with a fleeting opportunity is to readjust the spending plan. If the plan can be readjusted with other nonessential funds, then no harm no foul. For example, if a concert came into town unexpectedly that was deemed enough of a want to not pass up, what other funds are available to reallocate? Let's say you decide to use the rest of the eating out money to instead purchase concert tickets. That would not blow up your plan and would instead keep you on track for the month. Of course, that would also mean no more eating out for the rest of the month! This is where many fail. Any reallocations from one category to another have to equal a zero sum. Plus $100 into entertainment, minus $100 from eating out equals zero overall. Another note of caution... think twice about using money from your annual funds for popup expenses unless absolutely needed. Remember, the whole point of the annual funds is to stay on track for the annual expense! If we start robbing Peter to pay Paul, you will quickly find yourself off track for those annual expenses, reverting back to reactive mode instead of proactive mode.

The last resort for your contingency plan is to tap into the emergency fund. If you have a large unexpected expense popup that is a legitimate need, then that's what the emergency fund is there for. Before dipping in, be sure that you, together with your spouse, are in full agreement that it qualifies as an emergency need that cannot wait. If you find yourself justifying the use of the emergency fund for things like items going on sale, vacations, or tires for the car, you probably need to reassess exactly what the emergency fund is intended for. Again, for those that find themselves tapping into this fund for non-emergencies, consider moving the account to a different bank that makes it a bit more work to get to and keeps the fund out of sight and out of mind. If and when you do have to use your emergency funds, your first order of business next month should be to get back to step 3 and replenish the emergency fund.

It's equally important to have a plan for the opposite of a popup expense...unexpected income. This is clearly a better problem to have but equally important, if not more so, to be proactive on. It's way too tempting to see extra income as an excuse to revert back to our old spending ways. After all, it's just extra, right? Unexpected income has something in common with expected income...they are both soldier dollars. Even more than our regular monthly soldiers, unexpected income have a much higher tendency to run off leaving us wondering where they went! Have a plan, BEFORE extra funds show up in your account. Does that mean that all of the extra income has to be used for serious things? No, absolutely not. If you and your spouse decide that your plan with the next bonus is to put half into your vacation fund and save the other half for a house down payment or invest for retirement, no concerns with that. As with the spending plan, any plans for extra income are up to you! That said, my recommendation would be to always prioritize needs, debt payoff and emergency fund buildup, followed by your priorities for discretionary income. Because that's all that extra income is...more discretionary income. By having a plan before this good problem to have occurs, you will likely rely less on emotion in the moment, which will lead to having fewer regrets in the long run.

The bottom line with contingency planning is staying proactive to the max extent and providing yourself a higher likelihood to stay on track with the required discipline. Reactive decisions are made with emotion, the kryptonite to our discipline.... whereas proactive decisions invoke greater levels of discipline.

DO BETTER

REVISIT, REVISE & REPEAT

"Experience doesn't make you better –
evaluated experience makes you better."
- Howard Hendricks

37

Debriefing the Mission

While we don't want to stay focused in the rearview mirror, the past provides a potent tool to learn from. As highlighted in the Open Eyes section, the debrief is where every portion of the flight is dissected, and each objective is graded as either being met or missed. What went right, what went wrong, and why? In the event any objective was not met, contributing factors and root causes are identified and rolled up into lessons learned for future missions. The learning never ends, as there is always some level of lesson learned as a takeaway for the pilots. This process demands and enables our pilots to continually improve and aim higher, achieving new levels of effectiveness each mission.

Revisiting our spending plan at the end of the month is also a critical step to our financial success. Although it doesn't have to be hours long, like a flight debrief, taking some time to look back upon the previous month is absolutely crucial to making next month's plan even better. What did we miss or not execute per the plan last month? Why was it missed? What could have been better?   The key is not just recognizing what didn't go well, but more importantly why it didn't. Just like with our financial behaviors overall, if we don't take time to understand the why, the root causes, we are destined to repeat the same mistakes next month. Early on, the why is often that you just don't know how much was needed and therefore guessed. If so, that is an acceptable answer, but needs to be addressed. Or was there a lack of understanding of the plan? If so, why? Was it lack of tracking throughout the month? If so, why? Was it just a blatant disregard of the plan or the fact that it was too much of a challenge? If so, perhaps your "why" and goals aren't compelling enough and need a revisit.

An important note for married couples: the objective of this process is not about placing blame. If either spouse didn't hold up their part of an agreed-to spending plan, then hopefully they recognize it, take accountability, learn from it, and commit to doing better. The focus has to stay on what wasn't executed as planned, why this was the case, and then on improvements that can be made going forward. Most of the time when I see one spouse or the other not adhere to the plan, it goes back to their lack of buy-in and sense of ownership from when the plan was put together. If that's the case when you revisit how the month went, take a step back on your planning process and ensure that one spouse isn't holding control over the other. Buy-in from both is fundamental to putting the plan together. If one spouse is not on board with the plan at all, then take a further step back and go back to your "why," goals and how having a plan will best enable those and give you more freedom in the end.

At the end of every month, ask yourself, what can we learn from this month and improve upon? Continuous learning and improvement...that is the power of the debrief.

"Those who fail to learn from the past are doomed to repeat it."
- Winston Churchill

38

Adjust Fire

Even with all of the awesome technology on the latest generation of fighter aircraft, precision weapons can still miss the mark. If the pilot puts his aim on the target but the result is 20m left, they could try the same technique again. The result is almost always the same...20m left. In order to improve our results, the most effective pilots identify the need to adjust aim. If I aim a few mils to the right, what is the result? Still a miss but by less margin, now only 10m to the left. Continual adjustments to our aim, in smaller and smaller increments, is needed in order to shack the target. That process typically takes 2 or 3 adjustments in a jet. Once the desired result is achieved, the solution becomes a known.

The odds of you shacking all categories of your monthly spending plan the first time out the shoot are extremely low. You may get some categories right but will very likely be off on others. Don't beat yourself up and get frustrated! The need to revise and adjust fire on at least some of your spending categories is 100% normal and expected.

The key is recognition by revisiting, and then revising as needed, which is the whole purpose of revisiting in the first place. For example, if you were to plan on spending $200 on fuel for your vehicles in the coming month, but actually spent $250, then it should cause you to pause, assess and consider revising for the next month. Did fuel prices shoot up unexpectedly? If so, you probably have to adjust fire for the fuel category for the next month. Was the increase in expense due to taking an extra trip last month that wasn't considered in the plan? That probably doesn't necessitate changing our plan for next month but should make us question how we missed planning for it in the first place. If the trip was a popup contingency, was an adjustment made?

You also don't need to drive yourself bonkers by trying to get the plan perfect. The intent of the spending plan is not to get it down to the dollar and cent that we will spend. That would be maddening and unachievable. Remember, the whole purpose of the monthly spending plan is to put us back in control, being proactive versus reactive, and not wondering where any hard-earned income has run off to.

Once the plan has been revisited, lessons have been learned and revisions have been made, repeat the process for next month. Revisit, revise and repeat, every month, committing to never giving up and always striving to do better. Make the adjustments as needed, but most importantly, never lose sight of the purpose of spending plans in the first place. What will staying in control of my income make possible?

"You lose your way when you lose your why."
- Michael Hyatt

39

What's at Stake?

Changing our financial habits and behaviors is not an easy undertaking. As much as you may want to embrace the principles presented in these chapters, I will be the first to tell you that it will take work. But I'm not recommending that you do anything that can't be done. We've done it, and continue to, as well as millions of others who have achieved success after deciding to do better and making the necessary adjustments to do so. Don't be intimidated or overwhelmed – you've got this...one step at a time.

Don't allow your "yeah but" to win out over your "why." Remember that your "why" is what's at stake if you flake out and revert to your previous ways. Your "why" has got to be bigger and stronger than your "but." Changing your ways and then staying disciplined to maintain new ways comes down to how important it is to you. Constantly remind yourself of what's at stake if you don't. Your stress level? Your ability to comfortably provide for your family? Your relationships? Your marriage? Your ability to achieve financial independence after years of working? Your ability to be more generous and give consistently?

Even more important than revisiting and revising your monthly spending plans, is to do the same with your "why" and the goals that will get you there. If we forget why we are working at these ways, that are sadly counter-cultural, everything else will fall by the wayside. Soon after forgetting our "why," our goals will wither, followed shortly after by living like most do, in the here and now. Set a reminder on your calendar to revisit your written "why" and goals every few months, or, at a minimum, every year. If you are married, make it a point to do so together. Never lose sight of your "why." Remember, when you lose sight you will lose the fight!

It's also ok, and actually healthy, to allow your "why" and goals to change as you grow and go through life changes. Getting married, having kids, changing jobs and achieving financial independence are all life changes that present enough of a significant change to go back to square one to reassess your "why" and goals. Even if you don't go through one of these major life events, take the time to revisit and revise as needed. Also revisit your priorities on discretionary income from time to time, as they are likely to change and shuffle throughout our lives as we begin to look through different lenses.

Regardless of what they may be, it is essential to always know what your "why," goals and spending priorities are as a means to stay proactive and on the vector of your choosing, less you revert to a hot-air balloon approach!

Concluding Remarks

40

You Have the Aircraft

When an instructor pilot is teaching a new student pilot to fly, always knowing who is flying at any given time, referred to as who "has the aircraft," is of utmost importance. When one person is flying and wants to pass along control of the plane to the other, they say "you have the aircraft." The one taking over control of the plane then confirms the transfer, saying, "I have the aircraft." This positive transfer of control prevents multiple folks from thinking they are flying the plane at any given time, a situation which could quickly lead to disastrous results.

You have now completed your initial training as a personal finance student pilot, earning your personal finance pilot (PFP) wings. As your personal finance instructor pilot, I want to commend you for not just stopping at wanting or hoping to do better, but actually taking the time to learn proven principles that will produce results. Although you may be at the end of this book, that doesn't mean you should stop training and looking for ways to do better. It needs to be a continuous process that will bring you to greater heights. Keep taking steps, one at a time, always learning and striving to DO BETTER, both with your finances and in all areas of your life.

D – Decide
O – Open your eyes

B – Believe
E – Educate
T – Team and Talk
T – Task assets
E – Execute
R – Revisit, Revise and Repeat

Applying these principles will always bring you to a brighter financial path, without fail. Beyond with money, this same mantra to continually strive to DO BETTER will lead to future success in all endeavors. Whether it be becoming a better spouse or parent, improving your health or performance in the workplace, this acronym can be applied for increased effectiveness when you choose to raise the bar. Any aspect of your life that you seek to improve starts with deciding why your current path isn't good enough and then setting out to do something about it. Open your eyes to where you stand today and the root of what brought you there, then choose to believe in your ability to improve. Get educated - not by those with theories but instead by turning to mentors who have actually consistently succeeded in that area in their own lives. Know that you will always achieve higher altitudes when teamed with others that boost you up versus drag you down. Finally, put a plan in place, tasking your assets, whether it be dollars or our most precious commodity, time. Then execute, taking time to pause and reflect along the way to make continual improvements to the plan. Don't put off your goals to do better for one more day. Determine a new higher standard for yourself and then set out to make it happen!

In the first section, Decide, we highlighted the fact that many of us have set a low bar, or even no bar, for our finances. Each of us will achieve what we aim for and commit ourselves to, whether that be a high bar or low bar. These chapters have not only provided you with the proven principles needed to do better with your finances, but also a new standard. If you want to go above and beyond these standards, fantastic, but as a start, aim to set these standards as the minimum acceptable threshold for your personal finances:

MISSION READY
FINANCIAL STANDARDS

1. Written "why," short, mid and long-term financial goals that are revisited annually, at a minimum, and revised as required.
2. Emergency fund of at least 3-6 months of living expenses held in a separate account with clear boundaries on what constitutes a true emergency.
3. Debt-free aside from your mortgage, with a commitment to remain debt-free for good.
4. Consistently giving to a cause of your choosing each month.
5. Consistently saving, on a monthly basis, for any annual expenses that exceed a pre-determined threshold, utilizing an applicable number of funds.
6. Consistently and adequately investing, each month, as required to meet your financial goals for short, mid and long-term, prioritizing desired retirement goals.
7. On track to payoff home in accordance with goals.
8. All defensive measures in place: wills, adequate levels of applicable insurance coverages (medical, life, auto, long-term disability, etc.), credit accounts frozen and identity theft protection for all family members.

9. Established communication standards and on same financial page with spouse, if married; if single, have an accountability partner with whom you have shared your goals.
10. Plan for every dollar of monthly income, agreed upon with spouse if married, consistently built prior to every new period beginning, executed as planned with controls for any weak areas and contingency plans, revisited and revised as needed.

(Standards are provided on a single page following the appendices)

In this land of unmatched opportunity, freedom, and incredible incomes in comparison to the rest of the world, these ten standards should represent the minimum bar for every household in America. The standard has been set...the line drawn. So where are you today? Meeting or exceeding each? If not, instead finding yourself below the standard, what are you going to do, starting today, to put yourself at or above each standard? You have been armed with the principles needed to not just survive, but to thrive with your finances. Now it's up to you. You have to choose. Will you continue to conform or instead transform your ways? Will you go along with the winds of our culture or chart your own course against the winds?

Now that you know what needs to be done, it is time for action. **It's now time to not just want better, but rather to DO BETTER.** Using persistence and discipline, encouraged by and committed to your "why," it's time to step up, take ownership and do the work to make it happen.

It's up to you and it all starts with a decision to evaluate yourself. Where has your way taken you so far and why is that not good enough? What's at stake if you don't embrace a new way, your "why," and what are you willing to DO, to become BETTER?

What will your financial story be? You have the aircraft...fly your jet. In the words of the world's greatest Air Force...

Aim high, fly, fight and win!

Afterword

DO BETTER Revisited

You now have all the tools needed to DO BETTER with your finances. Once you decide to set your aim on higher standards and implement the principles, you will see improvements. Through your decisions, choices and financial discipline from here on out, you will be well on your way to achieving your goals and your "why." As we close, I would like to revisit DO BETTER from one additional perspective. As a Christian, I would be remiss to not highlight the guidance that the Lord has provided for our handling of money.

Our ultimate source of guidance and wisdom is God's Word, provided to us through the Bible. This book contains the guidance and answers to every segment of our lives, including how best to handle our finances. In fact, there are over 2,000 references on money and possessions in the Bible, more than any other topic.[1] Surprisingly, it's the last place that many Christians, myself included for many years, think to turn to for the handling of finances. The topics of money, finances and possessions don't even make the list of top fifty topics searched for biblical guidance![2] But that's the first place we should be turning for wisdom as Christ followers.

I believe that our Lord loves each and every one of His children unconditionally and does not want us to be weighed down by our finances, stressed out and just getting by, as this can cloud our relationship with Him. Instead, even more so than we want for our own children, God desires for each one of us to have hope and live fully and abundantly (Jeremiah 29:11, Romans 15:4, Matthew 7:11).

For any believer, it should come as no surprise that His ways work, every time, without fail. The Bible provides our ultimate thrust and vector with money along with all other aspects of our lives. So, what can we learn about how to DO BETTER with our finances from the Bible? The short version is that I truly believe all the principles covered in this book are in alignment with God's Word. But rather than take my word for it, I would challenge you to dig into His Word to see firsthand the wisdom that our Lord has provided for us. Below are references that I believe support the DO BETTER acronym, from a Christian perspective, along with a few of the verses that can help guide our decisions with the finances that we are blessed to have.

Decide
- If doing things our own way works best (Proverbs 3:5-6 & 21:2)
- To keep our sights forward with vision (Proverbs 4:25 & 29:18)
- Whether we are owners or simply the managers (Psalm 24:1, Luke 12:21,42-46, 1 Corinthians 10:26, Matthew 25:14)
- Choosing our ultimate "why" and calling in life (Matthew 5:16)
- Committing to His way with new intensity (Proverbs 6:1-5)

Open Eyes
- Tendency to fall for myths of the world (2 Timothy 4:3-4)
- Get-rich quick schemes (Proverbs 13:11 & 28:20, Matthew 13:22)
- Borrower becomes enslaved to the lender (Proverbs 22:7)
- Poverty to those who neglect discipline (Proverbs 13:18)
- Love of money, not money itself, is root of evil (1 Tim 6:10)
- Inability to serve two masters (Matthew 6:24, Luke 16:13-15)
- Never finding true satisfaction in the world (Ecclesiastes 5:10)

Believe
- What we believe becomes truth (Matthew 6:21)
- As we sow, we will reap (Galatians 6:7-9)
- All our needs will be met (Philippians 4:19, Matthew 28:20)
- All things are possible for those that believe (Mark 9:23, Luke 18:27, Matthew 19:26, Proverbs 30:5, Philippians 4:12-13, John 8:12)
- Finding purpose beyond pain (James 1:2,12, Luke 6:21, Deuteronomy 31:6, Romans 8:26-28, 2 Corinthians 4:8-10)

Educate
- Value of seeking wisdom (Proverbs 4:7 & 19:2,8,20, Romans 12:2, Matthew 7:24-27, 2 Peter 1:5, Ecclesiastes 7:12)
- Making the most of what we have been given (Matthew 25:15-30, 1 Timothy 5:8, Luke 19:15-26)
- Keeping perspective on wealth (Hebrews 13:5, Luke 3:14 & 12:34, 1 John 2:15-17, 1 Timothy 6:6-9,17, Matthew 6:24, Ecclesiastes 5:15)
- Living below your means (Proverbs 21:20)
- Savings to weather the storm (Proverbs 27:12, Ecclesiastes 11:2, Matthew 25:3-4)
- Avoiding debt (Proverbs 22:7, Romans 6:16 & 13:8, Galatians 5:1)
- Generosity and giving (Malachi 3:8-10, 2 Corinthians 9:6-12, 1 Timothy 6:17-19, Matthew 6:1-4 & 23:23 & 25:45, Proverbs 3:9 & 11:24-25, 1 Peter 4:10, Luke 6:38 & 10:25-37, Acts 20:35)

Team
- The benefits of teaming (Ecclesiastes 4:9-12, Proverbs 27:17, Hebrews 10:24-25, 3 John 1:8)
- Choosing our flock carefully (Proverbs 13:20, 1 Corinthians 15:33)
- Our ultimate wingman (Matthew 28:20, Isaiah 40:31 & 41:10)

Task / Execute / Revisit
- Proactive spending plans (Proverbs 10:4, 16:3,9 & 21:5, Luke 14:28)

The above references just scratch the surface on the many verses on money and possessions provided to us throughout the Bible. As with all the principles throughout this book, the intent is to now put them into practice in our own lives, pushing ourselves to not just be hearers but also doers (James 1:22).

I would like to close with one final thought on doing better. Doing better with our finances can only take us so far, ultimately falling short in the long run in two critical regards. First, no matter how well we implement proven financial principles in our lives and build wealth, the money itself will never bring us true lasting contentment. No amount of money, stuff or even giving will ever be able to fill the God-shaped hole in our hearts. Trying to do so serves as the ultimate root cause to our struggles with finances. Likewise, no matter how much better we do financially, we will never be able to bring our wealth with us beyond this world and it can never be great enough to secure our eternity. No amount of works, wealth or even giving can buy our ticket into Heaven (Ephesians 2:8-9, Titus 3:5, Romans 3:23).

The good news, make that the GREAT news, is that the work has already been done for us. There is nothing that we can or have to do, physically or monetarily, to earn eternal salvation. Thankfully, it's a free gift, provided by the Lord's grace and ready to be opened at any time. All it takes is making one decision. It's deciding whether to accept Christ as your Lord and Savior, acknowledging that He died for the sins of mankind and thereby paved the path for each of us to spend eternity with the one who loves us most, our Almighty God. Jesus is not a way, but rather the only way (John 14:6).

If you don't already have a relationship with Jesus, I highly recommend Him! All it takes is a decision to humble your heart, making yourself open to Him, then saying a prayer that you are ready to receive the gift of His love. If you are looking for more information before deciding, a good next step may be diving into the Bible to see if it speaks to you, or attending a service at Christian church of your choosing, whether that be one of the many denominations or a non-denominational service in your area. It's not about the religion or specific denomination of Christianity, but rather developing a personal relationship with Him and, ultimately, your salvation. And please don't fall for the fear that anything in your life prevents you from taking this next step. Our Father is one who forgives and loves unconditionally and wants nothing more than a relationship with you!

Acknowledgments

To all of the brave men and women who have answered the call to serve - you voluntarily put your life on the line to keep my family and I safe and in a position to enjoy all of the incredible opportunities and freedoms that we did nothing to deserve but are so thankful to have. Thank you for your service, dedication and commitment.

To all of the spouses of those serving our nation – our sincerest thanks. You provide unfathomable levels of support through your love. The work our guardians do would not be possible without you.

To all of the individuals and couples that I have had the distinct privilege of serving as a financial coach over the years – thank you. I commend you for taking the difficult first step of seeking help to improve your financial standing and entrusting me to be your guide. I have learned and grown from each and every one of you.

To Ms. Lyn Heady, my high school math teacher – thank you for taking the time to go above and beyond for your students. You believed in us and encouraged me to push myself farther than I thought possible. Thank you for years of dedicated service.

To Doc "Voodoo" Nelson and Dr. John Patterson – thank you for your example of selfless service and incredible support during my time of need. Our Air Force is incredibly fortunate to have professionals such as yourself...you make us a stronger and more formidable force.

To Christian artists...your lyrics provided inspiration, especially on all of those dark early mornings as this book was written. A special thanks to those whose songs really spoke to me as I wrote – Jeremy Camp's *Word of Life*, Mercy Me's *Greater*, Micah Tyler's *Even Then*, Casting Crowns' *Only Jesus*, and Elevation Worship's *Overcome*.

To Pastor Bill Ramsey - thank you for your example of faith and outreach as God's light. Your messages provided inspiration and your staff led us to renewal and strengthening as Christ followers.

To my siblings and the many friends who have supported me throughout the years, providing invaluable feedback along the way – thank you. I am blessed to have each of you in my life.

To my Mom and Dad – thank you for your unending support, always believing in my goals and dreams, no matter how far-fetched they may have seemed, and impressing upon me the power of hard work, determination, commitment, faith and prayer. Pop – you are missed.

To our four amazing children - I am beyond blessed to be your father and thank the Lord for each of you every single day. Thank you for your love and support throughout moves across the globe and for bringing true joy to my life. I pray that you glorify Him through the talents provided, find refuge in your faith, knowing that you can do all things through Him, and continue your walks as Christ followers.

To Courtney, my loving wife, best friend and amazing mother to our kiddos – my thanks cannot begin to describe the appreciation that I have for your unending love and backing from day one when we were kids ourselves. Without your support and patience throughout endless conversations, this project would not have been possible. Thank you for your encouragement and unwavering belief in me. Looking forward to continuing our walk with the Lord by your side.

To our loving Father and Creator – thank you for providing all of the incredible opportunities and experiences that I have been blessed to have in this life. I am grateful for every single one of them, to include the trials and tribulations, now seeing that they have formed me into who I am today. Thank you for leading me through a project that I had no intentions of taking on but felt called to do. Through your grace, you provided the guidance, wisdom and inspiration needed to see this undertaking through. Through your Word, we have all of the instruction that we will ever need in this life. May every one of your sons and daughters feel your presence and find comfort in your love.

Appendix A – My "Why"

<u>1. Circle all that apply:</u>
- An overall lower level of stress and worry
- Improved health and wellness due to having less stress
- A better marriage, with improved communication
- The security of being a more consistent provider for your family, both in the short-term and long-term
- Being more available to your family and a better parent when carrying less stress from month to month
- More effective in the workplace and in your career
- Having the opportunity to change jobs or careers to follow a dream and do something that you are actually excited to do
- Not being forced to work late in life unless choosing to do so
- For those serving in the military, no risk of losing clearance
- For all of our nation's defenders, being more effective and better situated to address and tackle the other unique stresses that come with the dangers of my occupation
- Having a comfortable retirement without relying on Social Security or our government in general
- Able to give more generously to causes near and dear to me
- The ability to have more of a positive impact in the lives of others, through donations of both time and money

- _____
  _____
- _____
  _____
- _____
  _____

<u>2. Items I am willing to give up or postpone to achieve above why(s):</u>
- _____
- _____
- _____
- _____

Appendix B – My Goals

Short-Term (within next five years):

- _____
  _____
- _____
  _____
- _____
  _____
- _____
  _____
- _____
  _____

Mid-Term (five years from today until financially independent):

- _____
  _____
- _____
  _____
- _____
  _____

Long-Term (once financial independence achieved):

- _____
  _____
- _____
  _____
- _____
  _____

Appendix C – My Financial Net Worth

Assets (+)

Things I Own:	Value	
House (your primary residence)		
Retirement Investments (current amount in all retirement accounts (401Ks, IRAs, TSP, etc.)		**TOTAL OWNED:** $
Non-retirement Accounts (cash, savings, emergency fund, and other investments not tied up in 401K, IRA, TSP, etc.)		
Vehicles/Toys (autos, boats, trailers, motorcycles, etc. if you owe on them, otherwise consider leaving out)		
Other items of value (land, rental property, business, cash value of insurance policies, etc.)		

Liabilities (-)

Items I Owe On:	Amount Owed	
House Mortgage (your primary residence)		
Vehicles/Toys (automobiles, motorcycles, boats, trailers, etc.)		**TOTAL OWED:** $
Credit Card Balances (including any store card balances)		
Student Loans (whether on deferment or not, total of what is owed back to federal or private)		
Personal Loans (include any amounts owed to family members, friends, 401K/TSP, etc.)		
Other Amounts Owed (cell phones, land, rental property, business debt, etc.)		

Total Assets (Owned) - Total Liabilities (Owed) = Net Worth

_____ - _____ = _____

Appendix D – My Max House Purchase Amount

House Purchase Multiplier Adjustments		
Baseline multiplier: 35 // My Multiplier: _____		
(multiply times total monthly take home income for household)		
Assumes a 4.5% 15-year loan with 20% down and average tax/insurance		
Adjustment Factor	*Number to **ADD** to multiplier*	*Number to **SUBTRACT** from multiplier*
Interest Rate	For every .5% lower interest rate, **add 1**	For every .5% higher interest rate, **subtract 1**
Down Payment*	If a 30% down payment, **add 4**	If only a 15% down payment, **subtract 2**
	If a 40% down payment, **add 9**	If only a 10% down payment, **subtract 4**
Property Tax and Homeowners Insur** (no adjustment for AK, FL, GA, ME, MD, MA, MN, MS, MO, NC, ND, OK, OR, SD, WA)	**Add 2 if in** AL, AZ, AR, CA, CO, ID, IN, KY, LA, MT, NV, NM, SC, TN, UT, VA, WV, WY	**Subtract 2 if in** IA, KS, MI, NE, NY, OH, PA, RI, VT and WI
	Add 3 if in DE or HI	**Subtract 4 if in** CT, IL, NH, NJ or TX

* Less than 20% down payment includes average payment for required PMI

** Based on average state property tax and homeowner's insurance rates (may vary)[1,2,3]

Two examples:

1. Buyer qualifies for a 15-year loan at 5% interest rate with a 30% down payment, purchasing in Kentucky:
   35 – 1 (for 5% rate) + 4 (30% down) +2 (KY) = 40 (40 x a total monthly take home pay of $6000 would be $240K house with $72K down, resulting in a mortgage amount of $168K.)

2. Buyer qualifies for a 15-year loan at 4% interest rate with only a 10% down payment, purchasing in Texas:
   35 + 1 (for 4% rate) – 4 (10% down) – 4 (TX) = 28
   (28 x $6000 take home is a $168K home with $17K down, resulting in a mortgage amount of $151K.)

Appendix E – Building My Monthly Spending Plan

1. Take Home Income

Source	Date Paid	Amount	Total (+)

2. Any Giving Off the Top

Given To	Date Due	Amount	Total (-)

3. Needs

Category	Date Due	Amount	Total (-)
A. Rent or Mortgage			(% of Income)
B. Food/Household Items			
C. Utilities - Electricity			
- Gas			
- Water			
- Trash			
- Sewer			
D. Transportation - Fuel			
- Public Trans.			
E. Clothing (May be funds)			
- Adults			
- Kids			
F. Insurance - Auto			
- Home/Renters			
- Medical			
- Life			
- Long-Term Dis.			
- ID Theft			
G. Other Needs - Childcare			
- Alimony			
- Child Support			
- Meds/prescrip			
- Phone/Mobile			
- Pet Needs			
- Hygiene/Hair			

4. Total Income Remaining After Meeting Monthly Needs: $

Total Income Remaining After Monthly Needs (last page):	$

5. Irregular Needs (Funds)

Fund Category	Annual Amount	Monthly (Annual ÷ 12)	Total (-)
Homeowners Association			
Vehicle Repair/Registration			
Vehicle Replacement			
House Repair/Upkeep			
Other			

6. Minimum Debt Payments

Category	Date Due	Min Amount	Total (-)
Credit Cards			
Vehicle/Toy Loans			
Student Loans			
Medical			
Personal Loans			
401K / TSP Loan			
Cell Phones			
Other Loans			

7. Total Discretionary Income Remaining (after all needs and all minimum debt payments accounted for)	$

Total Income Remaining After Needs & Debts (last page):	$

8. Plan for All Discretionary Income

If on steps 1-3:	Extra to Emerg. Fund or Debt Snowball	$ (% #7 Income)
Once complete with steps 1-3:	Investments	$ (% #1 Income)
	House Down Payment Savings Fund	$
	Kids' College Educ Savings/Investments	$
	Extra to House Principal (early payoff)	$

Monthly Wants

Category	Date Due	Amount	Total (-)
Any Additional Giving			
Internet			
Cable / Satellite TV			
Streaming Service #1			
Streaming Service #2			
Splurge Money - hers			
- his			
Dining Out			
Entertainment			
Clothing			
Gym membership			
Unique monthly expenses			
Unexpected pop-ups (small)			

Irregular Wants (Funds)

Fund Category	Annual Amount	Monthly (Annual ÷ 12)	Total (-)
Vacation / Travel			
Holidays (Birthdays, Christmas, etc.)			
Hobbies			
Kids' sports			
Other			

Total Income Remaining (needs to be zero):	$

278

Appendix F – Allocated Spending Plan

Spending Plan Period: _____

Bill/Expense	Amount Due	Due Date	Payday #1 Date: Amount: $	Payday #2 Date: Amount: $	Payday #3 Date: Amount: $	Payday #4 Date: Amount: $
Needed to carry over to next payday:						
Amount Remaining (should be zero each payday)						

MISSION READY
FINANCIAL STANDARDS

1. Written "why," short, mid and long-term financial goals that are revisited annually, at a minimum, and revised as required.

2. Emergency fund of at least 3-6 months of living expenses held in a separate account with clear boundaries on what constitutes a true emergency.

3. Debt-free aside from your mortgage, with a commitment to remain debt-free for good.

4. Consistently giving to a cause of your choosing each month.

5. Consistently saving, on a monthly basis, for any annual expenses that exceed a pre-determined threshold, utilizing an applicable number of funds.

6. Consistently and adequately investing, each month, as required to meet your financial goals for short, mid and long-term, prioritizing desired retirement goals.

7. On track to payoff home in accordance with goals.

8. All defensive measures in place: wills, adequate levels of applicable insurance coverages (medical, life, auto, long-term disability, etc.), credit accounts frozen and identity theft protection for all family members.

9. Established communication standards and on same financial page with spouse, if married; if single, have an accountability partner with whom you have shared your goals.

10. Plan for every dollar of monthly income, agreed upon with spouse if married, consistently built prior to every new period beginning, executed as planned with controls for any weak areas and contingency plans, revisited and revised as needed.

Endnotes

Chapter 1: Jets and Finances?

[1] Hill, Catey. "This Is the No. 1 Reason Americans Are so Stressed out." MarketWatch. December 17, 2018. https://www.marketwatch.com/story/one-big-reason-americans-are-so-stressed-and-unhealthy-2018-10-11.

[2] Amadeo, Kimberly. "5 Reasons Why America Is in So Much Debt." The Balance. May 12, 2019. https://www.thebalance.com/the-u-s-debt-and-how-it-got-so-big-3305778.

[3] "Credit Card Debt Surpasses $1 Trillion in the US for First Time." ABC News. March 08, 2018. https://abcnews.go.com/Business/credit-card-debt-surpasses-trillion-us-time/story?id=53608548.

[4] Ibid.

[5] "Here's How Much the Average American Pays in Interest Each Year." The Simple Dollar. March 23, 2017. https://www.thesimpledollar.com/heres-how-much-the-average-american-pays-in-interest-each-year/.

[6] "Credit Card Ownership Statistics." CreditCards.com. March 28, 2019. https://www.creditcards.com/credit-card-news/ownership-statistics.php.

[7] Corkery, Michael, and Jessica Silver-Greenberg. "Profits From Store-Branded Credit Cards Hide Depth of Retailers' Troubles." The New York Times. May 11, 2017. https://www.nytimes.com/2017/05/11/business/dealbook/retailer-credit-cards-macys-losses.html.

[8] "Total Household Debt Rises as 2018 Marks the Ninth Year of Annual Growth in New Auto Loans." Total Household Debt Rises as 2018 Marks the Ninth Year of Annual Growth in New Auto Loans - FEDERAL RESERVE BANK of NEW YORK. https://www.newyorkfed.org/newsevents/news/research/2019/20190212.

Chapter 2: Mission Ready

[1] Konish, Lorie. "US Median Household Income Climbs to New High of $61,372." CNBC. September 14, 2018. https://www.cnbc.com/2018/09/12/median-household-income-climbs-to-new-high-of-61372.html.

Chapter 3: Jet or Balloon?

[1] Felber, Terry. *Am I Making Myself Clear?: Secrets of the Worlds Greatest Communicators*. Nashville: Thomas Nelson Publishers, 2002.

[2] "Stretched Thin." U.S. News & World Report. https://www.usnews.com/news/the-report/articles/2019-01-11/stretched-thin-majority-of-americans-live-paycheck-to-paycheck.

[3] Torrieri, Marisa. "Why You Should Be Living Paycheck To Paycheck." Business Insider. January 18, 2014. https://www.businessinsider.com/why-you-should-live-paycheck-to-paycheck-2014-1.

[4] Caldwell, Miriam. "Practical Money Tips to Stop Living From Paycheck to Paycheck." The Balance. April 25, 2019. https://www.thebalance.com/stop-paycheck-to-paycheck-2385520.

[5] Nova, Annie. "A $1,000 Emergency Would Push Many Americans into Debt." CNBC. January 23, 2019. https://www.cnbc.com/2019/01/23/most-americans-dont-have-the-savings-to-cover-a-1000-emergency.html.

[6] Williams, Sean. "12 Facts the Social Security Administration Wants You to Know." The Motley Fool. August 28, 2017. https://www.fool.com/retirement/2017/08/28/12-facts-the-social-security-administration-wants.aspx.

[7] That's No Surprise. After Paying Bills. "66% of Millennials Have Nothing Saved for Retirement." CNNMoney. https://money.cnn.com/2018/03/07/retirement/millennial-retirement-savings/index.html.

[8] "Money Ruining Marriages in America: A Ramsey Solutions Study." Money Ruining Marriages in America: A Ramsey Solutions Study | DaveRamsey.com. https://www.daveramsey.com/pr/money-ruining-marriages-in-america.

[9] "Stress and Drug Abuse: The Brain Connection." Scholastic. http://headsup.scholastic.com/students/stress-and-drug-abuse.

[10] "Federal Poverty Guidelines." Families USA. July 25, 2018. https://familiesusa.org/product/federal-poverty-guidelines.

[11] "Global Rich List." Global Rich List. http://www.globalrichlist.com/.

[12] Ibid.

Chapter 4: Tunnel Vision

[1] "Financial Peace Military Edition." Daveramsey.com. https://www.daveramsey.com/military/.

[2] Ibid.

[3] "Politicians Seek Elimination of Financial Watchdog Lauded by Military Leaders · Consumer Federation of America." Consumer Federation of America. February 15, 2017. https://consumerfed.org/press_release/politicians-seek-elimination-financial-watchdog-lauded-military-leaders/.

Chapter 5: Yeah, But...

[1] Gallup, Inc. "Americans' Financial Worries Edge Up in 2016." Gallup.com. https://news.gallup.com/poll/191174/americans-financial-worries-edge-2016.aspx.

[2] Erb, Kelly Phillips. "Trustees Report That Social Security Benefits Are At Risk In 16 Years." Forbes. June 06, 2018. https://www.forbes.com/sites/kellyphillipserb/2018/06/05/trustees-predict-that-social-security-will-be-insolvent-in-16-years/#6f7f383d6120.

[3] Rae, David. "What Is The Most I Can Receive From My Social Security Retirement Benefits?" Forbes. April 18, 2018. https://www.forbes.com/sites/davidrae/2018/04/18/maximize-social-security/#493eaee59180.

[4] Jones, Charisse. "60% of Americans Have to Retire Sooner than They'd Planned." USA Today. June 03, 2015. https://www.usatoday.com/story/money/2015/06/02/majority-of-americans-have-to-retire-sooner-than-theyd-planned/28371099/.

[5] Frankel, Matthew. "20 Retirement Stats That Will Blow You Away." The Motley Fool. January 26, 2016. https://www.fool.com/retirement/general/2016/01/26/20-retirement-stats-that-will-blow-you-away.aspx.
[6] Davidson, Paul. "Jobs: 74% of Adults Say They're OK Financially, up from 70%." USA Today. May 22, 2018. https://www.usatoday.com/story/money/2018/05/22/74-adults-least-doing-ok-financially-up-70-year-ago/632757002/.
[7] Collins, Jim. "Good Is the Enemy of Great." https://www.jimcollins.com/media_topics/GoodIsTheEnemyOfGreat.html.
[8] "Monday Quote by Carl Bard." Leading U.S. Education Guide for All International Students. https://www.studyusa.com/en/blog/849/monday-quote-by-carl-bard.

Chapter 6: Aim High
[1] Ziglar, Tom. "If You Aim at Nothing..." Ziglar Inc. March 30, 2017. https://www.ziglar.com/articles/if-you-aim-at-nothing-2/.

Chapter 12: TTP
[1] Ramsey Solutions. "Tired of Keeping Up with the Joneses?" Daveramsey.com. June 20, 2019. https://www.daveramsey.com/blog/tired-of-keeping-up-with-the-joneses.

Chapter 13: Point of Departure
[2] White, Gillian B. "Do Americans Even Know How Much They Owe?" The Atlantic. September 01, 2015. https://www.theatlantic.com/business/archive/2015/09/americans-and-debt/403081/.

Chapter 14: Seat of the Pants
[1] All investment growth over time calculations throughout calculated utilizing the following reference: "Investment and Retirement Calculator." DaveRamsey.com. https://www.daveramsey.com/smartvestor/investment-calculator.
[2] Backman, Maurie. "The Average American Starts Saving for Retirement at This Age." The Motley Fool. December 17, 2018. https://www.fool.com/retirement/2018/12/17/the-average-american-starts-saving-for-retirement.aspx.
[3] "Median Weekly Earnings $783 for Women, $965 for Men, in First Quarter 2018." U.S. Bureau of Labor Statistics. April 20, 2018. https://www.bls.gov/opub/ted/2018/median-weekly-earnings-783-for-women-965-for-men-in-first-quarter-2018.htm.
[4] "Compound Annual Growth Rate (Annualized Return)." CAGR of the Stock Market: Annualized Returns of the S&P 500. http://www.moneychimp.com/features/market_cagr.htm.
[5] Ibid.

6 Konish, Lorie. "Consumer Debt Is Set to Reach $4 Trillion by the End of 2018." CNBC. May 21, 2018. https://www.cnbc.com/2018/05/21/consumer-debt-is-set-to-reach-4-trillion-by-the-end-of-2018.html.

7 "This Is How Much Debt the Average American Has Now-at Every Age." Money. http://money.com/money/5233033/average-debt-every-age/.

8 "Eight Dimensions of Wellness." Boston University Center for Psychiatric Rehabilitation. https://cpr.bu.edu/living-well/eight-dimensions-of-wellness/.

9 Konish, Lorie. "US Median Household Income Climbs to New High of $61,372." CNBC. September 14, 2018. https://www.cnbc.com/2018/09/12/median-household-income-climbs-to-new-high-of-61372.html.

10 Sullivan, Bob. "Once Again, Americans Are Not Saving Enough." MarketWatch. August 28, 2018. https://www.marketwatch.com/story/once-again-americans-are-not-saving-enough-2018-08-28.

11 "Real Median Personal Income in the United States." FRED. September 13, 2017. https://fred.stlouisfed.org/series/MEPAINUSA672N.

12 Bomey, Nathan. "Why Americans Are Suddenly Paying $550 per Month for New Cars." USA Today. March 07, 2019. https://www.usatoday.com/story/money/cars/2019/03/01/care-payments/3001818002/.

13 "Car Depreciation: How Much Value Will a New Car Lose?" CARFAX. February 05, 2019. https://www.carfax.com/blog/car-depreciation.

14 Fried, Carla. "Why It's Far Cheaper to Buy a Car than Lease." Barron's. May 01, 2017. https://www.barrons.com/articles/why-its-far-cheaper-to-buy-a-car-than-lease-1488585027.

15 "What Is the Best Age and Mileage for a Used Car?" U.S. News & World Report. https://cars.usnews.com/cars-trucks/what-is-the-best-age-and-mileage-for-a-used-car.

16 Hess, Abigail. "Students Who Work Actually Get Better Grades-but There's a Catch." CNBC. October 10, 2017. https://www.cnbc.com/2017/10/04/students-who-work-actually-get-better-grades-but-theres-a-catch.html.

17 "Student Loan Resources: Financial Aid & Loan Debt Management." Debt.org. https://www.debt.org/students/.

18 Friedman, Zack. "1 Million People Default On Student Loans Each Year." Forbes. October 01, 2018. https://www.forbes.com/sites/zackfriedman/2018/10/01/student-loans-default/.

19 "Here's How Much the Average American Pays in Interest Each Year." The Simple Dollar. March 23, 2017. https://www.thesimpledollar.com/heres-how-much-the-average-american-pays-in-interest-each-year/.

20 Konsko, Lindsay. "Credit Cards Make You Spend More: Studies." NerdWallet. June 01, 2016. https://www.nerdwallet.com/blog/credit-cards/credit-cards-make-you-spend-more/.

21 Perry, Mark J. "New Homes Today Have Twice the Square Feet per Person as in 1973 | Mark J. Perry." FEE Freeman Article. June 07, 2016. https://fee.org/articles/new-homes-today-have-twice-the-square-feet-per-person-as-in-1973/.

[22] "Here's How Much the Average American Pays in Interest Each Year." The Simple Dollar. March 23, 2017. https://www.thesimpledollar.com/heres-how-much-the-average-american-pays-in-interest-each-year/.

[23] Hostetter, Adam. "American Employees: Are You Leaving Money on the Table?" Financial Engines Education Center. January 04, 2019. https://financialengines.com/education-center/employer_match_results/

[24] Clements, Nick. "5 Reasons New Lenders Are Ignoring FICO Credit Scores." Forbes. October 12, 2015. https://www.forbes.com/sites/nickclements/2015/04/21/5-reasons-new-lenders-are-ignoring-fico-credit-scores/#a9dd02b28385.

[25] Lea, Brittany De. "How to Join the 800 Credit Score Crowd." Fox Business. April 04, 2019. https://www.foxbusiness.com/personal-finance/how-to-get-into-the-800-credit-score-crowd.

[26] Templeton, Deanna. "Will Paying off Debt Hurt My Credit Score?" MarketWatch. December 14, 2018. https://www.marketwatch.com/story/will-paying-off-debt-hurt-my-credit-score-2018-12-14.

[27] Luthi, Ben. "Credit-Based Insurance Scores: Do's and Don'ts for Getting the Best Rates." NerdWallet. February 21, 2018. https://www.nerdwallet.com/blog/finance/creditbased-insurance-scores-dos-donts-rates/.

[28] NerdWallet. "Why Employers Check Credit - and What They See." NerdWallet. June 18, 2019. https://www.nerdwallet.com/blog/finance/credit-score-employer-checking/.

[29] Konsko, Lindsay. "No Credit History (Probably) Won't Hurt Your Job Search." NerdWallet. February 25, 2019. https://www.nerdwallet.com/blog/finance/credit-score/credit-history-wont-hurt-job-search/.

[30] Kearns, Deborah. "Can You Get a Mortgage With No Credit History?" NerdWallet. July 23, 2018. https://www.nerdwallet.com/blog/mortgages/mortgage-no-credit-history/.

Chapter 15: How did we get here?

[1] Davidson, Paul. "Jobs: 74% of Adults Say They're OK Financially, up from 70%." USA Today. May 22, 2018. https://www.usatoday.com/story/money/2018/05/22/74-adults-least-doing-ok-financially-up-70-year-ago/632757002/.

[2] "Find Your Spot." Simply Self Storage. https://www.simplyss.com/storage-options/self-storage-statistics/.

[3] Martin, Emmie. "Here's How Much Money You Need to Be Happy, According to a New Analysis by Wealth Experts." CNBC. November 20, 2017. https://www.cnbc.com/2017/11/20/how-much-money-you-need-to-be-happy-according-to-wealth-experts.html.

Chapter 16: The Power of Belief
[1] Stanley, Thomas J. "BLOG: The Millionaire Next Door America Where Millionaires Are Self Made Comments. http://www.thomasjstanley.com/2014/05/america-where-millionaires-are-self-made/.
[2] Hogan, Chris. *Everyday Millionaires: How Ordinary People Built Extraordinary Wealth--and How You Can Too*. Brentwood, TN: Ramsey Press, 2019.

Chapter 17: Line In the Sky
[1] Ibid.
[2] Stanley, Thomas J. *The Millionaire Next Door*. New York: Pocket, 1996.
[3] Pennington, Randy. "5 Important Lessons from Immigrant Entrepreneurs." Entrepreneur. December 13, 2018. https://www.entrepreneur.com/article/324008.
[4] Hogan, Chris. *Everyday Millionaires: How Ordinary People Built Extraordinary Wealth--and How You Can Too*. Brentwood, TN: Ramsey Press, 2019.

Chapter 20: Scaling Mt. Wealth
[1] Jones, Charisse. "60% of Americans Have to Retire Sooner than They'd Planned." USA Today. June 03, 2015. https://www.usatoday.com/story/money/2015/06/02/majority-of-americans-have-to-retire-sooner-than-theyd-planned/28371099/.
[2] Hogan, Chris. *Everyday Millionaires: How Ordinary People Built Extraordinary Wealth--and How You Can Too*. Brentwood, TN: Ramsey Press, 2019.
[3] "Compound Annual Growth Rate (Annualized Return)." CAGR of the Stock Market: Annualized Returns of the S&P 500. http://www.moneychimp.com/features/market_cagr.htm.
[4] Ibid.
[5] Ibid.
[6] Best and worst performance graphs represent two standard deviations (95%).

Chapter 21: The Four Pillars
[1] Nova, Annie. "A $1,000 Emergency Would Push Many Americans into Debt." CNBC. January 23, 2019. https://www.cnbc.com/2019/01/23/most-americans-dont-have-the-savings-to-cover-a-1000-emergency.html.
[2] Hogan, Chris. *Everyday Millionaires: How Ordinary People Built Extraordinary Wealth--and How You Can Too*. Brentwood, TN: Ramsey Press, 2019.
[3] "Winston Churchill Quotes." Brainy Quote. https://www.brainyquote.com/quotes/winston_churchill_131192.

Chapter 22: Building Your Pillars
[1] "6 Reasons Credit Card Rewards Go Unredeemed -- and How to Change That." CreditCards.com. April 23, 2019. https://www.creditcards.com/credit-card-news/six-reasons-credit-card-rewards-go-unredeemed-1277.php.

[2] "A Quote by Zig Ziglar." Goodreads. https://www.goodreads.com/quotes/705178-we-all-need-a-daily-checkup-from-the-neck-up.

[3] "Dave Ramsey's 7 Baby Steps." Dave Ramsey's 7 Baby Steps | DaveRamsey.com. https://www.daveramsey.com/dave-ramsey-7-baby-steps.

[4] Berger, Rob. "Debt Snowball Versus Debt Avalanche: What The Academic Research Shows." Forbes. July 21, 2017. https://www.forbes.com/sites/robertberger/2017/07/20/debt-snowball-versus-debt-avalanche-what-the-academic-research-shows/#94df8da1454a.

[5] Boyer, Ray. "The 'Snowball Approach' to Debt." thttps://www.kellogg.northwestern.edu/news_articles/2012/snowball-approach.aspx. August 7, 2012.

[6] Trudel, Remi. "Research: The Best Strategy for Paying Off Credit Card Debt." Harvard Business Review. December 30, 2016. https://hbr.org/2016/12/research-the-best-strategy-for-paying-off-credit-card-debt.

[7] Ibid.

Chapter 23: Stand, In The Door

[1] Lea, Brittany De. "Social Security Shortfall: Trust Fund to Run Dry in 2035, Trustees Predict." Fox Business. April 22, 2019. https://www.foxbusiness.com/personal-finance/social-security-trust-fund-to-run-dry.

[2] "Compound Annual Growth Rate (Annualized Return)." CAGR of the Stock Market: Annualized Returns of the S&P 500. http://www.moneychimp.com/features/market_cagr.htm.

[3] Hogan, Chris. *Everyday Millionaires: How Ordinary People Built Extraordinary Wealth--and How You Can Too*. Brentwood, TN: Ramsey Press, 2019.

[4] Anderson, Tom. "Active Fund Managers Rarely Beat Their Benchmarks Year after Year." CNBC. February 27, 2017. https://www.cnbc.com/2017/02/27/active-fund-managers-rarely-beat-their-benchmarks-year-after-year.html.

[5] "5 Costly Investing Mistakes." Tonyrobbins.com. June 03, 2019. https://www.tonyrobbins.com/wealth-lifestyle/5-costly-investing-mistakes/.

[6] Hogan, Chris. *Everyday Millionaires: How Ordinary People Built Extraordinary Wealth--and How You Can Too*. Brentwood, TN: Ramsey Press, 2019.

Chapter 24: Department of Defense

[1] Konish, Lorie. "This Is the Real Reason Most Americans File for Bankruptcy." CNBC. February 11, 2019. https://www.cnbc.com/2019/02/11/this-is-the-real-reason-most-americans-file-for-bankruptcy.html.

[2] "Disability Statistics; Chance of Becoming Disabled." Council for Disability Awareness: Prevention, Financial Planning, Resources and Information. https://disabilitycanhappen.org/disability-statistic/.

[3] "Myths and Misconceptions." Employer Information & Resource Center - Council for Disability Awareness. https://disabilitycanhappen.org/employer/myths-and-misconceptions/.

4 Bischoff, Bill. "You Need a Will - Even If You're Not 'rich'." MarketWatch. February 04, 2019. https://www.marketwatch.com/story/why-wills-arent-just-for-the-wealthy-2015-03-17.

Chapter 25: Tac Admin
1 Hogan, Chris. *Everyday Millionaires: How Ordinary People Built Extraordinary Wealth--and How You Can Too.* Brentwood, TN: Ramsey Press, 2019.
2 Miller, Madison. "Average Cost of College in America: 2019 Report." Value Penguin. April 23, 2019. https://www.valuepenguin.com/student-loans/average-cost-of-college.
3 "BLOG." Thomas J Stanley The Millionaire Next Door Avoiding The Money Pit Comments. http://www.thomasjstanley.com/2009/10/avoiding-the-money-pit/.
4 Hogan, Chris. *Everyday Millionaires: How Ordinary People Built Extraordinary Wealth--and How You Can Too.* Brentwood, TN: Ramsey Press, 2019.

Chapter 26: Mutual Support
1 "Money Ruining Marriages in America: A Ramsey Solutions Study." Money Ruining Marriages in America: A Ramsey Solutions Study | DaveRamsey.com. https://www.daveramsey.com/pr/money-ruining-marriages-in-america.

Chapter 28: Birds of a Feather
1 Tebow, Tim, and A. J. Gregory. *This Is the Day: Reclaim Your Dream, Ignite Your Passion, Live Your Purpose.* Random House, 2018.

Afterword: DO BETTER Revisited
1 Brown, Chris. "3 Things the Bible Says About Money." Stewardship.com. May 22, 2015. https://www.stewardship.com/articles/3-things-the-bible-says-about-money.
2 "What You Look for in the Bible: The Top 20 Keyword Search Terms on Bible Gateway." Bible Gateway Blog. March 21, 2013. https://www.biblegateway.com/blog/2013/03/what-you-look-for-in-the-bible-the-top-25-keyword-search-terms-on-bible-gateway/.

Appendix D: My Max House Purchase Amount
1 Stebbins, Samuel. "Property Tax Varies by State. Here's a Look at What You'll Pay." USA Today. February 12, 2019. https://www.usatoday.com/story/money/2019/02/11/property-taxes-us-state-state-look-what-youll-pay/38909755/.
2 Moon, Chris. "Average Cost of Homeowners Insurance (2019)." Value Penguin. June 13, 2019. https://www.valuepenguin.com/average-cost-of-homeowners-insurance.
3 Masterson, Les. "Average Homeowners Insurance Rates by State." Insurance.com. March 27, 2018. https://www.insurance.com/home-and-renters-insurance/home-insurance-basics/average-homeowners-insurance-rates-by-state.

CPSIA information can be obtained
at www.ICGtesting.com
Printed in the USA
FFHW021804270719
53898874-59616FF

9 781733 215312